The Social Construction of Age

SECOND LANGUAGE ACQUISITION
Series Editor: Professor David Singleton, *Trinity College, Dublin, Ireland*

This series brings together titles dealing with a variety of aspects of language acquisition and processing in situations where a language or languages other than the native language is involved. Second language is thus interpreted in its broadest possible sense. The volumes included in the series all offer in their different ways, on the one hand, exposition and discussion of empirical findings and, on the other, some degree of theoretical reflection. In this latter connection, no particular theoretical stance is privileged in the series; nor is any relevant perspective – sociolinguistic, psycholinguistic, neurolinguistic, etc. – deemed out of place. The intended readership of the series includes final-year undergraduates working on second language acquisition projects, postgraduate students involved in second language acquisition research, and researchers and teachers in general whose interests include a second language acquisition component.

Full details of all the books in this series and of all our other publications can be found on http://www.multilingual-matters.com, or by writing to Multilingual Matters, St Nicholas House, 31–34 High Street, Bristol BS1 2AW, UK.

SECOND LANGUAGE ACQUISITION
Series Editor: David Singleton, *Trinity College, Dublin, Ireland*

The Social Construction of Age

Adult Foreign Language Learners

Patricia Andrew

MULTILINGUAL MATTERS
Bristol • Buffalo • Toronto

A Antonio, siempre

Library of Congress Cataloging in Publication Data
Andrew, Patricia.
The Social Construction of Age: Adult Foreign Language Learners/Patricia Andrew.
Second Language Acquisition: 63
Includes bibliographical references and index.
1. Second language acquisition. 2. Language and languages—Age differences. 3. Sociolinguistics. 4. Language and culture. I. Title.
P118.2.A55 2012
401'.93–dc23 2011048967

British Library Cataloguing in Publication Data
A catalogue entry for this book is available from the British Library.

ISBN-13: 978-1-84769-614-4 (hbk)
ISBN-13: 978-1-84769-613-7 (pbk)

Multilingual Matters
UK: St Nicholas House, 31–34 High Street, Bristol BS1 2AW, UK.
USA: UTP, 2250 Military Road, Tonawanda, NY 14150, USA.
Canada: UTP, 5201 Dufferin Street, North York, Ontario M3H 5T8, Canada.

Copyright © 2012 Patricia Andrew.

All rights reserved. No part of this work may be reproduced in any form or by any means without permission in writing from the publisher.

The policy of Multilingual Matters/Channel View Publications is to use papers that are natural, renewable and recyclable products, made from wood grown in sustainable forests. In the manufacturing process of our books, and to further support our policy, preference is given to printers that have FSC and PEFC Chain of Custody certification. The FSC and/or PEFC logos will appear on those books where full certification has been granted to the printer concerned.

Typeset by Techset Composition Ltd., Salisbury, UK.
Printed and bound in Great Britain by Short Run Press Ltd.

SECOND LANGUAGE ACQUISITION
Series Editor: David Singleton, *Trinity College, Dublin, Ireland*

The Social Construction of Age

Adult Foreign Language Learners

Patricia Andrew

MULTILINGUAL MATTERS
Bristol • Buffalo • Toronto

A Antonio, siempre

Library of Congress Cataloging in Publication Data
Andrew, Patricia.
The Social Construction of Age: Adult Foreign Language Learners/Patricia Andrew.
Second Language Acquisition: 63
Includes bibliographical references and index.
1. Second language acquisition. 2. Language and languages—Age differences. 3. Sociolinguistics. 4. Language and culture. I. Title.
P118.2.A55 2012
401'.93–dc23 2011048967

British Library Cataloguing in Publication Data
A catalogue entry for this book is available from the British Library.

ISBN-13: 978-1-84769-614-4 (hbk)
ISBN-13: 978-1-84769-613-7 (pbk)

Multilingual Matters
UK: St Nicholas House, 31–34 High Street, Bristol BS1 2AW, UK.
USA: UTP, 2250 Military Road, Tonawanda, NY 14150, USA.
Canada: UTP, 5201 Dufferin Street, North York, Ontario M3H 5T8, Canada.

Copyright © 2012 Patricia Andrew.

All rights reserved. No part of this work may be reproduced in any form or by any means without permission in writing from the publisher.

The policy of Multilingual Matters/Channel View Publications is to use papers that are natural, renewable and recyclable products, made from wood grown in sustainable forests. In the manufacturing process of our books, and to further support our policy, preference is given to printers that have FSC and PEFC Chain of Custody certification. The FSC and/or PEFC logos will appear on those books where full certification has been granted to the printer concerned.

Typeset by Techset Composition Ltd., Salisbury, UK.
Printed and bound in Great Britain by Short Run Press Ltd.

Contents

Acknowledgments		vii
Introduction: A First Glimpse of Age		ix

Part 1: Framing Age as Socially Constructed — 1

1 The Age Factor and Second Language Acquisition — 3
  Introduction — 3
  The Critical Period Hypothesis for Second Language
    Acquisition: A Critique — 3
  Sociocultural Approaches to Second Language Acquisition — 19
  Conclusion — 25

2 Present-Day Approaches to the Study of Age — 27
  Introduction — 27
  Social Constructionism — 27
  Recent Perspectives in Sociolinguistics on the Study of
    Social Dimensions — 32
  Conclusion — 42

3 Viewing Age through a Social Constructionist Lens — 44
  Introduction — 44
  Contemporary Age Discourses and Their Manifestations — 44
  Language and the Discursive Construction of Age Identity — 59
  Narrating Age — 62
  Conclusion — 65

Part 2: The Social Construction of Age in Mexico — 67

4 Constructing Age in Later Adulthood — 71
  Introduction — 71
  Hector's Story: A Tale of Progress — 71
  Felix's Story: A Tale of Discontent — 89
  Conclusion — 107

5 Constructing Age in 'Middle' Adulthood — 110
  Introduction — 110

	The Women Tell Their Stories	110
	Conclusion	130
6	Constructing Age in Young Adulthood	134
	Introduction	134
	David's Story	134
	Conclusion	149
	Final Reflections	152
	Introduction	152
	Age and Second Language Acquisition: What We Have Learned	153
	Implications of the Findings	156
	Concluding Remarks	159
	References	161
	Index	174

Acknowledgments

This book is the outcome of a kind of 'co-construction', for many people were involved in giving it shape. Certainly no one played a greater role than David Block, who expertly guided me through the research study on which it is based. His innovative approach to the issues has provided inspiration for me both then and now. I also benefited greatly from the critical insights of Jean-Marc Dewaele, Adrian Holliday, Margaret Lee Zoreda, Siân Preece and Javier Vivaldo, given at crucial moments in the process of clarifying my ideas. The following people generously devoted time to reading preliminary versions of the book and making helpful suggestions: Marcia Andrew-Camacho, John Gray, Jim Heinrich, Joy Holloway, Kathryn Kovacik, Rosa María Laguna and Emma Navarrete. I owe a particular debt of gratitude to the teachers who opened their classroom doors and to the students who so willingly shared their stories with me. Finally, Antonio Andrade gave gentle encouragement throughout. To all, I am deeply grateful.

Introduction: A First Glimpse of Age

The Age Dilemma

Felix, an English student, and I talk about age.[1]

F = Felix
P = Patricia

F: I ... I can tell you that I am not ... despite the fact that I am going on 70, I'm not old. I am not old. Why? Because I am still interested in life, OK.
P: And in the eyes of your children ... your friends ... your ... society in general, how do they see you, for example?
F: Look, they see me like ... I mean, 'Ah, you're retired. Now you're an old man.' Yes, but, no. I don't care ... I don't care anything about that.
P: Exactly, so you ...
F: I am young inside. I am still capable.

Young or old? In our interview, Felix constructs himself as 'young inside' and vigorously rejects being positioned as 'an old man' by his family and friends. I can readily understand the quandary this represents for him, for at the beginning of the new millennium I decided that I wanted to go back to school. I was excited at the prospect of spending the next few years of my life immersed in books and engaging with new ideas as I worked toward a doctoral degree. But I was also apprehensive, for I was nearly 60 years old and on the receiving end of discouraging messages from the society in which I lived about the deleterious effects of aging. So I wondered if I could succeed, if I was 'still capable', as Felix put it, if I could count on the same intellectual abilities that I had as a younger student and if I could muster the discipline and stamina needed for long hours of study. On the upside, I knew I was bringing many years of experience to the task, and I was convinced that this would count for something. I was curious about how others would view my return to the world of academia as an older student, and what impact the experience would have on me as a person, for I felt that it would surely change me irrevocably.

At the same time, I had been working for many years as an EFL (English as a Foreign Language) teacher in Mexico, where I had adults of all ages in my classroom. From the beginning I was intrigued by the significance of the age differences of my students, not only in terms of possible effects on their learning, but also, and perhaps more importantly, on the social interaction that takes place in the classroom. I also suspected that age might figure substantially in what the learners bring to and take away from the experience. Yet, second language pedagogy pays little heed to the diversity existing among adults of different ages, in essence adopting a generalized young-adult focus.[2] It has been mystifying to me that, in an era of learner-centeredness in education, and given the increasing importance of lifelong learning, such a narrow outlook should persist. I thought that perhaps it reflected the largely invisible status of older adults in cultures around the world which are increasingly youth-oriented. I hoped some day to discover answers to my concerns.

Once I decided to go back to school, I became doubly interested in the impact of age on the experience of being an adult learner. Having promised myself at the outset that I would choose a research topic that was meaningful to me both personally and professionally, the question of age and aging in adult learners emerged as an ideal subject to explore. My interest as an older learner in my own aging process dovetailed with my concern as a teacher with the undifferentiated treatment of adults in the language classroom. I wanted to find out what bearing age had on those of us who had added a learner identity to our other identities.

Accordingly, I set out to explore what it is like to be an adult language learner in Mexico. To accomplish this, I recruited seven students enrolled in English courses at the language center of the university where I work. Their ages, 23, 34, 36, 48, 59, 68 and 69, spanned a broad range of adult years. Four were women and three were men; one was a university student and the others members of the neighboring community. During one semester term, I attended their lessons, met with them periodically for interviews and received weekly audio-taped narrations from each of them. The close contact with these participants enabled me to learn much about the significance the language-learning experience had in their lives.

My interest was whether the experience coincided with the beliefs and expectations adults have about language learning, what different kinds of feelings it produced in them and in what ways they considered themselves to be changed by it. Most importantly, I wanted to know how they construct their age identity and what part they think age plays in the learning process and in their lives beyond the classroom. My concern was less with the issue

of linguistic attainment than with what the experience means in the larger context of their worlds. To this end, I endeavored to ascertain the significance the language-learning experience had for them at this precise moment of their lives in terms of their personal, academic or professional circumstances and aspirations. This connects importantly with the ways in which they constructed complex, new identities for themselves as a major nonlinguistic dimension of their language-learning experience.

English Language Learning in Mexico

Although English was studied by the elite in 19th-century Mexico, along with Latin, French and Italian, it was only in the post World War II era, when Mexico was catapulted from an agricultural to an industrialized nation, that the language took on special importance. By the 1960s, a broad spectrum of students from all social classes were receiving an education at the National University (*Universidad Nacional Autónoma de México*), and English was taught in many of its faculties. At the same time, bilingual schools, language institutes and private universities began to proliferate in urban Mexico, making the study of English even more widespread. For large sectors of the population, the customs, habits of consumption and aspirations of the United States constituted a model to emulate. In this sense, newly urbanized Mexico took on many of the values of the industrialized West.

A further upsurge in the learning of English in Mexico took place in the 1980s and 1990s as a result of the opening up of markets and the negotiation and signing of a free trade agreement with the United States and Canada. The desirability of knowing English was reflected in the increased demand for language courses both in educational institutions and in the work place. In addition, the proximity of the United States and Canada made travel to these countries a genuine possibility for many Mexicans and an aspiration for many others.

Now, in the 21st century, the importance of learning English goes relatively unquestioned; its status as a world language is universally acknowledged by all sectors of the population in Mexico, as it is elsewhere in the world. Characteristics of the current global context, such as the expansion of transportation and communication, the increase in international commerce and trade agreements, the internationalization of professional standards, training and accreditation, the need for intercultural communication at a personal level, the mushrooming of the internet and the presence of a new international political order as seen, for example, in the formation of new nations and the increased democratization of others, are cited as the most salient causes of the growing demand for opportunities to study foreign languages, and particularly English.

This demand is felt even more intensely in the case of Mexico, whose geographical proximity to the United States has had direct repercussions on trade relations and demographic movements, bringing about a pressing need for effective means of communication between the two countries. At the same time, it has engendered an ambivalent attitude toward English that is fairly common among Mexicans (Francis & Ryan, 1998). On the one hand, definite, though largely unacknowledged, prestige is associated with knowing English for it is imbued with the elevated status of the American and European worlds. On the other hand, an aversion to English and Anglophone culture is frequently found, even among students of the language, attributable to the asymmetrical relationship between Mexico and the United States. In my view, Mexicans are attracted by the technological and economic superiority of the United States, yet at the same time wary of the power it wields, the encroachment of American culture in Mexico and, consequently, the perceived threat to their national identity. Precisely because of the power associated with the United States, knowledge of English carries with it an aura of privilege, accomplishment and refinement, furnishing an entrée to both social and professional worlds in Mexico.

English is studied in Mexico as a foreign language rather than as a second language. This is because it is not a community language in Mexico. As such, learning takes place principally in a classroom setting as distinct from a naturalistic one. However, as Block (2003) points out, making broad generalizations about foreign-language contexts can be misleading for there are differences in the conditions surrounding the learning of different languages. For example, English has a higher visibility in Mexico than languages such as Korean or Arabic. The presence of transnational companies, the media and foreign visitors provide greater opportunities for contact with English outside the classroom. Nevertheless, the classroom remains the principal venue for learning the language.

The university where I work, and subsequently carried out my research, is a branch campus of the National University. The language center at the university regularly enrolls a small population of older people (25–70) returning to the classroom, who study alongside the university-age (18–22) students. The resulting amalgamation is an interesting one, for while the multiage group is drawn together by the shared goal of learning English, their reasons for wanting to learn the language are wide-ranging, as are the ways they go about it and participate in the process, and ultimately, what the experience means to them not only in terms of their learning but also of their broader life circumstances. While the tradition of lifelong learning is a relatively recent phenomenon in Mexico, the study of foreign languages has long been an acceptable activity for students of all ages. English courses are particularly popular among adults who, for personal, work-related or academic reasons, return to the classroom as older learners. In consequence, educators are facing issues about how best to fulfill the needs and expectations of such a varied population. Certainly, searching for methods to enable successful mastery of the language is an important goal, yet it is only part of the equation. Learning a new language, as I have observed, comprises vital experiences of a social nature that color this endeavor in significant ways. These, too, must be taken into account.

The Study of Age in Second Language Acquisition

Interestingly, age has been a highly visible topic in second language acquisition (SLA) research for many years. An important body of literature on the Critical Period Hypothesis (CPH) addresses the contentious issue of whether biological constraints operate on second language learning; that is, whether people are neurologically programmed for language at a predetermined period of time in childhood ending at puberty, and after which time they can acquire new languages only with great difficulty (Long, 1990; Singleton & Ryan, 2004). Researchers who believe that age is a determining factor in successful language acquisition take up any of several positions that vary according to the degree of stringency of the biological argument, but all based on the conviction that 'younger is better' (see e.g. Johnson & Newport, 1989; Marinova-Todd, 2003). Those adopting the counter-position draw on evidence from reported cases of older learners who outperform younger ones (see e.g. Birdsong, 1999; Ioup *et al.*, 1994). Because researchers involved in this debate are primarily interested in determining whether facility in language learning stops at around puberty or earlier, they compare language attainment of children of different ages or of children and adults, but they do not look at possible differences existing among adult second language learners. Differences in current language policy, particularly regarding the best time to initiate second language programs in schools in order to achieve optimum results, mirror the inconsistent findings of these studies.

In consequence of this focus, virtually nothing in the CPH literature makes distinctions between, for example, 30-, 40- and 50-year-old learners. Thus, while the CPH debate has proved interesting and informative in overall terms, it has not shed much light on adult second language learning nor has it broadened its scope beyond the issue of linguistic attainment. This is a concern to me as an English language teacher, for I have often wondered whether there are age-related differences among adult learners that I should be taking into account in my classroom teaching practice. One way I might have proceeded in my search for an answer is to have conducted a study of younger and older adults in the tradition of existing CPH research in order to determine whether age has an impact on success in adult language learning. Such an investigation would have filled a gap presently existing in the CPH literature. Nevertheless, I decided against approaching age as a biological factor precisely because it cannot tell me about the experiential side of learning a language. In the course of my work with mature students, I have on occasion observed the feelings of inadequacy, self-doubt and frustration, and of the concomitant threat to their identities, that learning a new language can engender. It is clear to me that the experience encompasses a broad range of concerns involving the social dimensions of age that are present in the classroom and that extend far beyond it as well. That is what I set out to explore.

Two Key Concepts: Age and Aging

The two central terms in this book are 'age' and 'aging'. Cognizant of the limitations inherent in any attempt to pin down such elusive concepts, I have adopted the following brief definitions that underscore the distinction between them. 'Aging' is a multidimensional process that is physiological, psychological, social and cultural. It entails movement through time and signifies change. 'Age', on the other hand, is a place or position a person has at a given moment in time. Age and aging are in reality two facets of the same phenomenon in that an understanding of one necessarily involves the other. The life course transpires as an ongoing process of change known as 'aging' and provides the backdrop for identifying any point along the way. 'Age' captures one of those fleeting moments; it is the point where we situate ourselves at a precise instant in the life course. It is important to clarify that at times 'age' is used as a superordinate term, encompassing the notions of age and aging, as in 'age theory' or 'age studies'. At other times, 'age' can refer to a stage in the life course, such as 'middle age'. I also recognize that in common parlance 'aging' is a euphemism for 'old age', an expression closely associated with decline and mortality in Anglophone cultures, and one which I have tried to refrain from using.

The Purpose of the Book

With the issues outlined above in mind, I embarked on the study of age from a social constructionist perspective, in line with many contemporary sociolinguistic approaches to social parameters, such as ethnicity and gender (see e.g. Blackledge, 2002; Cameron, 1999; Eckert & McConnell-Ginet, 1995; Wodak et al., 1999). Specifically, I explore the ways in which age as socially constructed is experienced by adult EFL learners in Mexico.

An increased awareness of how language learners construct their age identity and how it comes to bear on their involvement in the learning process can enable teachers to take into account not only what learners share in common but also how they differ from one another in their experience both in and outside of the classroom. People cannot fully understand each other without a sense of where they are in their lives – in the life course – relative to each other. Age is a core part of a person's identity. The age discourses[3] that people draw on to enact their identities can be perceived in their beliefs and attitudes about age and about language learning, in the way they position themselves and others, in classroom practices, as well as in the interplay of age identity and their other identities.

At the same time, the book contemplates the significance that taking a language class may have for people of different ages in terms of nonlinguistic aspects of the experience, such as working toward personal development, pursuing a fresh intellectual challenge, engaging in social encounters with other people or acquiring cultural capital and shaping a new identity. Understanding this can lead to more fruitful cooperation in building a classroom community that is dynamically connected and responsive to the real-world circumstances and aspirations of the learners.

Issues that have an impact on SLA research are also addressed. Our understanding of the age factor in SLA has until now been informed principally by research undertaken in the prevailing biological and cognitive tradition. The trend in the recent history of SLA research in the sociocultural tradition has been to view the social dimensions of identity, such as gender, social class and ethnicity, as socially constructed in discursive interaction, rather than as isolated variables. This has generated a more finely grained understanding of them as they are implicated in the construction of identities. For whatever reason, age has not been included in studies working from this perspective in SLA, although it is beginning to occupy an important place in research carried out in other fields. This omission is a serious one because age adds a temporal quality to the complex of a person's identities. A social constructionist approach, then, can round out our picture of age by providing a socially focused counterpart to work carried out with a psycholinguistic orientation to SLA.

On a broader level, the research on which this book is based sheds light on the ways in which age is socially constructed by adults in Mexico. A great deal of overlap exists between present-day urban Mexico and what might be termed 'generalized Western culture', yet there are some important differences in the construction of adulthood in Mexico that surface in the course of the study and that enhance our understanding of the social significance of age and aging in contemporary society elsewhere.

While research on age as socially constructed has been carried out in a variety of different contexts, it has not been studied in the foreign language classroom. This book brings fresh findings to the fledgling field of age studies and, by comparing and contrasting them with other research findings, it is hoped it will contribute to moving it forward.

Organization of the Book

The book is divided into two parts. Part 1 provides the conceptual basis for looking at age as a social construct. It begins with an examination of age in SLA in both the cognitive and the sociocultural traditions, followed by a discussion of social constructionist and contemporary sociolinguistic approaches to age and other social dimensions. In the final section of Part 1,

I explore the age discourses underlying the creation of age identity and giving meaning to the experience of aging in contemporary Western society.

In Part 2, the construction of age comes to life in the stories told by seven adult language learners in Mexico. The three data chapters revolve around their construction of later, middle and young adulthood as it links up with their experience as language learners.

Notes

(1) The interview extracts throughout the book are my translations from Spanish. Space does not permit the inclusion of the original Spanish texts.
(2) This appraisal is based on my own analysis of the characters, topics, settings and classroom activities in three English language textbooks used in Mexico at the time the research was undertaken: *Look Ahead* (Hopkins & Potter, 1994), *Interchange* (Richards *et al.*, 1991) and *American Headway* (Soars & Soars, 2001b).
(3) The term 'discourse' is used in two separate, but related ways in this book. In the present context, 'discourses' refer to ways of thinking, feeling, believing, talking about, behaving and valuing that are characteristic of specific communities. In short, they are 'ways of being in the world' (Gee, 1999: 7). At other times, 'discourse' denotes language in use, that is, language in interaction. The topic of discourse is treated more extensively in Chapter 2.

Part 1
Framing Age as Socially Constructed

The first part of the book analyzes the treatment of age in second language acquisition (SLA), sociolinguistics and cultural studies, and provides the conceptual foundation for the empirical study described in Part 2. Chapter 1 examines the broad literature on the Critical Period Hypothesis (CPH) as the primary source of information on age issues in SLA. After considering the current state of the debate, I argue that the CPH for SLA has not focused on the age factor in adults in any important way, at best providing a limited account of linguistic outcomes from a biological perspective. The impact of age as a social dimension and the nonlinguistic outcomes of adult language learning lie beyond the scope of the CPH and are better understood in light of sociocultural perspectives on SLA and by taking a social constructionist approach to age.

In Chapter 2, the research on which this book is based is positioned as a contemporary discourse-oriented sociolinguistic study. The key features of social constructionism that are relevant to the study of age from an interactional perspective are discussed. By tracing the links between contemporary sociolinguistics and social constructionism, I contend that they provide a coherent framework for the study of age and other social dimensions.

Following this, Chapter 3 takes up the question of how age is socially constructed in present-day Western society. I discuss the principal discourses that frame the way people give meaning to the experience of aging and create their age identity. Additional consideration is given to the existence of competing discourses which contribute to the multiple, changing and potentially contradictory nature of these processes in themselves and in relation to the other life experiences and identities with which they intersect. The fundamental role of narrative in discursive interaction and identity construction is a recurring theme throughout this chapter, furnishing a valuable link to the discussion of the empirical work which follows in the second part of the book.

Part 1

Framing Gro as Socially Constructed

1 The Age Factor and Second Language Acquisition

Introduction

To ascertain what part age and the age identity of adult language learners play in the process of acquiring and using English as a second language (L2), it is imperative to begin by considering how age has traditionally been treated in the field and what has been learned up to now. Given that questions regarding the importance of age in SLA have been restricted almost exclusively to the existence and nature of possible biological constraints on learning, a substantial part of this chapter is devoted to a discussion of the CPH. Following that, I offer an assessment of the existing orientation to the issue of age and SLA and suggest an alternative direction to take in exploring this topic. It involves adopting a sociocultural approach to SLA at the outset, a theoretical perspective in greater accord with the focus of the book. The sociocultural strand of SLA is the subject of the final part of the chapter and sets the tone for those that follow.

The Critical Period Hypothesis for Second Language Acquisition: A Critique

Any discussion of the age factor in SLA must necessarily give major consideration to the CPH. This is the most clearly articulated theory concerning age constraints on first language (L1) acquisition, and reflection on its applicability by extension to SLA logically precedes the exploration of alternate explanations of the relationship of age to the acquisition process. Questions of whether we are neurologically programmed for language acquisition at a defined period of time during our childhood, whether it is possible to acquire an L2 after this critical period has ended, what kinds of limitations might be entailed and what the ramifications are for teaching and learning languages comprise some of the issues of crucial importance in understanding the role that age plays in SLA.

The controversy surrounding this theory has been an animated one among SLA researchers in the 40 years since Lenneberg (1967) posited the existence of a critical period for language acquisition in *Biological Foundations of Language*.[1] According to the CPH, children have a special capacity for language development that is supported by an innate language-learning mechanism. The critical period ends around puberty, after which time the innate mechanism is no longer available and language development is virtually halted. This phenomenon is ascribed to the loss of neural plasticity of the brain and the establishment of hemispheric lateralization.[2] Central to Lenneberg's notion of age constraints on language acquisition is its biological bases, alluded to in the title of his book, namely, aspects of the child's neural structure involved in a fundamental way in the development of language. These are the key elements of the hypothesis as originally set forth by Lenneberg.

The CPH and L1 Acquisition

Evidence of the existence of a critical period begins with the commonplace observation that all normal children become fully competent in their L1, following a similar timetable through analogous developmental stages. Comparable critical periods are characteristic of different kinds of behavioral development in nonhuman species as well.

Studies of language recovery in adults and children who have suffered brain lesions indicate that children are clearly advantaged over adults. In addition, research into delayed L1 acquisition has tended to give substantial support to the concept of a critical period, in the sense that the linguistic competence ultimately attained by the subjects under study has proven to be deficient. Studies of feral children and others deprived of language input in early childhood as a result of abuse or neglect have offered valuable examples of the defective language that results (Curtiss, 1977, 1982, 1988). Another source of information has come from studies of congenitally deaf subjects whose first contact with American Sign Language, a fully functional language, occurred at different ages. Language development of Down's syndrome children has also proved a useful way to look at delay in L1 acquisition. However, possibilities for carrying out this type of empirical work have necessarily been limited by ethical considerations and by the fact that incidences of delayed L1 acquisition are relatively rare.

While the neurobiological basis of L1 acquisition is largely accepted, the CPH as originally set forth has come under closer scrutiny as more is learned about the structure and working of the brain. The ensuing debate on issues such as the age at which the critical period begins and ends, or when hemispheric lateralization occurs and whether this is significant, has given rise to alternate versions of the CPH. Some researchers suggest that, given the complex nature of language, there may be multiple critical periods for linguistic competence, or that some aspects of language proficiency may be subject to critical periods but others are not.

Furthermore, in view of research findings with delayed L1 learners, the strong version of the CPH, which holds that no learning would be possible if a child were not exposed to language before a certain age, usually understood to be puberty, has tended to give way to a weak version in which, according to Long:

> some learning would be possible beginning after that age, but that native-like abilities would be unattainable, and that the course of development would become more irregular and would fall further short of native levels the later the age of onset. (Long, 1990: 256–257)

The acceptance of the CPH for L1 acquisition, in either its strong or weak form, of necessity precedes any discussion of the more contentious issue of a neurobiologically based critical period for SLA, for it is unlikely that the latter could exist if the former did not. The foregoing considerations provide the necessary contextualization for looking at the CPH as applied to SLA, a task of more immediate concern here.

The CPH and Second Language Acquisition

Whereas L1 acquisition normally leads to full proficiency, SLA rarely does, and instead is characterized by a broad variation in outcomes. Divergent views regarding the potential of the CPH to explain this latter phenomenon have given rise to multiple ways of addressing a wide gamut of concerns about very specific aspects of language proficiency. This situation complicates a straightforward treatment of the CPH since there is only a minor area of overlap in the studies. Consequently, the present discussion will proceed along very general lines, with an attempt to tie in the various contributions where they seem pertinent.

The issues

Two broad claims about SLA furnish a point of departure:

- L2 learners rarely attain overall native-like language proficiency.
- Younger L2 learners are generally more successful than older ones.

On the whole, both these beliefs have a certain limited acceptance. Points of divergence derive primarily from considerations of what role the CPH plays, and whether it can be applied to all aspects of language proficiency and in all SLA contexts.

The fundamental questions to be addressed, then, are:

- Can the CPH account for the typically unsuccessful results of most L2 learners in achieving full mastery of the language?

- Does the CPH explain the better long-term achievement of younger learners in an L2 with respect to that of older learners?

A negative answer to either of the foregoing leads to the following question:

- What alternate theories are offered to account for these phenomena?

An affirmative response, albeit a qualified one, generates further questions, such as:

- How does the CPH explain the variability in SLA outcomes?
- To what extent can the CPH provide the sole explanation for this?
- Do distinct critical periods exist for different aspects of the SLA process?
- What other factors interact with the neurobiological ones in SLA, and to what extent?

These questions, in turn, will produce additional ones.

The viewpoints

The strong version of the CPH, that language acquisition can take place exclusively during the period of human development from infancy through puberty, maintains that once this period has ended, it is no longer possible, or exceptionally difficult, to learn a language. With regard to SLA, there is less support now for this extreme position, namely, that there exists an abrupt moment which ends any further language development. Were this true, post-critical period learners should not be able to learn an L2, patently not the case. Instead, supporters of a strong version of the CPH hold that after the close of the critical period, as a consequence of the loss of neural plasticity in the brain and because the biologically endowed faculty for language is no longer available, L2s are learned only with great difficulty. They point to findings that demonstrate a general tendency for younger learners to do better than older learners in the acquisition of an L2, claiming that these results are attributable precisely to the accessibility of the innate language-learning mechanism to younger learners but not to older ones (Johnson & Newport, 1989; Long, 1990; Oyama, 1976, 1978; Patkowski, 1980).

However, a number of research studies have reported findings at variance with these in specific language domains, thereby casting doubt on the soundness of the strong version of the CPH. Studies reporting incidences of highly successful late-starting learners have raised serious questions about the existence of maturational constraints on SLA (Abu-Rabia & Kehat, 2004; Bongaerts, 1999, 2005; Ioup *et al.*, 1994; Van Boxtel *et al.*, 2005). In view of a growing body of counter-evidence and as a consequence of an increasing awareness of the inherent complexity of the acquisition process and the impossibility of tracing the variation in outcomes to a single origin, a weak version of the CPH now has considerable credence among SLA researchers. In this version of the hypothesis, the term 'sensitive period' is often used in preference to the more rigidly deterministic 'critical period', denoting an optimal interval of time in which circumstances are favorable for developing a particular type of behavior, and after which efficiency gradually declines.

While few researchers completely reject any biological basis of observed age-related differences in SLA outcomes, the contention that proficiency in an L2 is contingent entirely or principally upon maturational factors implies causality for which, Bialystok (1997) insists, evidence must be provided unequivocally linking the two. This standpoint, in essence, is that the burden of proof is on those affirming the validity of the CPH, and not the other way around.

The evidence

Age-related effects on SLA are generally studied in terms of either the rate of acquisition or ultimate attainment, a distinction with critical implications for interpretation. In the first case, the underlying assumption is that a faster rate of acquisition demonstrates a greater facility for learning languages. In the second, the supposition is that a higher degree of achievement in the final outcome corresponds to a greater fulfillment of the potential for language learning. Both types of focus have been used to look at age of onset (AO)[3] or, less frequently, length of residence (LOR), as they relate to some measure of language proficiency. Interestingly, rate-of-acquisition studies, most of which were carried out in the 1970s and 1980s, found that older learners performed better than younger ones on measures of morphology, syntax and pronunciation. Long (1990) discusses this research in his survey of L2 investigation on age, and concludes that the initial advantage for adults is a transitory one. The consensus is that, in the long run, children outperform adults. Only two major studies of the rate of acquisition (Muñoz, 2006; Slavoff & Johnson, 1995) have been reported since the 1980s.

Ultimate attainment studies are considered more important in investigating maturational constraints on L2 development because of their long-term nature. Most of the earlier studies concluded that ultimate attainment declines as AO increases. These findings are interpreted as corroborating the strong version of the CPH. The most frequently cited are those of Oyama (1976, 1978), Patkowski (1980) and Johnson and Newport (1989). These studies found an earlier AO to be a strong predictor of greater proficiency in different aspects of L2 development.

Investigation that has attempted to disprove the broader claims of these earlier studies focuses on cases of highly successful older learners, adults who have achieved near-native proficiency in one or more language domains, despite a later AO. Studies carried out by Birdsong (1992), White and Genesee (1996) and Ioup *et al.* (1994) found subjects who performed at the same level as near-native speakers or native speakers of French, English and Egyptian Arabic, respectively. These studies have primarily explored the grammatical features of language. Several later studies of age looked at English as a third language in bilingual communities in the Basque Country and in Catalonia (García Mayo & García Lecumberri, 2003). Older learners were found to have an advantage over younger ones in formal instruction contexts in different language domains, including pronunciation. Another study reported attainment of native-like proficiency in Dutch by postpuberty learners, even those with a typologically distant L1 (Van Boxtel *et al.*, 2005).

The question of phonetics and phonology is perhaps even more important to the discussion of adult learner success than morphosyntax, for the reason that pronunciation is generally believed to be more susceptible to age constraints than other aspects of language, presumably because it involves neuromuscular skills. The widely held view is that late learners will have a more marked foreign accent than their younger counterparts. In separate studies that corroborate this standpoint, both Flege *et al.* (1995) and Moyer (1999) showed that age correlates negatively with phonological performance. Their research is representative of other studies that have found an age-related decline in end-state attainment in pronunciation, although not necessarily in other language domains. Singleton points out that 'the earlier an immigrant arrives in the host country and begins to be exposed to its language the more likely he/she is to end up sounding like a native' (Singleton, 1995: 8–9).

Nonetheless, some studies, such as those carried out in Spain, have demonstrated that older learners are not disadvantaged with respect to younger ones in pronunciation skills (García Lecumberri & Gallardo, 2003). Of particular relevance are cases reporting late starters who achieve a native-like accent (Bongaerts, 1999). In an early study, Neufeld (1978) trained 20 adult English speakers in the pronunciation of a set of utterances in two non-Indo-European languages, without giving them any corresponding syntactic or semantic information. The results led him to conclude that adults retain the potential for native-speaker proficiency in pronunciation. In the cases of the two adult learners of Egyptian Arabic studied by Ioup *et al.* (1994), both were judged to have accents indistinguishable from those of native speakers. Likewise, a number of older learners were reported to have attained native-like pronunciation of French and of English in studies undertaken with Dutch speakers (Bongaerts, 1999; Bongaerts *et al.*, 1997). Abu-Rabia and Kehat (2004) found similar cases of late starters, having different L1s, who were judged to have a native-like accent in Hebrew. The body of research findings describing instances of highly successful L2 learners in the areas of morphosyntax and phonology constitutes the principal counter-evidence used to challenge the theory that maturational constraints produce an age-related decline in proficiency.

Nevertheless, it is important to point out that, at present, evidence in support of the CPH is still forthcoming, principally from neuroscience research. Neurobiological findings have, for the most part, remained consistent with the earliest principles of the CPH, yet more is now known about the brain since the theory was first set forth. Weber-Fox and Neville (1996, 1999) used neural imaging techniques to reveal that linguistic processing is subject to maturational constraints, older L2 learners exhibiting slower processing than younger ones. In addition, the processing of grammatical aspects of the language was discovered to be quite distinct from that of semantic aspects. Stowe and Sabourin (2005) found evidence that the same areas of the brain are used in general for both L1 and L2, although not necessarily as efficiently in L2. They indicate that this may reflect an overuse of one part of the L1 processing system and an underuse of another. Mueller (2005, 2009) also compared L1 and L2 processing mechanisms in a variety of linguistic domains by looking at event-related potential (ERP) patterns. She found some similarities and some differences between L1 and L2 speakers, depending on the subprocesses involved, and suggested that the processing differences are attributable to age of acquisition and the level of proficiency. These findings are consistent with those of Hahne (2001), who studied ERPs of native Russians with differing levels of L2 proficiency in German. Slabakova (2006) suggests that because studies have tended to focus on how and where brain activity affects specific areas and subareas of linguistic competence, neurobiological research is especially compatible with the multiple CPH. While it is evident that a great deal still needs to be explored, these examples show the vast potential of modern neuroscience to help clarify our understanding of the inner workings of the brain and its role in SLA.

The interpretation

Interpretation of the evidence concerning age-related effects on SLA has proved as interesting as the outcomes themselves. As might be expected, where the evidence has been at variance with the notion of a critical period, alternate theories have emerged. On the other hand, where the data have been consistent with the CPH, this has traditionally been the preferred reading. However, increasingly, even when a later AO has been found to correlate with declining proficiency, this has not always been interpreted as a confirmation of the CPH, and other explanations have been tendered (Birdsong, 1999; Singleton & Ryan, 2004). Some of these draw attention to maturational constraints not associated with a critical period and others focus on nonbiological factors.

The role of L1

Bialystok maintains that L1 similarities and differences are more important for L2 attainment than AO, in the sense that 'the linguistic structure of our L1 sets important boundaries around subsequent linguistic structures that we attempt to learn' (Bialystok, 1997: 130). This was corroborated by Birdsong and Molis (2001) who, in their replication of Johnson and Newport's (1989) study, found evidence suggesting that the outcome of SLA may depend on L1–L2 pairings. Their study also pointed to a possible link between the amount of target language use and the level of proficiency. This is consistent with Abu-Rabia and Kehat's (2004) findings regarding L2 foreign accent. Nor does Flege consider the CPH to be the best explanation for the better pronunciation observed in younger learners. Instead, he claims that 'the L1 and L2 influence one another, and that this interaction constrains performance accuracy in both languages' (Flege, 1999: 108).

The environmental account

In another approach to L1 interference and transfer issues, Jia and colleagues (Jia & Aaronson, 2003; Jia *et al.*, 2006) explored the language preferences of Chinese immigrants to the United States. They found that the amount of rich language exposure they sought or received to either their L1 or L2 depended on their language preference as well as on a series of environmental factors, such as the language spoken by family and friends, and the language of the activities in which they engaged, the television they viewed and the books they read. The preference of earlier arrivals was shown to switch to the L2 sooner than it did for the later arrivals. As a consequence, the quality and quantity of L2 language exposure resulted in their greater proficiency.

The Universal Grammar (UG) perspective

Others have addressed the matter of age effects on SLA from the standpoint of UG theory (Cook, 1995; Martohardjono & Flynn, 1995; White & Genesee, 1996). The central question is whether the innate domain-specific faculty for language acquisition is still operative in the case of postpuberty SLA and, if so, whether parameters can be reset for the L2. The basic positions on the availability of UG for adult L2 learners are generally defined in terms of *full access, no access* and *partial access* (e.g. Skehan, 1998). Although this classification has been faulted for being overly simplistic (Eubank & Gregg, 1999), it illustrates the key UG approaches to the issue of age in SLA.

The position that full access to UG is not limited by age has obliged its supporters to provide an explanation for diminished attainment by older learners. Felix (1985) maintains that older learners have full access to UG, but suggests, in his 'competition model',[4] that the general problem-solving system available to postpuberty learners works in competition with UG, resulting in comparatively less success in SLA. This, he claims, is because problem-solving is an inadequate tool for processing more complex structures.

Those who hold the contrary position contend that poor achievement in SLA, as compared to L1 acquisition, can be explained by the fact that older learners no longer have access to UG, a view largely consistent with the CPH. Instead, according to Bley-Vroman's (1989) 'fundamental difference hypothesis', an essential distinction exists between L1 and L2 learning whereby older learners must resort to their L1 knowledge as an indirect source of knowledge about UG, as well as to general learning principles.

Among those who adopt a partial access position, some claim that the difficulty for older learners resides in resetting parameters for L2, for which they must rely on their L1 settings (Flynn, 1989; White, 1989). Others believe that UG is accessible to older L2 learners through their experience with L1, and that those principles not instantiated in the L1 remain available to them (Martohardjono & Flynn, 1995).

Classroom versus naturalistic settings

In her discussion of age effects on language acquisition, Muñoz (2006, 2008) makes an important distinction between naturalistic L2 contexts and foreign language classroom settings. Studies carried out in Catalonia and in the Basque Country (García Mayo & García Lecumberri, 2003; Muñoz, 2006, 2008) found that the limited amount of exposure to L2 that characterizes formal classroom instruction tends to favor older learners, who showed a faster rate of learning than younger ones. According to Muñoz, it is older learners' reliance on explicit learning mechanisms and their superior cognitive development and better test-taking abilities that enable them to outperform younger learners, who learn implicitly and thus require significant amounts of L2 input not normally available in classroom settings.

The role of cognitive, social and affective factors

The lack of any evidence demonstrating a discontinuity or sudden drop in language-learning ability at the end of the putative critical period is cited as a major flaw in the CPH by those who reject it (Bongaerts, 2005; Hakuta *et al.*, 2003; Singleton & Ryan, 2004). This has led to research that looks at noncritical period variables for an explanation of age-related effects on SLA. For example, lower end-state proficiency associated with a later AO has been attributed to declining cognitive abilities linked to the aging process (Bialystok & Hakuta, 1999; Birdsong, 2006; Singleton & Ryan, 2004). Others claim that distinct cognitive processes and styles are used to approach learning at different ages (Bialystok, 1997; Flynn & Manuel, 1991). Hakuta *et al.* (2003) found a significant connection between the level of education and ultimate attainment in L2.

A different interpretation of the age-related disparity in achievement in SLA is framed in terms of language aptitude components. Based on a study of L2 learners with different AOs, Harley and Hart (1997) found that verbal analytical ability is a predictor of success in adults whereas memory ability is in children. This is consistent with the view of DeKeyser (2000), who predicted that only those adults with a high level of verbal analytical ability would reach near-native competence, but that this would not be true of children. Findings in a recent study of near-native L2 speakers of Swedish led Abrahamsson and Hyltenstam (2008) to conclude that a high degree of language aptitude is an invariable component of native-like L2 proficiency, enabling exceptional adult learners to offset maturational constraints. For this reason, the authors contend that cases of near-native competence do not in themselves constitute compelling counter-evidence to the CPH.

In the matter of accent, Moyer (1999, 2004) suggests that the CPH alone cannot account for age-related differences found in pronunciation, and that further study of this problem should be expanded to include motivation and other sociopsychological factors as well as instructional variables, such as the type and extent of exposure to the L2. This is consistent with the environmental theory proposed by Jia and colleagues (Jia & Aaronson, 2003; Jia et al., 2006). In a similar vein, Leather (2003) points out that, because accent is a defining factor in social identity, phonological acquisition must be understood as both a social and a linguistic undertaking.

The extensive work by Dörnyei (see, e.g. Dörnyei, 2005, 2009) on motivation and individual differences in L2 development, as seen from a dynamic systems perspective, highlights the continuous interplay of learner characteristics, including age, with contextual or environmental factors. Other discussions of social and affective contributions to the acquisition of an L2, such as motivation and anxiety, abound in the literature. Their connection to the neurolinguistic aspects of SLA has been affirmed by Schumann (1997). Whether these social and psychological factors are believed to supplant the CPH or to work in tandem with maturational constraints as an explanation of varying learner outcomes is part of the ongoing debate.

Dynamic systems theory

De Bot and his collaborators (De Bot, 2008; De Bot & Makoni, 2005; De Bot & Schrauf, 2009) approach the age issue in L2 development from the standpoint of dynamic systems theory. From this perspective, both age and language are seen as systems consisting of subsystems and other interacting components, constantly changing in their interplay with cognitive, social, cultural and other environmental factors. L2 development is viewed as a nonlinear and dynamic process in which language and aging are linked and interact with multiple variables and subsystems both internal and external to the learner. The focus, rather than being on end-state attainment, is on the flux, growth and decline that characterize language proficiency at different points over the life span. In this sense, age is inexorably a part of L2 development, but one that is not easily separable from a cluster of other factors with which it is in a dynamic interaction throughout the life course.

Methodological issues

Other interpretations of the evidence revolve around the methods used in the research studies themselves. White and Genesee (1996) consider that the subject selection procedures and task types they employed in their study influenced the outcome. The artificiality of some types of tasks used to assess performance in other studies is questioned by Slavoff and Johnson (1995). They also point to the fact that age differences in test-taking ability are not controlled for in research studies, and that test training favors older learners. Marinova-Todd *et al.* (2000) criticize much of the existing research on the age factor in SLA because they believe that it taps differences in learning situations rather than learning capacity. Long (2005) identifies several design flaws in studies purporting to provide counter-evidence to the CPH, such as the instructions given to raters, the size of the language samples collected and the statistical interpretation of the data.

Birdsong (2005) questions the restricted focus of researchers on native-likeness as the principle criterion for judging L2 learner competence. He makes the point that 'the use of the monolingual native standard for falsification of the CPH is undermined by departures from monolingual nativelikeness that are artifacts of the nature of bilingualism' (Birdsong, 2005: 319). In a similar vein, both Cook (1995) and Harley *et al.* (1995) suggest that current research places undue emphasis on success, or product, rather than on possible differences in language processing mechanisms, thereby omitting an excellent source of valuable information. McDonald (2006), for example, found that L2 working memory capacity, decoding and processing speed better accounted for poor grammaticality judgment of late L2 learners than maturational constraints.

Finally, among supporters of the concept of a critical period, there is a general lack of agreement concerning the exact age at which it concludes. The commonly held belief among them is that puberty marks the end of the critical period, yet different researchers have set this as young as age 12 (Singleton, 1995), around 15 (Patkowski, 1980), over 16 (Weber-Fox & Neville, 1999) or 16–17 (DeKeyser, 2000), certainly too large an age span to be reliable in comparing the findings of different studies. For those who link the close of the critical period to cerebral lateralization, the evidence is also inconclusive, for it is now considered by some to occur much earlier in childhood than previously thought. Furthermore, there seem to be 'no known neurological correlates for a sudden decline in language ability at puberty' (Harley & Wang, 1997: 23). This has led some researchers to reject the notion that the critical period ends at puberty and to suggest instead that it is characterized by a gradual decline beginning as early as 6 or 7 for some language domains (Martohardjono & Flynn, 1995).

Multiple critical periods

In light of the complexity of the issues and the diversity of research findings, some researchers have adopted the multiple CPH proposed by Seliger (1978) and Long (1990). This theory maintains that there are distinct critical periods for different language domains, thereby providing an explanation for the apparent discrepancy between the age limit on the acquisition of phonology with respect to that of lexicon, for example. Scherag *et al.* (2004), in their study, found that while age constraints operate on certain aspects of SLA, others, such as semantic functions, remain intact. Other research findings consistent with this hypothesis are discussed by Singleton (1995, 1998, 2005) and Scovel (2000) in their critical overviews of the CPH. Eubank and Gregg (1999) suggest that 'language' is a cover term or an 'epiphenomenon' for a series of subcomponents, and that there may be one or more critical periods for the elements in it.

The state of the debate

It seems clear from the research findings to date concerning the age factor in SLA that a complete acceptance of the CPH is an untenable position. There is simply not enough neurobiological evidence to justify such a stance. Nor does the CPH provide a satisfactory explanation of how acquisition of an L2 does, in fact, occur after the critical period has ended. Yet it is plain that younger learners are generally better than older ones in the long run and in virtually all aspects of language performance, which lends some credence to the notion that maturational constraints are operating in some way. On the other hand, a total rejection of the CPH is difficult to sustain since no single factor or set of factors is able to completely account for these age-related differences in outcomes in nonbiological terms. Moreover, the general lack of success that characterizes SLA cannot be explained convincingly without providing reasons for the evidence of its unmistakable association with age. No such explanation has been forthcoming. It would appear, then, that the ramifications of the CPH for SLA are too complex to admit either such unembellished point of view.

Most recent research findings support a midway position in which age and biological factors are seen to have some degree of relationship to SLA, but not necessarily a causal one. In other words, a neurobiological program for human development is thought to exist, consisting of different stages that facilitate or constrain, but do not predetermine, the outcome of SLA. Ample evidence of this has been given in the studies of highly successful older learners. Yet the exact nature of the neurobiological component of the brain and how it exerts influence on human learning at different ages is far from being understood. A common viewpoint of SLA researchers advocating a weak version of the CPH is that the biological age factor operates in an attenuated way in conjunction with other factors, both internal and external to the learner. Harley suggests that 'a reasonable assumption on which to proceed is that second language acquisition involves a complex interplay of maturational and environmental factors of various kinds' (Harley, 2001: 635). Language aptitude, motivation, the relationship of the learner's L1 to the L2 and sociopsychological factors are among some that are considered in the studies described here, and have been seen to play a role in SLA (De Bot, 2008; De Bot & Schrauf, 2009; Dörnyei, 2005, 2009; Jia & Aaronson, 2003; Singleton, 2005). More than age, they are believed to be responsible for the variability in learner outcomes. However, not enough evidence exists at present to determine which of them are crucial to SLA, what their relative importance is, nor how they interact with each other. Part of the difficulty in resolving the debate is precisely the impossibility of isolating the age factor from these other variables.

To the extent that these issues continue to occupy the SLA research agenda, we can expect that more refined versions of the CPH as well as other competing accounts of age effects on language acquisition will be generated in the coming years that add to what is known about the age factor in SLA, as seen from a cognitive perspective.

Critical Assessment

As interesting as new developments in the CPH controversy may prove to be, the question remains whether this approach to the problem covers what can be learned about age and SLA, particularly adult language learning. I believe that it does not, and instead it offers only a limited perspective on the subject of age. I say this on the basis of the analysis carried out in the preceding section (see Table 1.1 for a brief summary of the studies discussed here). With few exceptions, the issues circumscribed by the CPH are concerned almost exclusively with child–adult differences in the ability to acquire an L2 (see 'AO or age of subjects' in Table 1.1). Such a binary distinction does not allow shades of difference to be sufficiently tapped. Because the concern is primarily with contrasting prepuberty and postpuberty learners, virtually no consideration is given to variations among adults of different ages, an area of obvious relevance to adult L2 learning, and to this book in particular, yet one that remains largely unexplored (but see De Bot & Makoni, 2005, for a treatment of multilingualism in older adults).

Certainly there is no incontrovertible evidence that a biologically determined critical period exists for adult L2 learners. If anything, maturational constraints operate in conjunction with a number of other affective, psychological and social factors. Moreover, to the extent that the issue of age differences among adult language learners receives any attention

TABLE 1.1 Pertinent studies of age effects on second language acquisition

Study	L1	L2	Language focus	AO or age of subjects
Oyama (1976, 1978)	Italian	English	Pronunciation/listening	AO = 6-20
Neufeld (1978)	English	Chinese/Japanese	Pronunciation	Adult
Patkowski (1980)	Various	English	Grammar	AO = ±15
Johnson and Newport (1989)	Korean/Chinese	English	Grammar	AO = 3-39
Birdsong (1992)	English	French	Grammar	AO = 11-28
Ioup et al. (1994)	English	Arabic	Overall proficiency	AO = (late); Age = adult
Flege et al. (1995)	Italian	English	Pronunciation	AO = 2-23
Harley et al. (1995)	Cantonese	English	Prosodic and syntactic processing	Age = 7-23
Singleton (1995)	English	French	Lexical proficiency	AO = ±12
Slavoff and Johnson (1995)	Various	English	Grammar	AO = 7-12
White and Genesee (1996)	French/other languages	English	Grammar	Age = 16-66
Bongaerts et al. (1997)	Dutch	English	Pronunciation	AO = 12+
Harley and Hart (1997)	English	French	Overall proficiency	AO = 5-12
Bongaerts (1999)	Dutch	English/French	Pronunciation	AO = 12+
Moyer (1999)	English	German	Pronunciation	AO = 11-27
Weber-Fox and Neville (1996, 1999)	Chinese	English	Semantic–syntactic processing	AO = 1-16 +

The Age Factor and Second Language Acquisition 17

Study	L1	L2	Area	Age
DeKeyser (2000)	Hungarian	English	Grammar	AO = 1–40
Birdsong and Molis (2001)	Spanish	English	Grammar	AO = 3–44
Hahne (2001)	Russian	German	Semantic–syntactic comprehension	AO = (late) Age = 21–34
García Lecumberri and Gallardo (2003)	Basque-Spanish	English	Pronunciation	AO = 4–11
García Mayo and García Lecumberri (2003)	Basque-Spanish/ Catalan-Spanish	English (L3)	Various aspects of proficiency	AO = 4–12
Hakuta et al. (2003)	Spanish/Chinese	English	Overall proficiency	AO = 1–60+
Jia and Aaronson (2003)	Mandarin	English	Overall proficiency	AO = 5–16
Abu-Rabia and Kehat (2004)	Various	Hebrew	Pronunciation	AO = 7–40
Moyer (2004)	Various	German	Pronunciation	AO = ±10
Scherag et al. (2004)	German	English German	Semantic–syntactic processing	AO = 10 +
Van Boxtel et al. (2005)	German, French, Turkish	Dutch	Grammar	AO = 12–35
McDonald (2006)	Various	English	Grammar	AO = 12+
Muñoz (2006)	Catalan-Spanish	English (L3)	Various aspects of proficiency	AO = 8–adult
Jia et al. (2006)	Mandarin	English	Perception/production	AO = 7–44
Abrahamsson and Hyltenstam (2008)	Spanish	Swedish	Overall proficiency	AO = 1–23
Mueller (2009)	German	Japanese	Semantic–syntactic processing	Age = 20–26

at all, the underlying assumption seems to be that aging is decremental, a supposition that reflects the discourse of decline[5] prevalent in contemporary Western culture, but one that thus far is not sustained by solid evidence.

A larger problem with the CPH studies is that age is invariably treated in chronological terms. Even those researchers who do not fully accept the biological determinism of the CPH and ascribe age-related differences to other factors connect them with chronological age. Such an essentialist notion of age can lead to a simplistic and unquestioned mode of categorizing people into groups by age-in-years or, more broadly, by life stages, that does not always dovetail with lived experience. Chronological age is not a reliable indicator of where a person is in the life course for, as Eckert points out, 'social and biological development do not move in lock step with chronological age, or with each other' (Eckert, 1997a: 154–155). Moreover, life stages, such as childhood, adolescence and middle age, are identified and defined differently from one culture to the next and from one moment in history to another. This explains in part why age can never be fully isolated from other social factors, such as gender, social class and ethnicity.

This stance is also consistent with the sociocultural perspective on SLA, one which gives greater prominence to social reality, in contrast to the mainstream cognitive strand of SLA, which has tended to neglect the social aspects of learning by focusing primarily on decontextualized cognitive processes. The principal thrust of research in the cognitive tradition has been on determining how individual learner factors, such as age, account for differential success among learners. The emphasis for the most part has been on universal properties of language and acquisition, on the formal aspects of language and on mental processes in the individual. The social side of language learning has largely been skirted by researchers adopting a psycholinguistic orientation to SLA. This is evident in the body of CPH research reviewed here (see 'language focus' in Table 1.1), which of necessity is grounded in cognitive-based theories of SLA. As a consequence, the contribution of the CPH and cognitive approaches is minimal at best in elucidating the social dimensions of L2 learning.

While recognizing the advances made in the field of SLA by research undertaken in the cognitive tradition, on balance I find that its limited scope has rendered it incapable of satisfactorily clarifying the social, dynamic and context-bound nature of SLA. In contrast, for SLA researchers working within a sociocultural framework, language learners are primarily social beings who engage in interaction and in the construction of their identities within the particular contexts of their social world (Hall, 1995; Larsen-Freeman, 2000; Larsen-Freeman & Long, 1991; Maguire & Graves, 2001; Norton, 2000; Toohey, 2000). The concerns of these researchers encompass both the linguistic and the nonlinguistic outcomes of the language-learning experience.

In sum, and given the aims of this book, I find a social constructionist view of age and a sociocultural perspective on SLA more adequate to the task. Furthermore, insofar as language is an active determinant of social identity, a study of narratives and social interaction can shed light on how people construct their age identity and experience the aging process. Accordingly, I propose this alternative path as a better way to explore the age factor and the acquisition of an L2 in adults, one which is able to reveal aspects about the interplay of age and the SLA experience not contemplated up to now.

Sociocultural Approaches to Second Language Acquisition

A parallel approach to cognitive-based SLA research, having as its source Hymes's pioneering work in sociolinguistics and anthropology, has taken up the analysis of the social and contextual aspects of language acquisition and use. It is to this tradition that I now turn my attention for it offers an excellent vantage point from which to appreciate the social dimensions of age in language learners. In essence, the social or sociolinguistic orientation to SLA regards the social context as assuming a key position in the language acquisition process, in view of the fact that acquisition invariably occurs in a social context. It focuses on language as a social and cultural phenomenon acquired and learned through social interaction. Since the early 1980s, an ever-growing number of SLA studies of an ethnographic nature have probed the interactional dimensions of language in an attempt to account for the processes underlying both SLA and use. Language learners are seen as social beings who actively participate in interactions with others in socially constituted communicative practices. According to Lantolf and Pavlenko, sociocultural theory 'moves individuals out of the Chomskian world of the idealized speaker-hearer and the experimental laboratory, and redeploys them in the world of their everyday existence, including real classrooms' (Lantolf & Pavlenko, 1995: 116).

In this sense, the sociocultural perspective is markedly different from mainstream cognitive approaches to SLA, in that the acquisition process is seen as originating in social interaction rather than in the individual mind. Consequently, the process of psychological development is considered to be embedded in and constructed through social interaction, impelling SLA researchers in the sociocultural tradition to seek possible links between social and cognitive concerns.

Approaches and Characteristics

The following are some of the key theories and ideas that have contributed in different ways to the sociocultural perspective on SLA, providing a framework that makes it possible to explore the social dimensions of learning a language more fruitfully.

Activity theory

Because of its interest in a more socially situated and linguistically mediated theory of cognition, the sociocultural tradition in SLA finds itself in harmony with much of 20th-century Soviet psychology. In Vygotsky's (1978, 1981) view, the mind is socially constituted, and higher forms of human mental activity are always mediated by symbolic means, the most important of these being language. Activity theory, inspired by the work of Vygotsky and articulated by his followers Leontiev and Luria, has been of particular importance in sociocultural explanations of the SLA process (Kramsch, 2000; Lantolf & Pavlenko, 1995, 2001; Lantolf & Thorne, 2006). From this perspective, the acquisition of language is believed to occur in much the same way as that of other higher mental functions, that is, external social knowledge is converted to internal cognitive knowledge. The following description of the development of L2 competence is based on Vygotskyan theory:

> Individual development begins in the social relationships both framing and framed by extended participation in our communicative practices, and proceeds from these to the psychological, that is, from intermental to intramental activity (Vygotsky, 1981). This movement from the social to the psychological is guided by assisted participation with other, more experienced participants. (Hall, 1997: 302)

Such assistance can take the form of scaffolding, modeling or training, and generally implies the presence of an expert. However, as Lantolf and Pavlenko (1995) point out, this can be obviated when individuals, none of whom is an expert, come together and collaborate, each person contributing something to, and taking something away from, the interaction. This is the idea behind peer-group work in the foreign language classroom. Ultimately, behaviors that were formerly executed conjointly become the psychological tools that mold the individuals' cognitive development.

Sociocognitive approaches

For Atkinson, language can never take on a completely internal mental function. He insists that 'although language may perhaps be seen from some points of view as more or less internalized and self-regulated – as the property of an individual, cognitive self – in actuality it always and everywhere exists in an integrated sociocognitive space' (Atkinson, 2002: 538). In his opinion and that of his colleagues, the social and cognitive aspects of language have developed concurrently and they operate interdependently and, very likely, inseparably (Atkinson, 2002; Atkinson et al., 2007).

In an attempt to bridge the gap between cognition and social action, they offer a social interpretation of connectionism.[6] From the connectionist point of view, meaning and knowledge exist only potentially in the human mind and rely for their formation on the activation of networks of neural associations, coming from past experience and embedded in a larger world of social significance. In any specific interaction, social products, practices and tools contribute to the realization of the speech event. Moreover, they contend that language acquisition, language use or even cognized linguistic knowledge cannot be properly understood unless their fundamental integration into a socially mediated world is taken into account, that is, mind, body and world are seen as linked in 'a continuous ecological circuit' (Atkinson et al., 2007: 170).

Language socialization research reveals similar interlocking ties between the social and cognitive aspects of language development. Traditionally investigating the interconnections between linguistic and cultural learning of children in different cultures, language socialization researchers are now looking at L2 learners. Their findings indicate that:

> Whether at home, in the classroom, at work, or in any number of other environments, language learners are embedded in and learn to become competent participants in culturally, socially, and politically shaped communicative contexts. The linguistic forms used in these contexts and their social significance affect how learners come to understand and use language. (Zuengler & Miller, 2006: 40)

The melding of language acquisition and use

Atkinson's notion of language and language acquisition as being constructed at the same time both 'in the head' and 'in the world' through interaction effectively blurs the sharp distinction made in the cognitive tradition between acquisition and use (see, e.g. Gass, 1998; Long, 1997). Most researchers adopting a sociocultural perspective tend to agree that the boundary between language learning and language use is disappearing (Firth & Wagner, 2007; Lantolf & Pavlenko, 1995). Similarly, Johnson (2004) contends that the Chomskyan notions of language competence and performance are not, in fact, divisible. In her model of SLA, based on Vygotsky's sociocultural theory and Bakhtin's dialogic view of language,[7] the origin of linguistic competence lies in language use, that is, language as it occurs in real social contexts. Thus, from her standpoint, no separation exists between language competence and language performance.

By the same token, Hall (1995, 1997) questions the very concept of 'second language acquisition', claiming that, from a sociohistorical perspective, it is inadequate in explaining how language is used and learned. Instead, she believes that because the acquisition process originates in socially constituted practices, individual development can never be understood apart from these practices. As she redefines it, the process of L2 development is 'one of becoming acculturated into these socially constituted webs of communicative practices' (Hall, 1997: 304). Concurring with Hall, Firth and Wagner call attention to the fallacy of the acquisition–use dichotomy in their initial treatment of central concepts in SLA research (1997) and then again in their more recent reflections on them (2007).

Such a stance on language acquisition and use leads logically to a further discussion of where then to set the boundaries of SLA as a discipline. Kasper, who argues for preserving the distinction between language acquisition and use, expresses concern that an open-ended position will undermine a clear and explicit definition of the aims of the field, by extending itself to such 'diverse endeavors as intercultural and cross-cultural communication, second language pedagogy, micro- and macrosociolinguistics with reference to second languages and dialects, societal and individual multilingualism, and SLA' (Kasper, 1997: 310). Yet an expanded agenda for SLA may be precisely what is needed, in the view of those, like Block (2003), who advocate a more socially informed approach to SLA. As Candlin comments:

> Thus, if we are to understand even partially the behaviour of learners in class, and appreciate their contributions, potential and actual, we need to explore a wider context, one which asks how the communicative practices in the crucial sites of classrooms relate to the practices in the crucial sites of the street, the workplace and the community. (Candlin, 2001: xx)

Such is the challenge to mainstream traditions presupposed by the sociocultural 'turn' in SLA.

Communities of practice

The notion of communities of practice is particularly helpful in understanding how learning, as an activity situated in specific circumstances, enables people to participate both in the contexts of their learning and in the larger social world in which these contexts are created. The term 'community of practice', first used by Lave and Wenger (1991), can be defined as a group of people who are bonded together by shared beliefs, values and ways of talking and acting, in the pursuit of a common goal. From the communities of practice perspective, rather than being given factual knowledge, learners themselves develop the necessary skills to perform by actually engaging in the process, that is, by participating with ever-increasing mastery in the sociocultural practices of a given community. Through the process called 'legitimate peripheral participation', newcomers move progressively toward full participation as members of a community of practice (Lave & Wenger, 1991).

Though not specifically concerned with language development, such a perspective is valuable for SLA in that it provides a broader view of learning as a complex social practice, a gradual process by which the learner becomes a member of a particular community of practice, learns to act accordingly and to communicate in the language of that community (Candlin, 2001; Norton, 2000; Pavlenko & Lantolf, 2000; Sfard, 1998), thereby adding the social dimension missing in mainstream cognitive approaches to SLA. Furthermore, because a multiplicity of relations operate within and between communities of practice, learning can best be understood in terms of the interconnections between persons, their actions and the larger world. It follows from this that issues of identity are accorded a central position in the sociocultural framework, for the learner is considered, in the broadest sense, to be a whole person participating in social interaction in the world. Lave and Wenger express it this way:

> Learning thus implies becoming a different person with respect to the possibilities enabled by these systems of relations. To ignore this aspect of learning is to overlook the fact that learning involves the construction of identities. (Lave & Wenger, 1991: 53)

In this wide-ranging conceptualization, learning always entails 'participation in relationship and community and transformation of both the person and of the social world' (Packer & Goicoechea, 2000: 239). Thus, learning signifies an ontological change, not just an epistemological one, in the sense that it brings about a restructuring of the person's identity in the process. Moreover, because learners' identities are multiple, they extend well beyond the classroom to other communities of practice.

Overview

In sum, I would argue that sociocultural theory and the concept of communities of practice offer a valuable alternative perception of L2 development that, while still in a relatively preliminary stage, is a radical departure from current mainstream SLA theory. From this viewpoint, the L2 learning process involves 'the copresence of intra- and interpsychological activity, environments with histories, and an ongoing negotiation of social identity' (Thorne, 2000: 224), and is grounded in a reinterpretation of the traditional notions of language, learning, interaction and context. Table 1.2 highlights the key points of departure between sociocultural and cognitive approaches to SLA.

TABLE 1.2 Points of difference between sociocultural and cognitive approaches to SLA

Sociocultural approaches to SLA	Cognitive approaches to SLA
• A foregrounding of the social over the individual	• An overriding interest in mental processes as an individual phenomenon
• A view of language as constructed socially and constructive of social reality	• A view of language largely focused on form
• A theory of communication as a coconstructed and negotiated social process	• A reliance on the transmission model of communication
• An understanding of cognition as relational, emerging from joint mediated activity and sociocultural practices that are historically and contextually situated within communities of practice	• A marked concern with universal properties of language and acquisition
• A conception of learning as change, a mutual transformation of the person and the social world, that brings about the construction of identities	• A static treatment and isolation of learner variables
• A dynamic view of context as integral to and constituted by human activity	
• An emphasis on the interdependence of language, interaction and context	• A relative lack of attention to social context

The Age Factor in the Sociocultural Perspective

Before concluding, I now return to the treatment of age in the sociocultural paradigm, where it appears as one of the individual learner attributes involved in the SLA process. However, in contrast to the traditional psycholinguistic stance, these individual characteristics take on significance only insofar as they are played out in social interaction within specific contexts (Block, 2003; Breen, 2001b; Pavlenko, 2002b). Rather than being considered separate and fixed background variables, learner attributes such as age, gender, class and ethnicity are held to be socially constructed and are interconnected in complex ways in the enactment of identity. Increasingly, issues of identity have come to occupy a prominent place in socially oriented SLA research, as an outcome of:

> a general push to open up SLA beyond its roots in linguistics and cognitive psychology. As a result of this pressure to open up SLA, it became

easy for some applied linguists to see links between theorisations of identity in social theory and sociology and the learning of languages. The result has been the aforementioned boom in publications linking identity and SLA. (Block, 2007: 864)

Nevertheless, it is important to point out that age has not been the focus of SLA research undertaken thus far from the sociocultural perspective, whereas other related learner characteristics, such as gender and ethnicity, have been the subject of studies carried out by competent scholars (see, e.g. Norton, 2000; Toohey, 2000). By looking to this research as a source for the study of age, it is hoped that the gap can be filled.

Conclusion

The age factor within mainstream cognitive-based SLA theory has been treated as an individual learner attribute, largely a fixed, biological or chronological variable. The core issue for researchers in the cognitive tradition is whether or not a critical period for learning an L2 exists. The debate surrounding this issue has been a lively one over the years and has generated an important body of literature, yet as the discussion in the first part of the chapter indicates, no definitive or irrefutable conclusions have emerged. More importantly, the CPH has not been concerned with variations among adults of different ages. Neither the CPH, in particular, nor cognitive approaches to SLA, in general, has addressed the social dimensions of age or L2 learning.

Sociocultural approaches to SLA are more pertinent to the aims of this book, for the reasons outlined in the final part of the chapter. Hall makes the following observation:

> Serious consideration of the premises of a sociocultural approach to SLA will lead us to contemplate new issues, and thus engage us in explorations of both theoretical and empirical regions that to date have gone largely unnoticed by a majority of us in the SLA field. Such pursuits, at the very least, should prove to be both stimulating and profitable. (Hall, 1997: 306)

This is the challenge I wish to take up with respect to age. In the specific context of the study of the social dimension of age in L2 learners of English, such an approach offers the promise of:

- A broader understanding of language learning as an experience that leads to both linguistic and nonlinguistic outcomes.
- An awareness of the learner as a complex person who lives in and participates in a world extending far beyond the classroom.

Notes

(1) According to some authors (e.g. White & Genesee, 1996), the hypothesis was first proposed by Penfield and Roberts (1959) and then developed more fully by Lenneberg.
(2) Lateralization is the process by which the two hemispheres of the brain become progressively more specialized for particular functions, such as language.
(3) The terms 'age on arrival' (AA or AOA), 'age of immersion', 'age of exposure' and 'age of initial acquisition' have also been employed to refer to the moment when contact with the L2 begins. For the sake of consistency, 'age of onset' (AO) is used in this book.
(4) This is not to be confused with the Competition Model proposed by MacWhinney (1998).
(5) The issue of decline discourses is addressed more comprehensively in Chapter 3.
(6) Connectionism is a cognitive approach to learning that veers from the traditional nativist course of symbolic models of cognition. Rather than being located in a single place, information is thought to be distributed throughout various parts of the brain, in networks of interconnections. Although not specifically restricted to language learning, connectionism offers a set of computational tools for understanding language acquisition as an emergent process (Ellis, 1998; MacWhinney, 1998).
(7) For Bakhtin, every utterance is the product of a 'dialogue' between the existing social uses of language and the new meaning created in the act of communication.

2 Present-Day Approaches to the Study of Age

Introduction

Framing age as social is consistent with recent trends in contemporary sociolinguistics that have brought more dynamic approaches to the study of language and the sociocultural context within which discursive interaction takes place. More precisely, discourse-oriented sociolinguistics has been at the vanguard of research addressing issues of social interaction, discourse and identity from a social constructionist perspective. This chapter begins by examining some of the philosophical and historical underpinnings of social constructionism that have particular relevance for the study of age. This is followed by a brief overview of recent work in sociolinguistics on the social dimensions of ethnicity, gender and social class, and attention is drawn to the treatment of age by sociolinguists. I argue that by shedding light on the way meaning is constructed through interaction, how people situate themselves in the context of their social relationships and what the local and historical framework contributes to the process, contemporary sociolinguistic work on social parameters provides a meaningful precedent for exploring age as socially constructed.

Social Constructionism

A Panoramic View

Social constructionism is a perspective on reality, a way of looking at ourselves and at the world. Simply put, reality is seen as constructed through discursive interaction. This perspective is situated in counter-position to the traditional 'picture theory of language' or 'mirror' metaphor, whereby the mind is presumed to reflect the world as it is (Gergen, 1999; Potter, 1996). For the constructionist, the world is not simply something that is found 'out there', but is what we make of it through language. In other words, language is the key to shaping and creating our social world rather than a means for merely describing phenomena thought to exist independently of us. The centrality of language and social interaction to the constructionist framework means that knowledge and understanding are grounded historically and culturally.

Social constructionists challenge many long-held assumptions about reality, such as Enlightenment beliefs in the individual mind, rationality, objectivity and truth. They contest the modern Western idea that knowledge of the world 'as it really exists' can be achieved through objective, scientific and empirical methods. Likewise, they reject the grand narratives of the past in favor of local narratives, in which claims to truth are more cautious and restrained. At the same time, social constructionists object to the focus on the individual as knowing, rational and autonomous, as well as to the sharp distinction made between the social and the natural, which they contend has become increasingly permeable as a result of the growth of techno-science. Such viewpoints position present-day social constructionism within the postmodern movement.

Key Themes

The following themes – the relational focus, language and discourse, dialogue, identity and narration – have special relevance to the social constructionist perspective in sociolinguistic research and specifically to the present discussion of age. For that reason, I have singled them out for further discussion, albeit briefly.

The relational focus

Social constructionism downplays individualism, in sharp contrast to the contemporary Western stance that places primacy on the individual. While recognizing that human beings live and behave in social contexts, the individualist tradition has focused initially on the self-contained individual in order to understand the human mind and its workings, and then, in consequence, the social world. Social constructionists reject the dichotomy between the individual and society that has permeated such traditional thinking. They deny that the individual can be artificially dissociated from the social, instead contending that human beings are 'the social', that is, both individual and society at the same time. As 'relational integers' (Gergen, 1996, 1999), people are part of a more collaborative vision of human life, one in which each of us is both constituted by and constitutes the other.

From this perspective, society is essentially relational in character in that it does not consist either of collectivities of individuals or of individuals, but is concerned with the relations between people. In the final analysis, the relational focus is an attempt to bridge the gap between self and other. This focus is important for the present discussion because it gives greater prominence to persons as social beings, participating in dynamic and mutually constituting relationships. In this sense, the construction of age is not an individual achievement but the outcome of the active collaboration of people in interaction with each other.

Language and discourse

The social constructionist movement is sustained by the belief that human social life is produced through discursive interaction. Discourse, the principal instrument of the social construction of reality, is generally conceived of as language in use, that is, language linked to situated action (see e.g. Austin, 1962; Blommaert, 2005; Gee, 2001, 2005; McCarthy & Carter, 1994; Schiffrin, 1994). Languages are used to categorize or classify our experience of the world; however, the world is not previously categorized for us. Instead it is constituted by people as they are involved in the process of performing actions through language in interaction with each other. People categorize or give things a specific sense, both fashioning and sharing their understanding of social phenomena. According to Burr:

> Through our linguistic exchanges with each other in our routine daily lives we construct and re-construct the concepts, categories and objects with which we are familiar. They form a kind of common currency with which we can meaningfully deal with other people who share the same culture. (Burr, 1997: 4)

Discourse, then, provides a framework that enables people to construct the phenomena of their world and to make sense of their lives and their personal experience. Different discourses do this in different ways. Alternatively called interpretive repertoires, they are available to speakers as resources, but are 'transindividual', in that they exist in a linguistic community rather than in particular people (Burr, 2003; Parker, 1992).

Gee (2001, 2005, 2008) sees discourse not only as connecting language to embodied experience and to situated action ('little d' discourse), but also as ultimately linked to the enactment of identity, in a broader understanding of the term ('big D' Discourse). He explains the latter notion this way:

> A Discourse integrates ways of talking, listening, writing, reading, acting, interacting, believing, valuing (and using various objects, symbols, images, tools, and technologies) in the service of enacting meaningful socially situated identities and activities. (Gee, 2001: 719)

In this sense, he suggests that the term 'Discourse'[1] closely parallels 'community of practice', 'actor–actant network' and 'activity system', in that, with minor differences, all refer to a set of relations among a group of people and the various ways in which they are bonded together through shared goals, values, beliefs, practices and activities (Gee, 2001).

The notion of discourse, in both its narrow and broad interpretations, is pertinent to the consideration of age as a social dimension on two accounts. First, it is through language-in-action or discursive interaction that age is constructed and given meaning. Second, age identity is enacted by recurring to available cultural discourses in particular sociohistorical contexts. This idea is developed more fully in Chapter 3.

Dialogue

It is in dialogue that relational being and discourse are joined. As Gergen puts it, 'there is a sense in which dialogue serves as the key organizing metaphor for social constructionist theory' (Gergen, 1999: 147). People construct understandings collaboratively through dialogue, and these understandings are shaped by the social and cultural context of the interaction. The work of Bakhtin (1981, 1986) has been indispensable in uncovering the intricacies of dialogue. He sees meaning as engendered through dialogue, a dialogue that takes place in a specific historical and cultural context. Each time people speak they draw on the existing language of their culture, yet at the same time language is dynamic; consequently the meanings of words and utterances change each time they are used. In this sense, utterances are double-voiced, deriving their significance both from the past and from the present context. Dialogue is central to the way in which the construction of age and other social dimensions is collaboratively accomplished against a particular sociocultural backdrop.

Identity

The social construction of identity is treated in some detail in Chapter 3. Therefore, in order not to be unduly repetitive, I wish to highlight only two key points important to the study of age that have grown out of the considerations made thus far in the discussion on social constructionism. The first is that identity is the outcome of social relations. Burr suggests that our identity arises out of interactions with other people and is based on language, that is, 'our identity is constructed out of the discourses culturally available to us, and which we draw upon in our communications with other people' (Burr, 2003: 106). Identity, then, can only be constructed within relationships, and all relationships are constrained by the specific cultural, social and linguistic conditions which are in existence at any given moment.

The second point is that socially constructed identity has a dynamic, changeable and multiple character. This outlook is in counter-position to essentialist views of identity as static, monolithic and in great measure predetermined. Gergen remarks:

> In the present context we concentrate on fluidity, the ways in which precisely who one is depends on the moment-to-moment movements in

conversation. Here we understand identity as precariously situated, subject to subtle shifts of word, intonation, and gesture. There is no final fixing of this process, as pragmatic uses are continuously evolving in society. (Gergen, 1999: 80)

Hence, people are involved in the ongoing, flexible and dynamic process of identity construction throughout their lifetimes. This view of identity, as dynamic, flexible, multiple and negotiated in discursive interaction, provides the groundwork for the study of age identity on which this book is based.

Narration
Narration is a core theme in social constructionism and one that is closely tied to the shaping of identity. Having found abstract, objectivist and empiricist approaches less than satisfactory in understanding the world, constructionists have turned to narrative approaches to elucidate human action and experience through storytelling. People have used narratives to make sense of their lives and themselves throughout history, structuring their experience in terms of stories. The role of narrative in identity construction is vital. 'We are often called upon to "tell our story", to recount our past, to identify where we have been and where we are going' (Gergen, 1999: 70). Thus, the self is seen in a certain sense as an ongoing narrative project (Giddens, 1991). The ability of human beings to create stories or narratives about themselves and their world offers countless possibilities to researchers working in a variety of disciplines to learn about the social construction of reality and of identity. Narratives play a fundamental role in the construction of age and age identity in this book, for the participants in the study recount events from their lives and share their experiences through stories.

Further Reflections

Social constructionists take the position that there are multiple, historically and culturally specific accounts of reality, all relative to each other, but no 'objective' basis for considering any one version to be more valid than any other. Yet, the multiple versions of reality are necessarily constructed from the specific perspective of those engaged in discourse. People come to know the world and understand their experiences through social practices, in effect agreeing on and constructing versions of what is 'real' or 'true' in their particular historical and cultural situations. At the same time, to the extent that they have agency, they are able to analyze critically the discourses which frame their lives, and to accept and reject them.

The openness to alternative orientations and the questioning of one's own traditions, approached reflectively, may be one of the most important benefits obtained from adopting a social constructionist perspective. This is among the reasons that many contemporary sociolinguists have found social constructionism to be particularly compatible with their research interests. By looking at key social dimensions such as social class, gender, ethnicity and now age, as social constructs, it has been possible to explore them in greater depth than that permitted by a descriptive perspective. Both social constructionists and discourse-oriented sociolinguists place substantial emphasis on the centrality of language, discursive interaction and the ongoing negotiation of meaning. Likewise, the social constructionist view of reality as historically and culturally situated is well suited to current trends in sociolinguistics that focus research on local, sociocultural contexts. Constructionist interest in the role of narration in the enactment of identity is another theme actively taken up by present-day sociolinguistics. Thus, the social constructionist perspective offers a basis from which to work that is clearly harmonious with the outlook and research interests of many contemporary sociolinguists, hence explaining why it has been embraced so wholeheartedly by them.

Recent Perspectives in Sociolinguistics on the Study of Social Dimensions

Sociolinguistics is concerned with the relationship of language and society. Within this broad field, the anthropological tradition, often referred to as 'ethnography of communication', harbors a number of loosely connected and overlapping research orientations, including discourse analysis, ethnomethodology, conversational analysis and interactional sociolinguistics (Mesthrie et al., 2000; Moreno Fernández, 1998). Of particular interest to the present study are discourse-oriented approaches to sociolinguistics, primarily those whose aim is to provide a 'micro description of the lived texture of situated experience' (Rampton, 2006).

Discourse-Oriented Approaches

The central concern of discourse-oriented sociolinguistics is on the way meaning is constructed and negotiated in discursive interaction. In the last several years, this strand has assumed a position of considerable prominence in the field of sociolinguistics. This has come about, in part, because many sociolinguists have changed their focus to the study of small group interaction in order to see how 'culture and social reality are both reproduced and created anew in the skilled activity of actors drawing on unevenly distributed resources in locally and historically specific circumstances' (Rampton, 2001: 279). This has signified a modification in their view of language, speech now considered only one element that contributes to meaning in the larger framework of communication. Moreover, the ongoing construction of meaning occurs through what Rampton calls 'a process of here-and-now inferencing' (Rampton, 2000: 105). Thus, the emphasis is on situated action and experience, in which the local and historical contexts are understood to play a constitutive role in communication. The impact this change of focus has had on methodology has been a turning away from long-established correlational studies toward more bottom-up, ethnographic descriptions of situated activity. At the same time, the research focus on language and social interaction located in specific contexts has given rise to a more relativist approach to theory, consistent with the breakdown of the grand narratives and the emphasis on diversity prevalent in postmodern approaches to other social sciences.

Furthermore, the question of how people position themselves in the context of their social relationships has brought the issue of identity to the forefront in recent sociolinguistic work. Identity is no longer seen as static inclusion in a social group whose defining characteristics determine those of its members but rather as something more fluid and variable, shaped through social interaction, and the outcome of a process of social construction. The social constructionist approach to identity is a key theme in contemporary sociolinguistics. It is in communicative interaction that people actively 'construct and project desirable versions of their identities, in a succession of performances targeted at specific audiences' (Jaworski & Coupland, 1999: 407). Social categories, such as social class, sex, age and ethnicity or nationality, conventionally considered to constitute an individual's identity, are now being redefined in more dynamic and flexible terms. Cameron, in referring to gender, explains:

> Whereas sociolinguistics traditionally assumes that people talk the way they do because of who they (already) are, the postmodernist approach suggests that people are who they are because of (among other things) the way they talk. (Cameron, 1999: 444)

The emphasis is on the process, on the performative aspect of identity construction, as well as on its flexibility and variability.

Studies of Ethnicity, Gender and Social Class

Three areas that have been treated in sociolinguistics research on identity construction are ethnicity, gender and, to a lesser extent, social class. Discourse-oriented and interactional sociolinguistics, particularly, have provided valuable ways to explore the intricacies of these social dimensions. The studies described below offer insights that can help clarify our understanding of the social construction of age identity. Moreover, because age identity is closely tied to and nuanced by these social dimensions, it is useful to give them some consideration.

Ethnicity

Ethnicity has rightly been called one 'of the most vexed and complex issues in post-colonial theory' (Ashcroft et al., 1995: 213). Part of the reason that it is such a difficult concept to elucidate is because of the interplay of the many characteristics associated with it. In different contexts and at different historical moments, factors such as shared heritage, language, language use, nationality, geographical boundaries, race and religion are used to characterize ethnicity. Yet no single or universal factor is present in all ethnic groups. At best we can venture to say that ethnicity refers to a sense of peoplehood or of belonging to a group that is defined and negotiated by both self and others, and by those both inside and outside the group. Precisely because of the changing sociohistorical context, the flexible and constructed nature of the traits which characterize a person's ethnicity, and the salience it may have in a given situation or interaction, ethnicity is more usefully considered in processual terms, as socially constructed.

The work of a number of prominent sociolinguists provides examples of different approaches to the construction of ethnic identity. Blackledge and Pavlenko, for instance, have both done extensive research on the negotiation of ethnic or national identities in multilingual settings by linguistic minority speakers (see e.g. Blackledge, 2002; Blackledge & Pavlenko, 2001; Pavlenko, 2001b). They argue that sociopsychological approaches, which regard identities as stable and unchangeable and view language users as members of homogeneous groups, no longer have credibility in the complex multiethnic world of today (Blackledge & Pavlenko, 2001). In cases where the dominant group in a heterogeneous society considers monolingualism or monoethnicity to be the ideal model for that society, questions of social justice are raised 'as such an ideology potentially excludes and discriminates against those who are either unable or unwilling to fit the norm' (Blackledge & Pavlenko, 2001: 243).

In an analysis of a single newspaper article published in Great Britain, Blackledge makes exactly this point, demonstrating how 'homogenization of news media contributes to the legitimation of the established order' (Blackledge, 2002: 68). In a different study, Pavlenko (2001b) explored the way in which contemporary American writers, for whom English is an L2, negotiate their identities in autobiographical narratives. The work of Blackledge and Pavlenko has helped corroborate their contention that 'the ideological assertion that one language equals one culture or one nation ignores the complexity of multilingual societies' (Blackledge & Pavlenko, 2001: 253).

In a study of Austrian national identity, Wodak et al. found that a diversity of discursive identity constructs were used to establish either 'intranational sameness and/or differences with other nations' (Wodak et al., 1999: 188). The emphasis on either sameness or difference as identity options varied according to the political and ideological orientations of the discourse, ranging from fully public to quasi-private contexts.

Schilling-Estes (2004) carried out research in a rural triethnic (Native American, African American and southern White) community in southern United States, in which she incorporated localized practice, in the form of a sociolinguistic interview, into a large-scale quantitative investigation on language use. Her in-depth analysis of the dialogue between the interviewer and interviewee reveals how ethnic identity is jointly constructed in ongoing discursive interaction. Moreover, ethnic identity is shown to be multifaceted, dynamic and not easily separable from an individual's other identities.

The diversity and flexibility of ethnic identity is also a central topic of Rampton's (1995, 2001, 2006) work in England. In a pioneering study of language 'crossing'[2] among adolescents of Indian, Pakistani, African Caribbean and Anglo descent in a working-class neighborhood, he examined the 'ways in which people use language and dialect in discursive practice to appropriate, explore, reproduce or challenge influential images and stereotypes of groups to which they **don't** themselves (straightforwardly) belong' (Rampton, 1999: 421, emphasis as in original). This study and other recent work on ethnicity highlight the complex and often unpredictable ways in which people use language to enact their ethnic, racial and other identities. Ethnicity forms an interesting part of the complex of identities of some of the participants in the study on which this book is based.

Gender

The study of the social construction of gender has also generated an impressive body of work, echoing many of the same themes that appear in research on ethnicity. Central to these studies is the distinction between 'sex' and 'gender', the former understood as a biological determinant denoting anatomical or physiological differences between men and women, and the latter referring to the sociocultural dimensions of human male and female persons, that is, the psychological, social and cultural differences between them. Femininity and masculinity are not seen as polar opposites, but rather as separate dimensions existing in the same person. Nor is there a single set of traits that epitomize masculinity or femininity; they are not monolithic constructs. Instead, a great diversity is to be found among men and women (Cameron, 2005; Mesthrie *et al.*, 2000).

Because information about a person's sex is normally readily observable, whereas analyzing the social construction of gender is infinitely more complex, the biological category of sex has conventionally been used in sociolinguistic studies in place of the more comprehensive, multifaceted one of gender. However, some researchers, who consider that working with fixed, *a priori* categories, such as sex, often leads to a superficial understanding of sociolinguistic phenomena, have opted to explore the nuances of gendered identity by looking at how it is constructed in social interaction, and how this construction is interconnected with speakers' other identities.

As with ethnicity, the construction of gender identity is seen as performance rather than a state of being (Butler, 1990). We perform gender identity by the repetition of acts that are associated with cultural norms of 'masculinity' and 'femininity'. Gender construction, or 'doing gender', varies broadly according to the social contexts in which women and men find themselves. Hence, people perform gender differently, availing themselves of different strategies, depending on whether they are with people of the same or different sex, in a formal or informal situation, in a public or private setting and on the nature of the social relationships they have with the other persons involved, among other possibilities (Cameron, 1999).

Social constructionist approaches to gender illustrate the way people construct and reinforce specific social identities through language. In the 1980s, Eckert (1988) carried out an ethnographic study of student culture in a Detroit high school, with a view to correlating instances of phonological variation with differences in social category. She singled out two principal peer groups, the 'jocks', middle-class students who identify with the institutional life of the school, and the 'burnouts', working-class students oriented toward local values. Although the original study did not focus on gender issues, as such, the extensive amount of information that was generated regarding gender construction allowed Eckert and McConnell-Ginet (1995) to reexamine the data at a later date in order to look at gender, class and power relations and how they are mutually constructed. They concluded that gender identity is constructed differently for each group, and that the relationship between gender and language variation is not a simple one, nor is that between social class and gender (Eckert, 1997b; Eckert & McConnell-Ginet, 1995).

The social construction of gender identity in fraternity men was the subject of a study by Kiesling (1998), who investigated the use of the vernacular (ING) variant to local identity construction, against the backdrop of larger cultural and community ideologies. Like Eckert and McConnell-Ginet, Kiesling acknowledges the centrality of power to masculine identity, pinpointing two cultural models as the source of male identity construction: the physically powerful, or working-class, cultural role and the structurally, or socioeconomically, powerful cultural role. His analysis revealed higher rates of the vernacular variant use among men having the working-class model and confrontational stances as part of their identity displays. He concluded that hegemonic masculinity impels men to construct powerful identities in which they actually or symbolically dominate others. In the case of working-class men, physical power is a substitute for the economic or structural power they do not have access to, and the use of vernacular language is commonly associated with this model of masculine identity.

Holmes (1997) looked at the construction of women and men's identities in a different context, that of New Zealand. One of her studies provides an illustration of how people use language not only to symbolize and construct their social identities but also to convey their compliance with or rejection of traditional norms and values. She emphasizes that the process of identity construction involves making choices based on an understanding of what these choices signify in a particular social context. In the first case, a woman constructs a very conventional gender identity in an everyday conversation with a friend. On one level, it is an unremarkable narrative description of her day's events. But on another level, through the narrative she presents herself as a good mother and a good daughter, constructing a predominantly conservative identity that conforms to society's notions about the way women should behave. In this particular instance, when the woman talks to a conventional and rather judgmental friend, she highlights a conservative aspect of her gender identity. However, in other contexts and with other participants, she may construct a very different identity. In a more recent study, Holmes and Schnurr (2006) examined the various ways in which working women not only perform conventional femininity but also parody and contest gendered expectations and suppositions in the workplace.

An ethnographic study of British high school students' classroom talk was carried out by Baxter (2003) to determine the extent to which institutional assessment of 'effective' talk was based on criteria associated with stereotypically masculine speech. Her feminist poststructuralist discourse analysis of the data indicated that a wide range of masculinities and femininities are constructed both by the students and by their teachers, based on prevalent local and global gender discourses. She found that the type of speaker likely to be judged as effective by peers, teachers and evaluators is 'one who is male, popular, and articulate, equally versatile in their use of the approved model of collaborative talk and the more "commanding" talk defined by the examination syllabus' (Baxter, 2003: 123). She also noted that the range of subject positions available to girls is limited because in conventional institutional discourses, boys are more easily conceived of as speakers in public settings than girls, who are expected to constitute a willing and attentive audience.

Several recurrent themes appear in these and other gender studies. To highlight only three: first, gender is diverse; there are significant differences not only between male and female identities but also between members of the same sex in the manner in which these identities are constructed. Indeed, the same person may display a variety of gender identities, depending on the contextual and interactional exigencies. Second, gender is interconnected with an individual's other identities. As with other social parameters, such as ethnicity or social class, it is infinitely complex in its interaction with all the other variables. Nor is gender always salient in every interaction; it fluctuates in accordance with the specific conversational context. Finally, in viewing gender as performance, it is important to emphasize that people construct their identities within the constraints of social and cultural norms, that is to say, individuals are not predetermined to act in a set, gender-specific manner, but rather are able to take into consideration the social significance linked to particular ways of speaking and acting and to choose among them according to their purpose. Gender played a much more crucial role in its interplay with age and other social dimensions in the identity construction of all of the participants in the study I undertook than originally anticipated.

Social class

If ethnicity is a knotty concept with which to contend, then grappling with that of social class is equally problematic. Labels, such as working class, middle class and upper class, have been used in distinct contexts to assess the 'worth' or position of people or groups relative to each other. Inherently 'a general principle of inequality' (Collins & La Santa, 2006: 9), social class involves positioning people or groups on a higher-to-lower 'prestige' continuum. The factors that serve as a basis for determining social class may include wealth, occupation, educational background, place of residence, language use and habits of consumption, among others. Again, like ethnicity, people rank themselves and others on the basis of a particular combination of these factors, and their relative weight, all of which are highly sensitive to the values and beliefs prevailing in local contexts.

Bourdieu's (1977) concept of symbolic capital is useful in comprehending the socially constructed and variable nature of social class. Symbolic capital encompasses three different forms of capital: economic capital (wealth, economic resources), cultural capital (knowledge, skills, education) and social capital (connections to others in social networks). The degree to which these capitals are valued is contingent on the social field[3] in which they are found. The symbolic capital that an individual has as a resource is understood as the prestige or status that comes from having acquired capital that is recognized or legitimized by others, be it economic, cultural or social, or a combination of these. People are positioned as superior or inferior to each other in a given field or context according to their relative symbolic capital. This idea works well with a view of social class as situated, flexible and constructed.

Social class as an identity inscription has received little direct attention in identity research, which has centered on the social dimensions of race, gender and ethnicity. Certainly, work focusing solely on social class is exceptional in contemporary sociolinguistics. Yet, social class is contemplated in many studies as part of the background or context, an assumed feature, although seldom addressed directly.

In the research described above, the close connection between social class and the enactment of both ethnic and gender identities manifests itself most plainly in the studies of urban youth (Rampton, 1995, 2001, 2006), 'jocks' and 'burnouts' (Eckert & McConnell-Ginet, 1995) and fraternity men (Kiesling, 1998). Rampton's work on language crossing pointed up the ways in which working-class adolescents switched into exaggerated posh and Cockney accents to accomplish a variety of social functions that reproduced their own social class and ethnic identities against the backdrop of the British class structure. In their study, Eckert and McConnell (1995) found that the 'jocks' and 'burnouts', two peer groups attending the same high school, operated in distinct social fields. Both social class and gender had a bearing on the types of cultural and social capital that were prized in each field. Similarly, Kiesling's study (1998) of fraternity men revealed the way in which power, as symbolic capital, took two different forms along social class lines, one physical and the other socioeconomic.

In a recent study, Preece (2009) looked at the enactment of social class and gender identities in multilingual university students from working-class black and minority backgrounds in London. Speaking about the construction of masculine identities, Preece noted that for many of the male students, 'laddish practices seemed to bestow status, expertise, sociability and a sense of well-being' (Preece, 2009: 130). These practices included resisting any overt identification with the norms of the academic community. In a different way, the female students chose to dissociate themselves from scholarly performance by striving to appear unexceptional and inconspicuous or by adopting a flippant 'ladette' femininity. The reinforcement of social class identity was clearly a factor in the establishment of important peer group networks among this population, although it was enacted differently by the female and the male students. For both genders, the accumulation of social capital took precedence over the cultural capital to be derived from academic performance.

Social class, and its associated symbolic capital, proved to be an important dimension in the identities of the adult Mexicans who participated in the study described in this book. The data (see Chapters 4 through 6) lend support to my contention that learning English signifies, above all else, acquiring cultural capital for this population. Social capital also emerged as a significant factor in the identity construction of both younger and older participants. In the course of the research, it became evident that social class is inextricably tied to gender, ethnicity and age. This is not surprising when considered in light of the studies discussed in this section.

Discourse-oriented sociolinguistic studies of gender, ethnicity and social class help illustrate how social constructionist approaches have enabled researchers to explore identity issues in greater depth than before. This leads to the conclusion that age identity can also be considered more meaningfully as a social construct.

Sociolinguistic Approaches to Age

Age as a sociolinguistic dimension has generated only mild interest over the years. Although age has routinely been included along with social class and gender as one of the three principal demographic categories used in studies of linguistic variation, it has seldom been accorded a central place in sociolinguistic research, unlike ethnicity and gender. It appears in sociolinguistic studies chiefly because it may reveal dialectal variation within speech communities over apparent time. In these studies, age is invariably expressed in chronological terms, measured as an accumulation of years since birth, a trademark of our industrial society in which a societal dating system determines a person's place in the society. The fact that social and biological development do not always coincide with chronological age is acknowledged in the main, yet it is chronological age that counts as valid in Western industrialized society, although not necessarily in others. In an era where gender roles are more fluid, and it is possible for people to move from one social class to another in the course of their lifetime, age has essentially remained a fixed, inflexible category.

Eckert (1997a, 1997b) was among the first to recognize the limitations of using chronological age in sociolinguistic studies, and to explore alternatives for defining age categories and grouping age cohorts. 'The age continuum is commonly divided into equal chunks with no particular attention to the relation between these chunks and the life stages that make age socially significant' (Eckert, 1997b: 213). She noted that while a number of landmarks, such as certain birthdays or attaining legal majority, are associated with the passage of calendar time, they are endowed with special significance by each society. Other markers are less directly linked to chronological age and more to life events, such as graduation, marriage or retirement. These life events are connected with more general life stages that are relevant for each culture, for example, childhood, adolescence, adulthood and old age. They may also be associated with major historical events that occur during the age span of a population and are perceived as shared experiences, such as the Vietnam War or the Great Depression. Eckert recommended 'directing our focus away from chronological age and towards the life experiences that give age meaning' (Eckert, 1997a: 167).

Eckert also recognized that age interacts with other social variables such as gender, class and ethnicity, though undoubtedly in ways that vary from culture to culture. Although her primary interest remains the study of variation, her analysis of age as a socially constructed category has added depth to and focused attention on a relatively neglected topic, yet one that should be given due consideration in sociolinguistic research of many kinds.

Coupland calls age 'sociolinguistics' under-developed social dimension' (Coupland, 2001: 185). He regards the present involvement of sociolinguists with age as too narrowly circumscribed, too restricted to the study of linguistic change and overly reliant on the apparent-time method. Instead he believes that contemporary social theorizing about the lifespan should be less limited to chronological age and more attuned to the ways in which age is socially constructed by people in their interaction with each other. Thus,

Present-Day Approaches to the Study of Age   41

he would extend the narrow scope of sociolinguists' treatment of age to cover a much broader range of concerns.

In work spanning nearly two decades, Coupland and his colleagues, principally among them J. Coupland, Giles and Nussbaum, have addressed many of these issues in some of the most thought-provoking studies of age and aging in sociolinguistics to date (see e.g. Coupland, 1997, 2001; Coupland & Nussbaum, 1993; Coupland *et al.*, 1991; Giles *et al.*, 1991).[4] Their research has focused on old age as a significant life stage, an area previously overlooked by sociolinguistics, and has led them to study the discursive construction of age by the elderly in one-on-one conversations, group discussions, interviews and long-term interactions, as well as in a variety of contexts, including day centers, nursing homes, geriatric medical outpatient consultations and home visits.

In general terms, their findings indicate that the expectation of decline or decremental change is an integral part of the 'mythology of ageing' (Coupland *et al.*, 1991: 4) in our culture. 'Decrement' is understood in this context to be progressive decline in health or competence. The overwhelming presence of ageist discourses is evident both in the ways people talk about the old, either disparagingly or using simplistic and romantic images, and in the ways people talk to the old, for example, using secondary baby talk, overaccommodation or patronizing talk. Coupland (2001) has also delved into questions of age appropriateness, the legitimacy of old age and what he calls the 'inverted U' stereotype of the life course, one that infantilizes both the old and the young as physically small, incompetent, dependent and socially marginalized individuals.

Coupland (2001) has identified four main reasons for the neglect of old age by other sociolinguists. First, he points to a reluctance to study old age based on the fear of aging ('gerontophobia') and its implications, prevalent in contemporary Western society. A second reason he cites is that research issues dealing with aging have been taken over to a large extent by social policy makers, social welfare institutions and the like, as an 'applied' concern. This has had the double disadvantage of excluding relevant theoretical aspects and of implying that old age is inherently problematic. Third, the social environments of old age in our society are widely divergent, that is, the old may find themselves being either powerful or powerless, and living either a time of fulfillment or one of penury. Old age defies simple generalizations. Finally, he contends that sociolinguistics does not have a satisfactory social theory of aging, and has worked up to now in the framework of a limited and somewhat makeshift one.

The view of late life as a problem is only one indicator of the ageism common in present-day Western culture. Because of its importance, the topic of age discourses is treated more extensively in the following chapter. However, I would like to single out two key points in the work of Coupland and his colleagues that have a fundamental relevance for the present discussion. The first is their rejection of the notion of age as 'a *determinant* of language competence and language behaviour' (Coupland *et al.*, 1993b: xi, emphasis as in original). This supposition underlies most research on children's 'developing' language as well as on linguistic 'decrement' in the elderly. Yet the findings of studies of older subjects are inconclusive, some reporting diminished performance and others, contrary to predicted outcomes, comparable or superior performance. It would appear, then, that at best only a tenuous association can be made between biological age and communicative competence, and certainly not a causal one.

The second point they make, closely related to the first, is that the assumption that aging follows a 'normal' and unwavering path of decline is unfounded (Coupland *et al.*, 1991). Again, research evidence does not demonstrate that decrement is the 'natural' and inexorable outcome of aging, but instead suggests that the experience of aging is characterized by considerable variability. Furthermore, people of the same age cohort do not necessarily age in the same way. Although their research focuses primarily on language and communication in later life, it has contributed significantly to elucidating the theoretical and methodological issues surrounding age and aging throughout the life course, as seen from the perspective of contemporary sociolinguistics.

Finally, Coupland has done major work on the discursive negotiation of life course identities, analyzing how people construct their own and other people's age identities in interaction. In his words:

> Sociolinguistics can explore the extent to which, and ways in which, age is (re)negotiated in different settings, under what constraints and with what consequences. This dynamic perspective on identity and age-identity in particular has an established pedigree. It can be found very explicitly in Mead's (1932) process model of identity, which assumed that the self emerges through interactional experience. (Coupland, 2001: 195)

Recent work on the social construction of identity in discursive interaction has changed the way many sociolinguists view ethnicity, social class and gender. There is every reason to believe that this same approach can and should be extended to age, an area of vital importance to contemporary sociolinguistics.

Conclusion

I have set out to establish that discourse-oriented sociolinguistics offers the most satisfactory approach to the study of age because of its focus on the ways in which people construct meaning through social interaction in specific sociocultural contexts. In particular, I regard the social constructionist perspective adopted by many contemporary sociolinguists as having the greatest potential for exploring the question of age and identity. It seems particularly well suited to do so. For one thing, if language is considered part of a larger communication system, then it is the study of social interaction that holds the key to unlocking the complex, interwoven relationship between language and the sociocultural context within which communication occurs. This puts the spotlight on the way meaning is constructed through interaction, how people situate themselves in the context of their social relationships, and what the local and historical framework contributes to the process. Such a process is necessarily a dynamic and ongoing one. In this sense, social parameters such as age, social class, gender and ethnicity, rather than being considered as broad, static categories, are best regarded as socially constructed through discursive interaction in specific communicative contexts.

Notes

(1) The concept of Discourse, as Gee defines it, plays a fundamental role in the study described in this book. However, I have opted to use the lowercase spelling ('discourse'), now in common currency, henceforward.
(2) 'Crossing' is a particular kind of code-switching, in which speakers use apparently outgroup linguistic styles, that is to say, they move outside the language varieties they normally employ and briefly use the codes of other groups to which they do not belong (Rampton, 1997, 1999).
(3) Bourdieu (2002; Bourdieu & Wacquant, 2005) uses the term 'field' to refer to a site or network of social interaction in which individuals strive for more favored positions on the basis of possessing capital that is valued in that setting.
(4) It should be noted that these studies have been undertaken only in industrialized countries.

3 Viewing Age through a Social Constructionist Lens

Introduction

The social construction of age is a discursive process whereby people give meaning to the experience of aging and create their age identity through their interaction with each other. This chapter highlights the principal features that are brought into play in the process. I begin by considering how cultural studies and contemporary sociolinguistics complement each other in their approach to age. A major portion of the chapter is devoted to singling out the principal age discourses in present-day Western culture, for these discourses furnish people with a framework for interpreting their experience and enacting their identities. Following this, I address the question of identity from a poststructuralist perspective, as multiple, fragmented, changeable and a site of struggle, and draw attention to the complexity of age identity. I then turn to the issue of narration, focusing on how people use stories to tell about their lives and to understand the experience of aging. Finally, the various themes of this first part of the book are tied together in order to bring to a close the conceptual foundations of the study of age as a social construct.

Contemporary Age Discourses and Their Manifestations

From the standpoint of social constructionists, aging is not simply a natural, preordained process, but one that is to a large extent shaped by sociocultural factors. The first prominent exposition of the idea that different 'ages of life' vary over history and culture is generally attributed to Ariès, whose groundbreaking work, *Centuries of Childhood* (Ariès, 1962), outlines the social construction of childhood. The view of aging as a socially constructed event has since been taken up by researchers in a variety of fields, such as political economy, critical gerontology, communication sciences and the humanities, each operating within its own conceptual and methodological framework. Working from a culturalist perspective,[1] their theoretical and research concerns have begun to converge in a single field called age studies. While retaining their own particular objects of study and goals, they engage in age research with the same shared conviction that human beings are aged more by culture than by biology and that the 'natural' process of aging has been overemphasized at the expense of the cultural. This new field is endeavoring to denaturalize the construct of age much as feminist theory and critical race theory did for other body-based categories. Yet, at this juncture, age continues to be an impoverished concept and age studies theory is as underdeveloped as gender theory and critical race theory were a few decades ago. However, it is likely that the coming years will see advances in this direction because of the amount of interest being generated by a host of age-related issues, such as intergenerational relations, adult education, employment practices and health care for the elderly.

In the absence, then, of a wholly developed age theory, this book draws extensively on two main sources for its foundational support: cultural studies, for a broad conceptual base, and discourse-oriented sociolinguistics (treated in Chapter 2), for a more focused approach to age and identity. By making use of these complementary approaches, a solid basis for framing the discussion of age can be established.

The two principal components in the discussion, 'age' and 'aging', defined in the introduction, are linked to two other important concepts: time and change. Whereas some societies in Africa and in other nonindustrialized parts of the world have little notion of age as measured in years from the date of one's birth, Western industrial society has invariably placed primacy on chronological age (Ariès, 1962; Makoni, 1997). This view, harking back to the first of the two schools of thought that are identified with Western conceptions of time, is the 'objective', mechanistic notion of time, coming from the writings of Aristotle and Newton. It was adopted by the sciences and is characterized by being quantifiable and ontologically prior to our consciousness of it. Most research on aging equates the aging process with the linear flow of objective time. A second, more subjective and existential idea of time, flowing from Augustine through Einstein and Bergson to present-day phenomenologists, treats time as multifaceted, qualitative and based on subjective perception. This latter orientation is more closely aligned with a social constructionist perspective on age.

Discourse-oriented sociolinguistics blends well with age studies, highlighting the dynamic process in which the meanings attached to age and aging emerge from the ongoing construction of social reality, primarily through discursive interaction. Age is located in our discourse because, as Green remarks, 'it follows from the principle that social reality is made in and of language that there is no such extralinguistic thing as aging or the aged (or any other sociological category)' (Green, 1993: 15). From a discourse perspective, then, aging is considered to be an interactive process rather than an individual one, and can be analyzed by looking at how it is constructed through communicative practices, both verbal and nonverbal. Likewise, the study of communicative practices reveals the underlying cultural narratives or discourses through which people make sense of their experience of aging.

A common backdrop to age research is the life course perspective. This approach views the entire life course as a whole with the idea that, in order to understand an individual's present position in the lifespan, it is imperative to take into consideration their past life history and, if possible, their future aspirations. It also locates them in a particular cultural and historical context, where specific moments or life stages are experienced and shaped through language and participation in social interaction within the frame of the life course.

The life course perspective is important for the research study described here on two accounts. First, the use of narrative inquiry encouraged the participants in the study to talk about their lives as a seamless whole. Their narratives about present events were interspersed with stories of the past and shared hopes for the future, and these connections made it possible to come to a better understanding of where they positioned themselves in the life course. Second, by including persons from different age groups in the study rather than concentrating on a single life stage, the similarities, differences and ambiguities that characterize the experience of the life course could be distinguished with greater clarity. Putting people of diverse ages side by side also casts light on the fluidity of the life course, and circumvents the lack of precision inherent in using global designations for diverse groups of people.

The Discourse of Decline

The meanings with which we imbue age and aging come to us initially through the prevailing discourses or narratives in our culture. The way a specific culture envisions age and the passing of time permeates every aspect of life, including attitudes, beliefs, feelings, values, social practices, ways of talking, as well as social institutions, and these discourses are internalized by the members of a given society from an early age. In most of the industrialized West the dominant discourse is one of decline, yet this is not necessarily the case in other parts of the world. China, Japan, India, certain African societies and Islamic cultures have traditionally placed a high value on aging, associating it with increased wisdom, authority, status and freedom. Older people are esteemed and considered 'custodians of the traditions and history of their people' (Nelson, 2005: 208). Nevertheless, it must be pointed out that many of these same societies are currently experiencing changes in attitudes toward age as a consequence of increasing urbanization and industrialization. This is what can be observed in Mexico, a country that has only been industrialized for the past 50 years

(Haber, 1989). The kinds of discourses available, then, depend crucially on how age is represented at a given historical moment in the specific context of each culture.

The prevailing discourse of aging in present-day Western culture is one of inevitable and irreversible decline. In *Aged by Culture*, Gullette claims that we accept and internalize an age-as-decline discourse to such an extent that it colors 'our expectations of the future, our view of others, our explanatory systems, and then our retrospective judgments' (Gullette, 2004: 11).[2] She goes on to say that what began as the decline narrative of old age has now moved steadily backwards to younger and younger ages, so that it is now the predominant discourse of people below 40, 30 or even 20 years of age. The decline discourse is strongly supported by institutions and commercial interests and is manifested overtly and covertly in societal ageism.

The decline narrative must be understood with respect to its counterpart, the progress narrative, which depicts aging in terms of growth and progress, occurring before the onset of decline. It is the fitting narrative for childhood, in that children are seen as moving through the life course in progressive stages of physical, psychological and social development that prepare them for the adult world. The progress narrative accounts for their increased status, based primarily on age, as they advance through the school system and other organizations or institutions. The basic theme of the progress narrative is one that envisions aging as positive and leading inexorably to a propitious future.

This narrative has also been used, inconsistently, for adults. It used to be part of what was called 'the American Dream', associated with continuing upward advancement in the workplace. However, Gullette (2004) argues that the progress narrative is disappearing from the narrative of adulthood because, despite increasing longevity, decline is believed to take place at ever younger ages in the industrialized West. Thus, the narrative begins as a story of progress, reaches a peak and is then transformed into a decline story. The result is a progress-versus-decline binary that has effectively covered most of the available narrative possibilities, thereby limiting the emergence of alternative discourses for understanding or explaining age. Although there is general agreement about the prevalence of the decline discourse in contemporary Western culture, not everyone would share Gullette's dark view of a midlife now being removed to an early stage of old age. Both the general populace and the academic research community have tended to fix the culminating point of the life course somewhere in the middle adult years (Eckert, 1997a; Featherstone & Hepworth, 1989). This is also the case for urban Mexico.

In general, the vision of aging as decline is consistent with prevailing age discourses in Mexico, intensified by the fact that poverty and aging are linked throughout the life course in that country (Giraldo Rodríguez & Torres Castro, 2006; Treviño Siller *et al.*, 2006; Zúñiga Herrera, 2004).

With respect to old age, Bijarro Hernández and Mendiola Infante make the point that:

> to bring together the role of poverty and that of later life is to analyze the very history of Mexico's colonial period.... where the first preoccupations and activities in this regard were focused on old age, considered as a condition of life in which sickness and dependence predominated.[3] (Bijarro Hernández & Mendiola Infante, 2009: 86)

Other Discourses and Their Manifestations

To bring the discussion of age ideology into the more familiar arena of everyday experience, I next look at some of the prevalent discourses in contemporary Western culture that are offshoots of the decline narrative, along with their overt and covert manifestations. Some topics are broader than others, and, as might be anticipated, a certain amount of overlapping is unavoidable.

Ageist discourses

The decline discourse is closely associated with societal ageism. 'Ageism', a term first used by Butler (1969), is commonly understood as a set of prejudicial attitudes and discriminatory practices that target the elderly as an age group and which endorse their subordinate and marginal positions in society. However, 'ageism' can be expanded to include any age group that is discriminated against on the basis of age and deprived of access to material and social resources, such as education, medical services or employment opportunities. Ageism may be explicit, as in the case of laws that establish upper or lower age limits, for example, for obtaining employment. It can also take more subtle forms, as, for instance, in the way physical illness in midlife may be understood to signal the onset of the 'natural' biological aging process. Such an interpretation is permeated with tacit ageist discourses.

Behind societal ageism lie stereotypical beliefs that attribute selected, and generally unfavorable, characteristics to individuals on the sole basis of their belonging to a particular age cohort. Ageist myths, attitudes and practices are part of the age lore of Western culture and are rationalized by problematizing a targeted age group on the basis of negative stereotypes. The most prevalent ones are those referring to old people.[4] As a case in point, I report in the research study that one of the teachers made ageist jokes on more than 25 occasions during the 20 lessons that were observed, frequently singling out the 70-year-old member of the group as the target of his humorous remarks.

One belief, built on the notion that later adulthood brings with it the end of change, is that the elderly are inflexible and set in their ways. Another is that they are long-winded and rambling, displaying an 'off-target verbosity unrelated to present contextual stimuli' (Cicirelli, 1993: 221). They are also characterized at times as egocentric and cantankerous. The vision of old age as a 'second childhood' is another popular stereotype in which the 'declining' competence, increased dependency, lack of productivity, social marginality and physical smallness of the elderly are likened to similar characteristics in young children, in what is aptly described as the 'inverted-U' model of the life course (Coupland, 2001; Coupland *et al.*, 1991). Stereotypes in Mexico are similar in characterizing old age as 'a period of poor health, economic instability, loneliness and declining physical and mental capacities' (Franco Saldaña *et al.*, 2010: 989).

Among the most damaging is the discourse or narrative of disengagement, in which older people are seen as alienated from mainstream society, to a large extent detached from a world in which they no longer have an active role. This idea has clearly identifiable roots in the establishment, following World War II, of voluntary or mandatory retirement from the workforce at a predetermined age (Phillipson, 1998). Retirement is thought to signal the end of an individual's economic productivity, a key value in industrialized societies, and to entail a concomitant 'retirement' from the community and a loss of status. In the ensuing years, the system of retirement has placed increasingly heavy burdens on society and the economic, political and social consequences have been serious. Not surprisingly, older people are both affected by and blamed for the critical situation that has resulted. In all fairness, it must be pointed out that, when analyzed on a case-by-case basis, retirement can be seen in a positive light as affording freedom, leisure and new opportunities to individuals in some sectors of the population. However, to numerous others, retirement signifies economic constraints and marginalization from society. This is particularly true in the case of Mexico, where only about 20% of the retired population receives a pension, one which for most retirees is meager at best (Ham Chande, 1999; Zúñiga Herrera, 2004).

Closely bound to the issue of productivity is a depreciation of the accumulated experience of aging. This is especially evident in the workplace, where the value formerly accorded to seniority and the rewards that accompanied it have been eroded in modern times. Gullette (2004, 2011) reports that it is increasingly commonplace in the United States for experienced workers to be edged out of their jobs to make room for younger untried replacements. Older persons are often unceremoniously moved into retirement, and midlifers are encouraged to follow them, or are locked into their current positions, or even relegated to inferior ones before they have developed a sense of professional accomplishment.

It must be noted, however, that the phenomenon of forced early retirement pertains to developed countries, where it can serve various purposes, such as keeping salaries from escalating by the replacement of experienced workers with younger, cheaper ones or, in those nations where the private sector assumes a large responsibility for pension funds. Government policy in some countries may also promote early retirement as a way to combat unemployment by opening up positions in the job market to younger workers.

This situation does not hold true for developing nations such as Mexico, where the unemployment rate in the formal sector is so high that the large number of people competing for the limited number of jobs guarantees that salaries will remain low. Pension systems, as mentioned before, cover only a small percentage of the population. Consequently, there is little incentive for employees to retire early in Mexico. Moreover, older people who want to find work face a labor market which is virtually closed to them (Robles Silva *et al.*, 2006). As García Rendón explains:

> At the present time Mexican institutions do not hire people over forty and much less older people. Despite the fact that there are multiple activities in the production process that do not require precision or speed and could be performed by older persons, the institutions or companies prefer not to hire them in order to avoid assuming the costs of the social benefits that they would be partially responsible for in conjunction with the subsidy that the federal government provides. (García Rendón, 2006: 6)

Certainly, the devaluation of experience is as prevalent in Mexico as it is elsewhere in the industrialized world. The consequences go far beyond the economic, for there is psychological and social damage as well. Older people in that country 'experience a social and symbolic expulsion from the spaces and social relations which were part of their identity in previous stages of their lives' (Robles Silva *et al.*, 2006: 288). Thus, aging is no longer seen in terms of gains, a building up of experience or cultural capital, but primarily as loss and decline.

Ageist discourses concerning other age groups can be perceived in stereotypes about the midlife crisis, loss of physical attractiveness, depression and the empty-nest syndrome (Clay, 2003; Shweder, 1998). Interestingly, not all of these stereotypes have relevance in Mexico, where notions of 'middle age' do not form part of the narratives of age at the present time (this point is treated below in the section '*Age-category discourses*').

Different stereotypes of adolescents portray them as violent, rebellious, criminal, reckless, complaining, lazy and valueless. Stereotypes of young children represent them variably as helpless and vulnerable or as devilish and dangerous.

It is not only popular or folk beliefs, such as these, that are ageist. Ageism has found its way into academic discourse as well. The research agenda in age and communication studies has a decidedly ageist slant (Coupland *et al.*, 1991). A clear example is the debate surrounding the CPH for SLA, discussed in Chapter 1, in which participating researchers have commonly launched their studies from the initial supposition that children will perform better than adults because increased age brings with it a loss of ability to learn a new language. In view of the considerable counter-evidence reporting better performance by older L2 learners, such a presupposition seems unnecessarily precipitate. In addition, relatively few studies focus on differences among adults of distinct ages, yet an underlying assumption exists that adult L2 learning ability continues to diminish throughout the life course, a position that cannot, in any case, be explained by the CPH (Singleton & Ryan, 2004).

Furthermore, the research evidence to date has identified comparatively few areas in which increasing age may be accompanied by the loss of capacities considered critical for successful language learning, such as auditory acuity and efficiency of memory processing. Singleton and Ryan (2004) point out that training and teaching procedures can compensate for many of these difficulties, which are, moreover, frequently offset by favorable motivational and experiential factors characteristic of older learners. In view of the fact that research findings on older versus younger L2 learners are inconclusive and the CPH debate is no closer to being resolved today than it was 30 years ago, one is hard put to account for the ageist tack taken by ostensibly neutral academicians.

Yet, not all stereotypes are negative. Positive stereotypes also form part of societal ageism by making simplistic generalizations that do not take into account real variations among people in an age group. Favorable images of older people portray them as warm, nurturing grandparents or as singularly wise or dignified. Young people are represented as possessing physical attractiveness and sexuality, and children are stereotyped as cute and angelic. In fact, experience tells us that we draw on multiple, and often conflicting, discourses to categorize people of different age groups. The use of 'sanitised one-dimensional benign stereotypes' is 'an ageist trap', for it locks people indiscriminately into roles such as 'granny' and 'grandpa' 'which do not do justice to the richness of their individual experiences and multi-facets of their personalities' (Featherstone & Hepworth, 1991: 382).

Furthermore, ageist discourses are commonly interwoven with gender, ethnic and racial differences. For instance, old women in medieval times were believed to be witches and often appear in fairy tales as crones, shrews or nags, an image that has persisted to our times. Midlife women are portrayed as spiteful mothers-in-law, yet few corresponding images exist for men.

All these stereotypes have been discredited by evidence from research, despite the fact that elements of truth may be found in some of them. However, the issue is not to determine the extent to which they present an accurate portrayal of particular age groups. That misses the point, which is that people age in far different ways, a fact that stereotypes, both positive and negative, overlook. As a result, ageist discourses engender prejudicial beliefs and practices that have potentially detrimental effects on every age group. Perhaps the most serious consequence is that people tend to internalize negative discourses and to adopt the very traits they believe to be prototypical of the age group to which they belong (Cruikshank, 2003; Gullette, 2011; Hazan, 1994; Levy, 2001).

Age behavior and talk

Discourses of aging have a strong effect on the way people act. The norms for acceptable behavior for each age group are clearly understood by the members of a society, yet rarely explicit. These unwritten rules of age-appropriate behavior govern the manner of looking, sounding and dressing, as well as of making choices. Those who violate the norms by acting either 'older' or 'younger' are sanctioned. Although there have been efforts to break through certain age barriers, for example, in the case of people returning to school after retirement, the stereotypes of age-appropriate appearance and behavior in most cultures remain very powerful.

The marketers of consumer goods rely on such accepted age-related images for targeting different segments of the population, such as teenagers or 'yuppies'. With the affluent older adult markets, this has required treading a fine line between recognizing their needs and interests and at the same time skirting the more negative stereotypes and images of bodily aging which produce anxiety (Katz, 2001; Sawchuk, 1995). Age anxiety also stems from what Gullette (2004) calls the 'speed-up' of the life course, that is, the feeling of urgency that arises out of the pressure of time to get things done. It is the sensation of being perpetually behind schedule that drives people to work harder and longer hours, to neglect family and friends and to skip leisure-time activities in a futile effort to catch up. Nor are adolescents and children immune to 'speed-up'. Young people worry years ahead of time about getting a job or accomplishing enough before it is 'too late'. Children are pushed at ever earlier ages into acquiring skills considered 'essential' for their future success in the adult world. The feeling of being 'too late' is readily transformed into the feeling of being 'too old'. The irony, then, is that, in an era of unprecedented longevity, premature decline is making inroads in the life course at earlier stages.

Ageist attitudes are evident in the way people talk about age and aging. The words and expressions they use reflect conventional cultural stereotypes. For example, pejorative terms, such as 'over the hill', 'old-timer', 'old bag', *'anciano'* (aged person), *'chocho'* (doddering old person) or *'ruco'* (old fogy), form part of the popular discourse referring to older people in English and Spanish. The lexicon also contains euphemisms for this age group, like 'golden-ager' (*adulto en plenitud*) or 'mature person' (*persona de la tercera edad*), which attempt to cover up the negative overtones of the 'taboo' subject of old age. Countless examples of ageist verbal expressions are also found in clichés, adages, humor, popular fiction and the media (Palmore, 2005). While the use of disparaging language is clearly offensive to members of the targeted age group, interestingly enough, the use of flattering terms and complimentary expressions, such as 'You look wonderful,' may be equally demeaning to an older person if what is implied is that it is somehow a surprise, given the circumstances of age, health or fortune (Coupland et al., 1991; Cruikshank, 2003).

Ageist attitudes can also be revealed by the way people adjust their speech to facilitate or hinder comprehension when talking to others. In the context of intergenerational talk, 'overaccommodation', exemplified by the use of simplified languages such as baby talk or elder speech, can be patronizing. 'Underaccommodation', resulting from some style or quality of talk being underplayed such as the use of 'ingroup' language, can be exclusionary (Giles et al., 1991; Nussbaum et al., 2005; Williams & Giles, 1996).

Age-category discourses

The discussion of 'ingroups' and 'outgroups' and intergenerational talk makes sense only in the context of a life course that is divided into different stages. Historically, every society separates the life course into the stages it believes correspond to progressive 'natural' sequences of development. However, age categories, such as 'childhood', 'adolescence' and 'old age', are in fact arbitrary divisions, varying between as well as within cultures. This is illustrated by the fact that in some cultures there are as few as two classifications, old and young, and in others as many as 10 or more (Keith, 1984). The idea, then, that lifespan development can be seen as a 'natural' process consisting of a series of universal stages is faulty and obscures the socially constructed and historically specific nature of age categories. Moreover, age grading is potentially ageist 'in that it segregates younger and older people into "us and them"' (Nelson, 2005: 217).

'Childhood', as a distinct age group, emerged in American and Western European culture in the early part of the 19th century as a result of historical changes that shifted the focus from kinship groups or lineage to the modern conjugal family (Ariès, 1962). At the same time, a decline in infant and child mortality and a greater proliferation of conscious birth-control practices contributed to the increased interest in the child-centered family.

Childhood and adolescence, as we now know them, were undifferentiated until the latter part of the 19th century, when 'adolescence' became a recognized age category in industrialized Western cultures. Factors that contributed to its emergence were the exclusion of adolescents from entry into the adult world, the lengthening of formal education through secondary school and the extension of age limits for child labor. This led to the custom of young people banding together and adopting styles of peer-group behavior that were felt to pose a threat to society.

Adolescence has now been extended at both ends of the spectrum. On the one hand, the media and peer pressure propel 10- to 12-year-olds into a world in which body image, sexual behavior and the adoption of older role models mark an early entrance into adolescence. On the other hand, adolescence is not considered to have ended until a person has finished school, gotten a job and started a family, events much more likely to occur nearer to 30 than to 20. 'Both stages of life [childhood and adolescence] emerged into public consciousness as a result of the social crises associated with those age groups in a manner similar to the emergence of old age later on' (Hareven, 1995: 124).

Adulthood remained a relatively amorphous category, bounded only by adolescence at one end of the continuum, until early in the 20th century when 'old age' became a distinct new stage of life at the other end. Whereas in preindustrialized societies, the latter part of adulthood was associated with the survival of the fittest, in the urban industrialized world, old age soon became identified with physical and mental decline, dependence and obsolescence. In addition, the proportion of older people in the population grew as a result of a decline in fertility and an increase in life expectancy attributable to advances in medicine. Furthermore, older people were fazed out of productive roles in the economy to a much greater extent because of retirement practices.

The term 'middle age' or 'midlife', the newest addition to the list of age categories in English, draws a distinction between the social problems of midlife and those of late life. The problems of forced early retirement and the empty-nest syndrome have given rise to the adoption of the middle age category; yet at present this does not have a counterpart in much of the developing world, including Mexico, where people falling in the vast range between adolescence and old age are subsumed under the broad indeterminate category of 'adults'.[5] As mentioned previously, forced early retirement is not an issue in Mexico.

Likewise, the empty-nest syndrome has not appeared to any great extent in Mexico, where the family structure is based on close economic and affective ties across generations. The trigenerational family, which includes a couple, their children and their grandchildren, is the prototype for all social levels (Adler Lomnitz, 1999; Leñero Otero, 1999). Furthermore, as more women have entered the work force in recent years, it is grandparents, and primarily grandmothers, who have come to aid working mothers in the care of their children (González de la Rocha, 2005; Malacara, 2006; Zermeño, 2005). There is no empty nest.

Hareven observes that there is 'an increasing segregation of different stages of life – and of their corresponding age groups – in modern American society' (Hareven, 1995: 132). As a case in point, in recent years, the 'old age' category has been further segmented to distinguish the 'young old' from the 'old old'. Other newly minted terms reflect the subdivision of an expanded adolescence into 'tweenies' (7–12-year-olds), 'teens' (13–19) and 'middlescents' (20–30).

When viewing aging as a diachronic process, we expect that a person will belong to each of the age groups, from childhood to old age, at different moments over the course of a normal lifetime. Yet by looking at age from a synchronic perspective, it is possible to see another kind of age division, one that is brought about by naming age cohorts or by making an allusion to a shared historical moment or experience, such as 'Baby Boomers' or 'Generation X-ers'. People typically are members of both a cohort and an age group. However, belonging to an age group is always temporary whereas membership in a cohort is lifelong. Cohorts are generally characterized in terms of popular stereotypes. The rise of named age cohorts has hardened these stereotypes and put emphasis on age divisions. While the construction of age categories and cohorts has provided people with a framework for interpreting their experiences and for understanding life change, it has also been a means of power and social control (Bourdieu, 2003; Cruikshank, 2003).

Invoking age categories or cohort membership in talk, everyday conversation or in humor, is a practice tinged with ageism for it reproduces age stereotypes. Even the simple mention of chronological age calls up age images, as is evident in the journalistic convention of 'age-tagging' in character descriptions (Coupland *et al.*, 1993a). Age salience is a pervasive feature of the contemporary Western world.

> From birth to death we all age, and from womb to tomb our chronological progress is obsessively and meticulously recorded: on our driver's licenses, on our passports, in the newspapers (if we are unfortunate enough to be celebrities), on the end papers of our books, and at our birthday parties. (Deats & Lenker, 1999: 9)

The body and biomedical discourses

Culturally endorsed images of physical attractiveness and age-appropriate behavior highlight the centrality of the human body to the discussion of age, for it is the body that makes us part of the physical and temporal world, enabling us to be social beings and to create a social world. This does not imply that the biological, psychological and social dimensions are discrete segments that add up to the whole person; we are at the same time fully physical and fully social beings (Ainlay & Redfoot, 1982). Aging is our passage through time, and it is an embodied social process inseparable from its social context. As Featherstone and Hepworth point out:

> Whilst the biological processes of aging, old age, and death cannot in the last resort be avoided, the meanings which we give to these processes and the evaluations we make of people as they grow physically older are social constructions which reflect the beliefs and values found in a specific culture at a particular period of history. (Featherstone & Hepworth, 1995: 30–31)

Our embodiment is fundamental to understanding not only the experience of aging, but also the process of identity. The body is a signifier; it makes a statement about who a person is. We both 'have' a body and 'perform' our body, that is, our bodies are simultaneously real and constructed (Harper, 1997). People may consciously choose to rework bodily appearance and behavior through, for example, adornment or cosmetic surgery, or by adopting postures or facial expressions. In today's Western world, the young body is the norm, romanticized through advertising and the visual imagery of the media and 'bolstered by a consumer culture with its images of youth, fitness and beauty lifestyles' (Featherstone & Wernick, 1995: 7). In Mexico, the mass media and the cosmetic industry have been instrumental in fostering the need to distance oneself from the aging process by playing on the fears that are particularly prevalent in the female population (Montes de Oca, 2001).

While many changes in appearance may be brought about intentionally, others can be attributed to involuntary biochemical processes or to outside factors, such as illness, accident or stress. Powerful links are made between aging, sickness and death. Yet this seemingly natural connection is in reality a historical phenomenon. Up until the end of the 19th century, death was associated with newborns and young children, and old age was seen as a sign of physical strength rather than weakness. However, because of the demographic changes brought on by industrialization and urbanization, beginning around 1880, aging became a 'medical problem' for which science is expected to provide a solution (Vincent, 2003, 2006). Since that time, the biomedical model has dominated the understanding of aging in Western culture. It has assumed the task of preventing, hiding or halting the aging process via the biotechnological advancements that foster reconstruction of the body, such as plastic surgery, organ transplants, hip replacements and other similar procedures.

In general, the medical model focuses its attention on the pathology of aging, considering sickness to be the 'natural' consequence of biological decline. Yet the fact is that, even within the scientific–medical community, there is no universal agreement on how biological aging comes about. Moreover, the fear of aging and of death, so prevalent in contemporary Western culture, has augmented the significance of illness. Here, two points must be made. First, although biological decline may predispose older people to illness, it does not in itself cause it. Indeed, many older people live in good health. The second point, one that has been stated before, is that biological aging cannot be artificially separated from the sociocultural framework within which it is experienced and given meaning.[6] Because the medical profession has taken upon itself the task of eradicating illness and prolonging life – indeed, its primary objective is seen as preventing death – some believe that a disproportionate amount of time and resources are channeled to preserving life and avoiding death (Cruikshank, 2003; Nelson, 2005; Vincent,

2003, 2006). The effect is to divert attention from a consideration of possible ways to bring old age to a satisfactory close.

Anti-ageist discourses

In a broad sense, the counter-position to the deficit model is the discourse or narrative of change, in which aging is seen as change, understood in terms of difference rather than decrement and free of the pejorative values associated with the latter. Challenge or resistance to decline ideology has emerged since the 1970s in the form of 'anti-ageist' discourses. The two main approaches, subsumed under the banner of 'positive' aging, stand in stark contrast to each other. One tendency is the quest for eternal youth or the pursuit of 'agelessness'. The other is the construction of aging as a meaningful process through a variety of alternative images and lifestyles that change throughout the life course.

The first approach, characterized by a search for ways to stave off the 'negative' manifestations of aging, has flourished in the present-day consumer culture, where the 'aging industry' (Cole, 1992: 222) provides a plethora of products and services for the affluent that promise to erase the signs of aging. What is more, methods to prevent aging altogether are offered in self-help courses and advice books, such as Deepak Chopra's best-selling *Ageless Body, Timeless Mind* (1993). Even the large segment of the population whose economic possibilities limit their participation in this consumer culture, defines their aspirations in terms of an affluent lifestyle and set of values (Gilleard & Higgs, 2000).

Anti-aging products and surgical procedures are now routinely in demand by midlifers and even young people. In other words, the preferred method of successful aging is to curtail the internal and external signs of aging, or better yet, not to age at all. Trying to 'pass' as younger is a temptation throughout the adult life course 'in a culture where youth itself appears to be for purchase' (Andrews, 1999: 307), but it is an endeavor ultimately destined to fail. A more serious consequence is that older people are held accountable for maintaining their health, active lifestyle and independence permanently, thereby relieving the social institutions and medical profession of much of their responsibility in this regard (Calasanti, 2005; Cole, 1992; Cruikshank, 2003; Latimer, 1997; Vincent, 2003). Thus, despite certain benefits, such as the promotion of fitness and health, this version of positive aging discourse does not, in the final analysis, resolve the 'problem' of aging. It only delays it.

A contrasting, more centered discourse of positive aging has emerged as a result of the growing economic power of older people and their ability to self-organize. They have been joined by midlifers in assuming greater control of their lives and fashioning alternative narratives of aging. This approach to positive aging has begun to take hold in less developed countries, such as Mexico, as well (Brigeiro, 2005). Rather than adopting images of the young or searching for means to prolong youth, people are finding value for every stage of life in its own right. Many older people have come to question the work ethic and the value of productivity, so endemic to Western culture, that have left them feeling devalued and marginalized. Instead, new discourses and narratives have been shaped that discard these cultural values and place priority on personal happiness, self-fulfillment and what Cruikshank calls 'comfortable aging' (Cruikshank, 2003: 3). In addition, many older people are seeking to take charge of the circumstances of the final stage of their lives rather than relinquishing control of their bodies to the medical professionals (Vincent, 2003). In short, positive aging from this perspective signifies that people of all ages, young and old, are relying on themselves to negotiate and define the issues of aging and to articulate new discourses and narratives. It entails adapting to ongoing change and then choosing to live well within the limits set out at any point in the life course (Tulle-Winton, 1999).

Interlinking age with other discourses

The age discourses that come into play in the enactment of identity are invariably colored in particular ways by other discourses. For instance, expectations and opportunities affecting the life chances of young adults are drawn from discourses of social class, as Bourdieu (2003) observed in considering differences between young workers and students of the same age in France. The construction of age identity is sensitive to discourses of ethnicity at every stage of the life course in Mexico (Fortes de Leff, 2002). With regard to gender, discourses of bodily appearance are more salient in the case of midlife and older women than of their male counterparts (Calasanti, 2005; Cruikshank, 2003; Dumas *et al.*, 2005; Montes de Oca, 2001). Gender discourses have an impact on professional aspirations in the crucial adult years, during which women may interrupt their work history to have children or where the 'glass ceiling' hinders their career advancement. Unequal pay scales and employment opportunities bring about inequitable retirement situations for men and women in later adulthood, in both developed and developing nations (Arber & Ginn, 1995; Cruikshank, 2003; Gullette, 2011). These few examples illustrate the dynamic interplay of discourses and point to ways in which the aging process can be shaped by gender, class and ethnicity.

Final Considerations

In this section, emphasis has been placed on the lifelong character of aging and the conviction that age theory must necessarily be a whole-life theory. Aging, as a process of continuing development, involves choices and opportunities at different moments throughout the life course. As people make choices, they construct their age socially, framing it within the discourses available to them. In present-day Western culture, ageist discourses in many guises, including a deceptive antiageist one, have been generated by the prevailing ideology of decline and are so pervasive that people generally adopt them unwittingly. Positive aging discourses attempt to counter ageism by calling attention to its inherent fallacies and by promoting the construction of 'our own age stories from the choice of narratives that reflect a "true age consciousness"' (Gullette, 2004: 154).

Gullette (2004) asks if it is possible to feel at home in the life course at every age. This is the crux of the matter, and doing so depends on the ability 'to conceive of aging at any age as an issue of consciousness and a relationship to personal change informed by age culture's devices' (Gullette, 2004: 65). Ultimately, the particular ways in which people exercise their choice and agency across the life course will vary according to the cultural values they share and the age discourses they draw on or generate. An awareness of, and an acceptance of or resistance to, the prevailing age discourses make it possible to encounter a significance for each moment in the life course.

Discovering how the meaning and experience of age are constructed throughout the life course entails a better understanding of how age identity and age narratives are created. In order to pursue these issues more comprehensively, I discuss age identity in the following section and take up the topic of narration in the final part of the chapter.

Language and the Discursive Construction of Age Identity

The exponential growth of the literature on identity in recent years has occasioned a corresponding lack of precision in the discourse and terminology surrounding this topic. To avoid getting submerged in these murky waters, it is important to make clear at the outset that the position I am taking here with respect to identity is a poststructuralist one. The social constructionist focus on identity as discursively constructed has found strong theoretical support in different strands of poststructuralism, particularly in feminist poststructuralism (Weedon, 1997). Poststructuralist approaches to the study of gender and power relations have served as an effective model for research not only on gender but also on other social dimensions, such as ethnicity (see e.g. Blackledge & Pavlenko, 2001; Norton, 2000). In this section, I draw largely on Weedon's (1997) work to argue that poststructuralism also provides a valuable way of understanding age identity or subjectivity.[7]

Subjectivity and Subject Positions

Poststructuralists define subjectivity as our sense of ourselves, our conscious and unconscious thoughts and emotions and our ways of understanding our relation to the world (Weedon, 1997). Subjectivity is formed in our relationships with others through our identification with particular subject positions, or ways of being an individual, within discourses, in an ongoing process constantly being recreated in discourse each time we speak or act. The range of subject positions open to an individual is necessarily limited to those made available by the specific discourses operating in a particular historical and social context and people can actively take up a position, try out others and accept, reject or challenge positions conferred on them by others (Harré & van Langenhove, 1999b).

Furthermore, because subject positions are often in conflict with each other, subjectivity is seen as a site of struggle between competing yet interlinked discourses. It is precisely the greater attention given by feminist poststructuralists to 'the unresolved tensions, competing perspectives, shifts of power, ambiguities and contradictions inherent within all texts' (Baxter, 2003: 2) which distinguishes their approach from the closely related social constructionist one to identity.

Characteristics of Subjectivity

Both social constructionism and poststructuralism underscore the multiple, fragmented nature of subjectivity, its changeability over time, its cultural and historical dependence, as well as the key role of language in its construction. For poststructuralists, identity is not something people 'have' or 'are', but rather something they 'perform' or 'do' (Baxter, 2003; Butler, 1990; Cameron, 1999). This perspective is diametrically opposed to the liberal-humanist or essentialist account of identity, which theorizes a unified, conscious, rational subject, possessing a unique essence that remains constant throughout all contexts. For poststructuralists, human nature is not essential nor do biological attributes 'have inherent "natural" or social meaning. Their meanings, which are far from uniform, are produced within a range of conflicting discourses' (Weedon, 1997: 123). Subjectivity is conceived as discursively produced in an ongoing social process in which the individual is multiply located in a number of different discourses rather than possessing a single, unitary identity.

Moreover, the impossibility of maintaining a stable subject with a set identity makes subjectivity an eminently changeable process. Because the self is constructed through language and social interaction, meaning is always specific to the particular historically and culturally located discourses in which it is produced; hence, it can only be temporarily fixed. Continuity is achieved by connecting our past and present selves or, more precisely, our embodied selves in space and over time, through discursive processes. For Giddens, such continuity is the outcome of the reflexive project of the self, which 'consists in the sustaining of coherent, yet continually revised, biographical narratives' (Giddens, 1991: 5). Identity construction is thus seen as an ongoing 'narrative' project, in which the stories we tell about ourselves, jointly produced in our interaction with others, furnish our sense of continuity.

A Poststructuralist View of Age Identity

Poststructuralism offers a number of constructive insights into language, discourse practices and subjectivity that are directly relevant to the study undertaken here. In what follows, I single out three aspects that impinge most immediately on the issue of age in adult L2 learners as I engage with it. First of all, the poststructuralist understanding of experience as having no meaning except that constituted in language is an important move away from the liberal-humanist supposition that experience is basically the same for all individuals, a way to know the world, and a guarantee of truth, as expressed in language. In contrast, poststructuralist views allow for varied and contradictory interpretations of experience that are sustained by social interests rather than by an elusive 'objective truth'. In this sense, the meaning of age is contingent on the ways individuals interpret the world and on the discourses available to them at any given moment. In other words, it is not the biological and material reality of aging as such that is the issue, but rather how it is understood or given meaning through the competing discourses existing in a particular culture. Consequently, the experience of aging and the construction of an age identity can only occur through language and never outside it.

A second area of interest linked to the question of age is the poststructuralist notion of subjectivity, particularly as multiple, changing and a site of struggle. The idea that we have a multiplicity of potential selves that are not always consistent with each other, and which change as the context changes, is a far cry from the traditional concept of a single, unified and fixed self. At the same moment in time, a person may conceivably take up or be assigned a number of positions as part of their age identity, depending on the specific circumstances. For instance, a mature student, returning to the classroom, may be positioned as 'old', 'incompetent', 'experienced', 'inflexible' and 'dignified' by university-age students, and be positioned in still other ways by family members or friends. In addition, our multiple selves are diachronic as well as synchronic, in the sense that the ongoing process of constructing identity involves connecting our past and present selves. The notion of subjectivity as changing and flexible is perhaps easier to appreciate in the case of age than for our other identities, such as gender, for the very definition of aging as 'change over time' is something that is generally acknowledged. It also makes it easier to see subjectivity as a site of potential conflict, given that the subject positions open to an individual at a particular historical moment will be those offered not only by the dominant discourses, but also by the alternative, oppositional ones, all of which have different political implications.

Furthermore, discourses of aging may not only be in conflict with each other, but they may also compete with other discourses at work in a given context, such as gender or social class. This leads to the final consideration to be made regarding the pertinence of poststructuralism to the present study, namely, that identities are so intricately intertwined that there can be no simple reading of any single variable. Norton affirmed this in her research on identity and language learning:

> I take the position that ethnicity, gender and class are not experienced as a series of discrete background variables, but are all, in complex and interconnected ways, implicated in the construction of identity and the possibilities of speech. (Norton, 2000: 13)

In the same way, age and its corresponding subject positions and power relations cannot be experienced in isolation from other factors, such as gender, ethnicity and social class. Moreover, discourses of age will likely intersect with other discourses in the language classroom, such as those comprising models of teaching and learning, peer relationships among students or teacher–student interactions, among different possibilities. A complex, nuanced age identity is one of the outcomes of the intersection of identities.

Narrating Age

Age identity, like other identities, manifests itself importantly in the stories people tell about themselves and use to make sense of their experiences. The narrative form is 'ubiquitous throughout human cultures ... fundamental to what it means to be human' (Burr, 2003: 142). But, what exactly is narrative? A concise definition is that it is a discourse or way of using language to construct stories (Bruner, 1990). Although the term 'narrative' is often utilized interchangeably with 'story', in point of fact it is much broader in that it encompasses both the narrative structure and the manner and circumstances of the telling. Because both the construction of age identity and the experience of aging occur through language, they are closely bound up with narrative. First, as seen in the previous section, narrative is a means by which people define and recreate themselves in the social world through the discursive construction of identity. In a narrative, 'people present themselves, and others, as actors in a drama' (Harré & van

Langenhove, 1999a: 8) in which they take up certain subject positions. Second, we understand and interpret our human experience narratively, that is, we organize our experience in terms of stories. Narrative is the principal means by which people confer meaning on their lives over the course of time. We communicate our experience to others and create new ways to be in the world. 'We have something to say, we have experience to bring to language, experience to share' (Ricoeur, 1995: 149).

Characteristics of Narration

The following are some of the key features of narration that are crucial to a better understanding of how it relates to the study of age and aging.

Interactivity

An important facet of narrative is its interactive character. As Pavlenko points out:

> Recent research convincingly demonstrates that narratives are not purely individual productions – they are powerfully shaped by social, cultural, and historical conventions as well as by the relationship between the storyteller and the interlocutor (whether an interviewer, a researcher, a friend, or an imaginary reader). (Pavlenko, 2002a: 214)

There is, then, the sense that the construction of a narrative is 'an "achievement" of our joint production and understanding of stories through our dialogue with each other' (Mishler, 1999: 18).

Temporality

Narrative has a central role in shaping the human experience of time. Its function is not so much to remember the past but to retrieve it and reenact it in the present (Cilliers, 1998). 'The past is not set in stone, but the meaning of events and experiences is constantly being reframed within the contexts of our current and ongoing lives' (Mishler, 2006: 36). Narrative also provides a link to the future:

> Temporal existence draws the past and its possibilities into the present through tales and histories, and it imaginatively anticipates the future consequences of activity by seeing them as reenactments of its repertoire of stories. (Polkinghorne, 1988: 135)

Thus, the past is connected to the present, and both condition a person's expectations of the future.

Coherence

A fundamental feature of narration, coherence refers to the way a narrative is organized in order to be meaningful and understood, that is, its inner logic. Gubrium *et al.* point out that 'much of the work of assembling a life story is the management of consistency and continuity, assuring that the past reasonably leads up to the present to form a lifeline' (Gubrium *et al.*, 1994: 155). Coherence is especially difficult to achieve in the case of life-story narratives, for a life story is neither linear nor noncontradictory. Multiple storylines compete with varying, and often contradictory subject positions; inconsistencies are found; and multiple participants and their individual stories intersect with the life story being told. Furthermore, the circumstances of the telling may give rise to multiple coherences, discontinuity or nonlinearity. For instance, nonlinearity may be the outcome of the narrator's determination of the best way to tell the story in order to capture the interest of the audience, or it may emerge as a consequence of the coconstruction of the narrative.

Truth

Narratives aim at life verisimilitude rather than historical truth. Coherence, both internal and external, is the key to creating believable stories or accounts. Hence, narrative truth is seen as the consistency or likelihood of the elements within the story as well as the compatibility of the story with other accounts or narratives. Most importantly, narrative truth is revealed or discovered, for the construction of a narrative is a hermeneutic process in which we come to understand and make sense of the world in new ways. Through our stories, ordinary things appear in a new light. Events are imbued with meaning by being selected, included or omitted in the narrative and by the way they are woven together to make a single story. As such, any narrative is necessarily incomplete for no one can tell the full story, or even the 'only' story.

Linking Narration and Age

The life-story narrative is inevitably a story of aging for it articulates and gives meaning to the human experience of change over time by highlighting and interpreting the significant happenings in our lives. As people construct their stories, they connect the past to the present to the future in their life course. Through culturally shared discourses, life stories are told, enabling people to move toward greater self-understanding and to make themselves intelligible to each other.

In this sense, narration interconnects with age on two accounts: the construction of age identity and the experience of aging. With regard to the former, contemporary perspectives on identity view it as an ongoing narrative project, as aptly described by Giddens (1991), and one that is inherently a lifespan concern. When people narrate their life story, something new emerges in the telling and affects their life; it becomes part of their identity. Their sense of where they are in the life trajectory, or their age identity, emerges from the narratives they tell and listen to. As such, it can never be fully separated from the specific experiences that are given meaning by and integrated into the plot that constitutes their life story. That story is first and foremost an account of the aging process because of the reciprocity existing between narration and temporality (Ricoeur, 1995). Moreover, both aging and narration are ongoing processes, for our life story is an open-ended and unfinished one. 'We are in the middle of our stories and cannot be sure how they will end; we are constantly having to revise the plot as new events are added to our lives' (Polkinghorne, 1988: 150).

Conclusion

A social perspective on age provides a far richer framework for understanding how people give meaning to the aging process and construct their age identity through discursive interaction. A broader and more complex picture emerges when we look at age as socially constructed, for it reveals to us not only how people experience aging, but also how age plays into their other life experiences. At the same time, it illustrates the ways in which people create their age identity and, equally important, how this identity intersects with their other identities. When considering the lived experience of age, it is clear that a social approach is more valuable and far-reaching than the more limited, essentialist view of age.

The social construction of age is a dynamic enterprise, ongoing throughout the life course. It is accomplished by means of discursive interaction, primarily through narrative, in accordance with the particular discourses offered by a specific culture at a given historical moment. In present-day Western culture, these discourses are largely generated by the predominant age ideology of decline. The storylines and subject positions available for the narrative construction of aging and age identity are chiefly derived from decline discourses and their manifestations, including ageist stereotypes, attitudes, behavior and talk, as well as body and biomedical discourses. At the same time, counter-discourses of positive aging furnish alternatives to decline narratives. Because of the existence of competing discourses, the interpretation of the aging experience and the construction of age identity are multiple, changing and potentially contradictory processes in themselves and in relation to the other life experiences and identities with which they are interwoven. This occurs both on a synchronic and a diachronic plane, for narratives bring to light our multiple selves at a precise moment in time and also link our past and present selves in the life course.

Notes

(1) From this perspective, the phenomenon of aging is understood in terms of the cultural contexts surrounding it and the cultural repertoires used in constructing its meaning.
(2) Although her book specifically addresses decline ideology in present-day American culture, by and large her reflections are applicable to most other Western industrial societies, including Mexico. Therefore, the distinction in the treatment of her ideas is not made here except where it is relevant.
(3) All translations are mine.
(4) People in this age group are referred to as 'old people' or 'older people' throughout the chapter in an effort to use the most neutral terms available. However, precisely because of societal ageism, all terms are offensive to some degree.
(5) I confirmed this by examining a sample of about 15 studies on age in Mexico.
(6) An example is the medicalization of menopause, treated by the medical establishment as a 'deficiency disease', purportedly accounting for sickness, depression, frigidity, osteoporosis and other maladies affecting midlife women (Gullette, 1997, 2004; Shweder, 1998). Interestingly, it is reported that the Mayas of Yucatán, Mexico, do not experience hot flashes or other symptoms typically associated with menopause (Malacara, 2006). Moreover, in Japan, India and some other cultures, no equivalent term for 'menopause' is found (Shweder, 1998). It is not considered in and of itself a life-marking event, or even an 'event' at all. By biologizing menopause, the pharmaceutical industry succeeded in opening up a lucrative new market in hormone replacement 'therapy'. The widespread public menopause discourse shows 'culture impinging on the midlife – a clear case of women being aged by culture' (Gullette, 1997: 98–99).
(7) While the feminist poststructuralist preference for the term 'subjectivity' conveys important distinctions with regard to traditional essentialist notions of identity, 'identity' is still the more commonly used term, even among many poststructuralists. Therefore, 'identity' and 'subjectivity' are used interchangeably here, unless otherwise specified.

Part 2
The Social Construction of Age in Mexico

The remaining part of this book is devoted precisely to the task of exploring age in the particular context of language learning in Mexico and of fleshing out the skeletal frame of age discourses outlined in the previous chapter, with the aim of providing a more complete picture of how age and L2 learning interconnect. For the study, I adopted a broadly ethnographic approach to the research, consisting primarily of narrative inquiry, as developed through a series of periodic interviews with the participants during a language course. This was complemented by classroom observations, audiotaped narrative accounts made by the participants and an interview with the classroom teachers at the end of the term.

The five semistructured in-depth interviews furnished the main wellspring of data for this study. My aim was to collect stories and identify critical moments or events that would enable me to understand the meaning the participants gave to their language-learning experiences and how age factored into their lives. The number and content of the interviews was not established beforehand, but responded to my need as a researcher for ever greater understanding of the participants' beliefs, attitudes and experiences, as they came to light over the course of the term. In them, I addressed the basic issues identified in the research questions, including the participants' prior and present experience studying English, their language ideology, their beliefs about age and aging and the significance of age in learning a new language. However, the coconstructed nature of the interviews often led to interesting digressions in which the participants took control of the conversations and moved them in unforeseen directions.

I became a fixed part of the participants' language-learning world as a permanent observer in the classroom, attending virtually every lesson during the term. My interest was in observing the language-learning environment, how participants went about learning languages, how they related to the other students and to the teacher, the extent of their participation and how age surfaced in this setting. I designed a simple format to record noteworthy moments, describing the activities taking place, the time involved and what I observed about the participants. It should be mentioned that my presence was readily accepted by the students and teachers as the language center at the university is regularly used for teacher training, supervision and frequent classroom observations.

For the audio-taped narrative accounts, I provided each of the participants with a small tape recorder and instructed them to make an informal reflection on each week's lessons in Spanish. I instructed them to talk about their feelings regarding the activities, their difficulties and achievements with respect to specific language points, their participation, their relationship with the other members of the group and any critical moments which arose in the classroom, but I also emphasized that they were free to talk about whatever they considered important and wanted to share.

Three broad questions guided the search to discover what the language-learning experience is like for adults of different ages:

- How is age coconstructed in the EFL classroom context and in the personal narratives of adult language learners?

I was particularly interested in finding out what can be observed about the ways that age is played out in the classroom activities and in the relations among the learners and with the teacher. I was also interested in discovering what perceptions the learners have of themselves and of others and what perceptions they believe others have of them.

- What beliefs and attitudes do adult language learners have about age and about language learning, and how do these beliefs and attitudes intersect with the way age is enacted?

This question covers three more detailed ones. First, in what ways do adult learners believe that age constrains or enhances their language-learning experience? How can prior life experiences be seen to have impacted on their attitudes and beliefs regarding both age and language learning? Finally, in what ways does their language-learning experience carry over into their lives outside the classroom and vary according to where each person positions herself/himself in the lifespan?

- How is age as a subject position interlinked with other subject positions in adult language learners?

This question arose out of my interest in exploring the ways in which age identity is seen to be nuanced by other identities, such as gender and ethnicity.

Chapters 4 through 6 contain first-hand data generated by a group of seven adult EFL students of different ages in Mexico and discuss their significance in terms of the questions set out above (see Table P2.1). Two principal sources furnished access to the participants' construction of age: the language lessons I observed and the stories they told me in the interviews and narrative accounts. Because of the ongoing nature of the data collection process, it was possible to combine both sources advantageously, either corroborating in interviews what had been observed in the classroom or confirming in the observations something expressed earlier in the

TABLE P2.1 Profile of the participants

Name	Age	Gender	Course level	Profession	Academic background
Adela	48	F	6	Middle-school teacher	Some university studies
Berta	59	F	3	Physician	University graduate
David	23	M	6	University student	Some university studies
Elsa	34	F	2	Salesperson	Some university studies
Felix	68	M	2	Accountant (retired)	University graduate
Gilda	36	F	6	Actuary	University graduate
Hector	69	M	3	Physician	University graduate

interviews or narrative accounts. At the end of the course, the opportunity presented itself to interview the five teachers who taught the English classes in which the participants were enrolled (see Table P2.2). The three chapters which follow present the most significant findings to emerge from the study, and highlight what was unique and what was shared in their experience of age and language learning.

Chapter 4 describes the construction of age in later adulthood by two older men, Hector and Felix. Although their life stories converge in many ways, they are markedly distinct in others. The social consequences of retirement are seen to be particularly significant in their different experiences and understanding of age. Also notable are the manifestations of ageist discourses that they have each internalized.

Chapter 5 interweaves the stories of Adela, Berta, Elsa and Gilda, four 'midlife' women who carefully position themselves as neither old nor young. The lack of a corresponding term for 'midlife' or 'middle age' in Spanish is one of the more interesting findings to emerge in this part of the study. The age identity of these midlife adults is closely interlinked with their identities as women, professionals and mothers, among others. Their stories relate how these competing positions are often a source of conflict in the patriarchal society of contemporary Mexico.

In Chapter 6, I present the narrative of a university student as a case of the construction of young adulthood. David's story brings to light the way in which his desire for emotional independence is at variance with his continued economic dependence on his family, illustrating very poignantly how competing discourses of age vie with one another in the enactment of his identity.

TABLE P2.2 Profile of the teachers

Name	Age	Gender	Course level	Responsibility	Academic background
Martin	35	M	6	Team teacher with Ramon	Undergraduate coursework in English language teaching completed
Nidia	43	F	2	Head teacher and supervising teacher	University graduate in communication. Master's studies in education in process
Ramon	46	M	3	Team teacher with Martin	University graduate in education Master's studies completed in applied linguistics
			6	Head teacher	
Simon	25	M	2	Practice teacher	Completing undergraduate coursework in English language teaching
Tomas	26	M	2	Practice teacher	Completing undergraduate coursework in English language teaching

The stories of the seven participants highlight the significance the language-learning experience has for them at this precise moment of their lives in terms of their personal, academic or professional circumstances and aspirations. This connects importantly with the ways in which they construct complex, new identities for themselves as a major outcome of their language-learning experience. In broad terms, the two most important findings coming out of the study are, first, the experience of learning a language varies according to each person's position in the lifespan and involves both linguistic and nonlinguistic dimensions, and second, the age identity of foreign language learners is closely interwoven with their other subject positions.

4 Constructing Age in Later Adulthood

Introduction

This chapter contains two stories, first Hector's and then Felix's, which bring to light their enactment of age, that is, their performance of age through discursive practices. Each story is divided into four parts, beginning with a panoramic view of their lives to date, followed by a picture of what learning English has meant to them. This is followed by some scenes from the classroom language lessons in which Hector and Felix participated, and it ends with other scenes depicting their lives in the world beyond the classroom that illustrate the construction of their age identity. My concluding remarks point out how these two stories, at times remarkably parallel and at other times vastly divergent, contribute to our understanding of the construction of age in later adulthood and to the formulation of responses to the questions that were posed.

Hector's Story: A Tale of Progress

Hector's story can aptly be titled 'A tale of progress' because the main thread that ties his story together is that of success or progress. Hector sees his life as a series of conquests that have enabled him to move upwards in the world. This is a part of a progress–decline narrative, in that life is envisioned as having a binary mode, progress or decline (Gullette, 2004). Implicit in the idea of progress is that the alternative is decline; one is either progressing or declining. There is a drive in Hector's case to keep the progress narrative going as long as possible.

A Thumbnail Sketch of Hector's Life

At the time of the fieldwork Hector was 70 years old, a physician specializing in occupational medicine. He had retired from his job in a teaching hospital in the Mexican public health sector five years previously, but still maintains his private practice. He is married and has four adult children. Hector's description of his upbringing in a family of shopkeepers referred as much to the paucity of culture in the home as it did to the economic limitations to which he was subject. Although he grew up in straitened circumstances, he now enjoys a comfortable and privileged lifestyle that includes frequent trips to the United States. He attributed this change in socioeconomic status to his triumphs in the academic and professional worlds. Academic success represents the highest value for him; the interviews abound with stories of his educational and career achievements and the corresponding social prestige these brought him. In Extract 1, he credited this success to his mental capacities and to 'destiny', claiming:

Extract 1

```
1   I was born under a good star. . . . Under this good star were . . . my[1]
2   capabilities . . . mental capacities, obviously . . . that enabled me to
3   advance . . . because it is very difficult to move from one social station
4   to another . . . another one. (Hector, Interview 3)
```

Repeated allusions to his academic background and his status as a professional permeate all the interviews, and carried over to his comments about his children. Hector mentioned with evident pride that all four are university educated and speak several languages, but did not refer to any other aspects of their lives.

Hector also spoke at great length about the famous and influential people he has known over the years, many of whom have served as 'connections' for advancement at different points in his life.

The Goal of Learning English

At the time I interviewed him, Hector explained that retirement had brought the academic and professional aspects of his life course to a virtual halt. Learning English then has become part of his desire to reach new educational and social goals. When asked to tell me more about this, he made the comments that appear in the following extract:

Extract 2

H = Hector; P = Patricia

```
1   H:  Yes, I'm interested in . . . in learning the language . . . as fast as
2       possible. But not because I am in a rush for institutional reasons.
3       If . . . if I don't hurry up, I won't have time to learn the language.
4   P:  What do you mean?!
5   H:  Yes, it's not . . . it's not a drama . . . but now at . . . at this age . . . at
6       my age . . . you have to do things more quickly.
7   P:  OK . . . OK.
8   H:  No . . . no . . . no . . . I'm doing it and enjoying it . . . and moreover,
```

9	I feel 'alive' ... doing it ... because at this point in time, what
10	for? If I've lived my whole life without the language ... I can
11	keep living whatever time I have left ... no, no, no ... it's a
12	personal ambition ... but, yes, I have to hurry up to keep
13	progressing. (Hector, Interview 2)

Hector brought up the issue of age himself when we first talked about his reasons for wanting to learn English, explaining that he is 'interested in learning the language as fast as possible' (lines 1 and 2) and that if he does not hurry up, he will not have time to learn it. He added that at his age 'you have to do things more quickly' (line 6). This can be seen as an enactment of an old age identity and an expression of age anxiety. He went on to say in line 9 that studying English makes him 'feel alive', an interesting choice of words, suggesting that he is moving forward, advancing and, by remaining 'productive', staving off decline. It is important to note that retirement in industrialized societies is a life-marking event, understood by many to signal the end of advancement and productivity. For Hector, then, studying English would seem to signify a way to continue his progress narrative.

The fact of the matter is he does not really need to learn the language for any practical purpose. As he pointed out, he has managed to live his whole life without knowing English (lines 10 and 11). Rather, it is a personal ambition and allows him to remain active now that he has retired. He recognized that there is a prestige factor as well; knowing English signifies an increase in cultural capital (Bourdieu, 1977). In Extract 3, he gives voice to this idea.

Extract 3

1	I'm Mexican and ... and ... and proud to be Mexican. So, I am someone
2	who speaks another language besides Spanish, OK? Yes, it makes you feel
3	that ... that there is a cultural value that is more ... that is higher ...
4	because I speak [two languages]. ... It increases my self-esteem ... my
5	status. (Hector, Interview 1)

Besides the 'cultural value' (line 3) and greater self-worth and status (lines 4 and 5) that knowing English affords, Hector viewed it as 'another step upwards' and 'added value' for himself on a personal level (Hector, Interview 3). This has provided him with ample motives for studying the language.

The Construction of Age: In the Classroom

Hector maintained that the best time to start learning another language is in childhood, expressing, in the next extract, the commonly held notion that 'younger is better.'

Extract 4

H = Hector; P = Patricia

```
 1  P:  What is the ideal age to begin learning a language ... in your
 2      opinion?
 3  H:  There is a very 'Mexican' expression that says 'sooner than
 4      soon' (desde denantes) ... that's correctly expressed, eh ... it's old
 5      Spanish ... in other words, as soon as possible.
 6  P:  Uh huh. At what age?
 7  H:  Learning to speak it as a second language? Immediately ...
 8      because ... because you learn ... faster and you can see it in the
 9      bilingual communities near the United States that use two
10      [languages].
11  P:  And why is that? Why do they learn so quickly?
12  H:  Because they do it naturally. There are no inhibitions ... there are
13      no prejudices ... there are no ... besides there are no rules.
        (Hector, Interview 1)
```

Given that Hector received only minimal exposure to English in *secundaria* (equivalent to US middle school), he now feels that as an older learner, 'a handicap exists with respect to the younger students' (Hector, Interview 2). He claimed that this is because most of them have studied English in bilingual kindergartens and primary schools; however, on the basis of my own knowledge of this population, I believe this is unlikely to be the case. Hector argued that their early contact with the language has put them ahead of the older members of the class. In his opinion, the younger students, whom he calls 'children', are also sharper, less inhibited and more self-confident, whereas mature students become blocked more easily and lack self-assurance.

Later, in an about-face, he questioned whether success in learning a new language is a matter of age-related learning ability, for he said that, 'if it were, I wouldn't be here. ... What you need is motivation ... and that is internal' (Hector, Interview 1). He pointed out that learning a language is not a priority for the younger students because they are focused on their academic studies. He believes that mature students, on the other hand, have more experience and resources to fall back on, and also more time to dedicate to language learning.

In assessing his own progress over the course of the semester in his narrative accounts, Hector cited listening as his principal problem, maintaining that his auditory memory is not as good as his visual memory. Interestingly, he did not attribute this to any age-related decline, but rather to the limited number of opportunities he has had to practice the language in conversation, compared to those he has had to read it.

Some of these beliefs and attitudes underscored Hector's enactment of age in the classroom activities and in his relationship with his fellow students and with the teacher. It is necessary to clarify that the lessons were generally teacher-fronted, with virtually no small-group work taking place. The teacher talked a great deal of the time and the interaction was principally between the teacher and individual students. Notwithstanding the rather constrained communicative environment, Hector proved to be a highly vocal participant; I recorded numerous occasions on which he volunteered responses, asked questions or requested clarification from the teacher. He made frequent humorous remarks and displayed an upbeat attitude, despite the fact that he often failed to provide the correct answer or to respond with the facility he desired. Even so, in my estimation, his proficiency in English at this stage was comparable to that of the other students in the group.

Enactment of Age: Examining Classroom Activities

The classroom activities followed the textbook, *American Headway 2* (Soars & Soars, 2001b), very closely. As an affluent professional and a frequent international traveler, Hector could undoubtedly relate to the global perspective of *American Headway 2* more easily than the younger students in the group, few of whom have had the opportunity to travel abroad. Yet he would not have encountered much in the textbook that engaged him as an older adult. Consequently, in those classroom activities having an explicit orientation to the world of young people, Hector generally modified the exercises to fit his circumstances as an older person. For example, Hector made the substitutions that I recorded in the following classroom observation notes:

CLASS 8, MARCH 18, 2004

Time	Activity	Hector
10'	Exercise 1 from textbook: 'My mother/father drives me crazy when...'; 'I hate it when my boyfriend/girlfriend...'; and 'It really annoys me when...' (*American Headway 2*, Unit 2, 16) Teacher – Whole group	Hector [H] changes the structures to 'My children drive me crazy when...' and 'I hate it when my wife...,' then makes a joke.

When the occasion arose, Hector was positioned as or actively took up the part of an older person. For instance, in a class discussion about teenagers, Hector talked about raising children, giving the viewpoint of a parent. He also recounted how he had had to wear short pants as a young child, as was the custom years ago, and then how he was finally allowed to wear long pants, a symbol of his transition to maturity. Volunteering this story suggests that Hector wished to serve as a historical witness, sharing the perspective of an older person who has had the benefit of living in other times. Clearly, he places a value on his accumulated life experience. At another level, the routine practice whereby Hector took up or was assigned the subject position 'older person', illustrates the extent to which age salience is a defining feature of our culture.

At the same time, Hector evinced a desire to maintain a vital connection with the contemporary world of young people. He commented that the teacher's references to current movies and songs compel him to stay abreast of the times. In addition to listening to young people's music in class, he goes to the movies often, although he confessed that he does not always enjoy the films he sees. However, in his opinion, this enables him to keep up with the interests of young people. He remarked:

Extract 5

1   And given ... my ... my personal circumstance of age ... the teacher
2   is up-to-date and he is talking to young people ... well, I ... I
3   personally must be ready to talk about a movie. If they ask me what
4   movie ... and I say 'Casablanca' ... that's ancient history. (Hector, Interview 2)

Nonetheless, on the various occasions in which songs were used as a classroom exercise, Hector either did not participate or made only token attempts to sing along with the other students. I sensed in Hector an internal tension between a glorification of youth culture, on the one hand, and a satisfaction with the place where he finds himself in the life course, on the other.

Enactment of Age: In Relations with Fellow Students

In my observations, I noted that while Hector got along well with his classmates, it was he who invariably took it upon himself to develop a cordial relationship with them, and not the other way around. Hector admitted this, pointing out, in Extract 6, that because he is 'different' from the other students, a clear reference to his age, he must be the one to adapt to the present environment and to bridge the gap between himself and the younger members of the class.

Extract 6

1   There is a … a … a biological maxim … 'Animals that don't adapt
2   perish.' So, in this case I am the one who is different. … Well, the others
3   are in their … in their own environment … in their situation. I am the one
4   who comes in … so, I definitely have been the one who has made the effort
5   to … to understand everyone else. (Hector, Interview 5)

One of the ways Hector endeavored to fit into the group was by positioning himself as the classroom 'expert' in vocabulary, a place he carved out for himself in which he could establish himself as a person worthy of respect. He brought his electronic dictionary to every class and was pleased when his classmates asked him for help with the meaning of unknown words because, as he said, 'they treat me … just like any other classmate' (Hector, Interview 2).

Even so, on most occasions in which the activities were carried out in pairs or small teams, Hector chose to work with the two students who normally sat next to him, both from the outside community and slightly older than the other members of the group. He explained to me that he had formed his own small group of the more mature students in the class. This act of self-segregation suggests that, despite his claims to be well-accepted by the group, there is a perceptible defensiveness in Hector's manner. In fact, he used that very expression, remarking, 'I defend myself by showing [the younger students] that I am here to learn' (Hector, Interview 5).

Yet at other moments he adopted a more accommodating posture. In the same interview, he imagined that he was being positioned by his fellow students as 'a little old man taking a class and not doing too badly' (Hector, Interview 5). His use of the ageist term *viejito* (little old man) in a self-deprecating display of humor seems to imply that a good performance in language learning is not expected from an older person.

Enactment of Age: In Relations with the Teacher

Hector's attitude of accommodation extended to his relationship with the teacher as well. In my classroom observation notes, I registered a series of episodes which took place over the length of the course in which Ramon, the teacher, made disparaging references to age and joked about age and aging, most often singling out Hector as his target. For example, he made humorous remarks about Alzheimer's, about the 'older generation' and their incapacity to use the internet, about Hector, saying, 'Hector is just a little older than me!' and to Hector himself, joking, 'You're a little old for that.' The following excerpt from my classroom observation notes illustrates this kind of ageist humor:

CLASS 18, MAY 4, 2004

Time	Activity	Hector
30'	Exercise 'Talking about you' from textbook. Questions and answers about hopes and ambitions. Informal conversation. (*American Headway 2*, Unit 5, 35)	When called on, H explains that while he is officially retired, he still works at home and has his private practice.
	Teacher – whole group	Ramon [R] asks if he still does surgery. H answers that he does not because (1) he finds it difficult to stand on his feet for so many hours, and (2) the new technology requires learning how to operate a great deal of equipment that he is not familiar with. R comments that he thought maybe it was because he [H] had a shaky hand.

In the fifth and final interview, I asked Hector how he felt about the teacher's remarks. He started out by claiming that instead of being bothered, he felt it was 'a compliment' and was flattered because it meant that he is 'a unique person' (Hector, Interview 5). When asked to explain this further, he made the lengthy commentary that follows:

Extract 7

1   What I'm saying is, no ... no ... age has never been a ... problem ...
2   for me ... starting with the fact that I have always looked much
3   younger than I am. When I began to practice, people said to me, 'You
4   are very young, Doctor' ... and for a long time after that, I looked
5   younger than I was. What's more, my voice, by some quirk of fate ...
6   people still confuse mine with my son's and I just take it as a joke.
7   'Hey, son.' 'Yes, mom, what do you want.' ... And my wife's
8   friends begin to talk, until they realize that they're not talking to my
9   son ... they're talking to me. But, no, not in the least. Even more, it's
10 ... it's a motivation for me because I think the teacher is very
11 motivating. He may have, like any human being, a lot of ... repressed
12 or unrepressed psychological issues ... because in that case he can

13   show them, right? ... the ... the ... source ... attitudes ... of ... very
14   deep-seated ... very difficult to appreciate. I'm not ... not a
15   psychologist ... because I'm a doctor ... and at any given moment he
16   can show them [attitudes]. He has a pony tail. He's not a typical
17   teacher. Moreover ... he's up-to-date because just like me he wears
18   jeans. No ... he doesn't come dressed with the formality of other
19   times. This man ... it seems that he has an inclination towards
20   motorcycle culture. Maybe he is a ... a rebel in another personality
21   ... because he likes motorcycles, but as a teacher he is a good English
22   teacher. He brings a lot of enthusiasm ... he takes his role seriously. ...
23   No ... because you can't ... you can't ... and you shouldn't deny your
24   age, OK? A person should be more or less satisfied. (Hector,
     Interview 5)

Although Hector insisted that age has never been a problem for him (lines 1 and 2), he gave this reason, 'I have always looked much younger than I am' (lines 2 and 3). He then related how people have always perceived him to be younger than he is, switching to their voices to show how he is seen by others. 'You are very young, Doctor' (lines 3 and 4). He added that, to this day, he is mistaken on the telephone for his son, using a constructed dialogue to illustrate his point (line 7). He clearly likes 'passing' – being considered younger than he is. This would seem to contradict his initial statement that he has no problem about his age. He then went back to his original claim, saying that he was not in the least disturbed by the teacher's comments (line 9).

At that point, the conversation took an interesting turn. Hector launched into a commentary about the teacher that, while not overtly critical, indicates that he felt the teacher might have some unresolved psychological issues, perhaps even concerning his own aging process (lines 11–14). He also questioned the teacher's appearance and behavior in terms of age-appropriacy, mentioning the teacher's hairstyle, a pony tail, and his informal and modern way of dressing, which Hector associates with motorcyclists and rebels (lines 16–20). He then counteracted these negative remarks by praising Ramon as a good and enthusiastic English teacher who takes his role seriously (lines 21 and 22). Finally, he returned to his starting point and commented that we should accept our age (and aging), saying, 'you can't ... and you shouldn't deny your age, OK? A person should be more or less satisfied' (lines 23 and 24).

The contradictions in this extract are interesting. First, it is clear that Hector places great value on looking young, or 'passing' as young. In this, he is manifesting his own ageist attitudes by distancing himself from who he really is. At the same time, he shows some ambivalence about the norms of age-appropriacy, both with regard to the teacher's appearance and behavior, and his own choice to wear jeans. In the end, his remarks advocate accepting aging as a fact of life and finding a sense of life satisfaction. These are discourses of positive aging, in that a value is placed on continued development over a lifetime and 'age is [seen as] an accomplishment, something one has worked long and hard at' (Andrews, 1999: 310).

But more to the point, at the end of the day it is hard to know to what extent Hector resented the teacher's constant ageist jokes and either chose not to or did not feel free to express his feelings. It may also have been Hector's personal way of handling being positioned as the target of 'good-natured' ridicule because of his age. Whatever the reason, he seemed to be accommodating to or colluding with the blatantly ageist behavior of the teacher.

The Construction of Age: Beyond the Classroom

To come to a better understanding of how Hector constructed his age as a language learner, it is helpful to explore the wider context of his life, for the significance of learning English at this precise moment in his life course is part of a much larger story. In it, Hector's age identity connects with his other identities, and together they flow in and out of the classroom, shaping his experiences. The interviews, and to a lesser extent the narrative accounts, allowed me to share in the construction of Hector's personal narrative and to focus on the interplay of his multiple identities.

In this section, I draw attention to some of the more illustrative moments in the complex, and often conflicting, construction of Hector's age identity. It is important to mention that part of the social setting of the interviews included the particular positions we took up in relation to each other. Hector and I ostensibly belong to the same age group of older adults, and share similar academic qualifications and socioeconomic status. Significant differences are our gender, nationality and particular areas of expertise. For example, many of Hector's digressions during the interviews seemed intended to position himself as a well-respected academic and professional. Because no similar incidents were observed in his interaction with his classmates or with the teacher, there was the sense that he was attempting to put himself on an equal footing with me, as a fellow academic. Also, on various occasions, Hector spoke favorably of the United States, never once criticizing American culture. In view of the complexities of the relationship between the two countries, it is possible that things would have played out differently had the interviewer been a Mexican rather than me, an American. An awareness of these circumstances operated at some level during the interviews, and I have tried to take them into consideration in the discussion and interpretation of the data.

Competing Discourses of Age

When asked for a description of the life course, Hector separated it into four stages: birth, growth, reproduction and death, a view that owes much to his medical training. He went on to state that the biological, psychological, familial, social and academic aspects of these events exist concurrently, beginning at birth and first peaking at 35–40 years of age (see Figure 4.1). The life course then moves upwards more gradually during maturity until, at around 60, a biological and psychosocial decline commences that continues until one dies. Although Hector referred very dispassionately to aging after 60 as a process of degeneration and involution, on a personal level he denied that he himself is at a point of decline, despite his being 70 years old.

What is more, Hector referred explicitly to his chronological age on various occasions during the interviews. According to Coupland et al. (1991), age-telling is a means of identity-marking that may reveal a person's positive or negative self-appraisal of their contextual aging, as well as the extent to which they perceive their chronological and contextual life positions to be in or out of phase. In Hector's case, and considering the pride he took in passing as younger, it is likely that the disclosure of his age was a stratagem to elicit confirmation from me of his 'youthfulness' and to underscore his favorable life position when weighed against the circumstances of other 70-year-olds. This type of interplay between discourses of decline and of positive aging is woven throughout Hector's narrative.

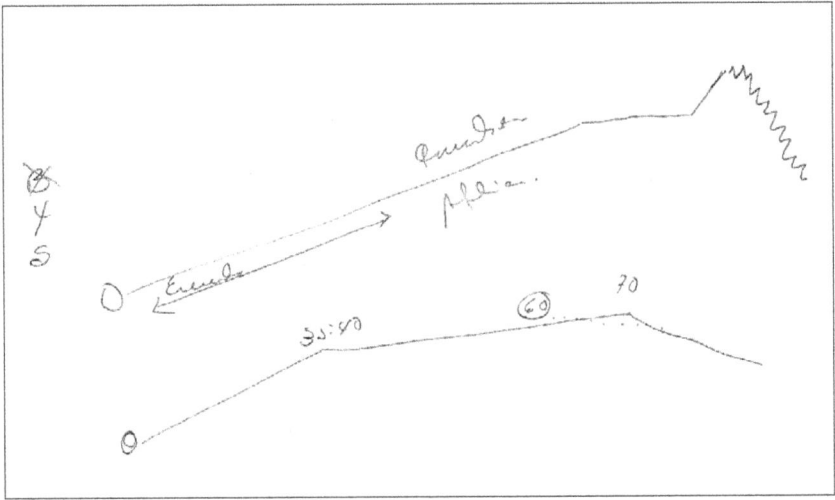

Figure 4.1 Hector's sketch of the life course

Living in the Past and Living in the Present

A case in point is the ambivalence Hector shows about the past and present. Coupland *et al.* (1991) indicate that references to past times, or temporal framing processes, provide an indirect way of constructing an elderly age identity, to the extent that they locate a person in a particular lifespan position. Hector recounted stories of his past experiences in every interview that generally worked to build the image of a successful person and that displayed a largely positive aging attitude. He insisted that all stages of life are good, although they invariably have ups and downs, and he could not identify any particular moment as the best in his own life. When considering how his life might have been different had he made other decisions, he declared that he is satisfied with the choices he has made and emphasized the pointlessness of having regrets.

At the same time, his tales are often tinged with a measure of nostalgia, as can be perceived, for example, in his accounts of having worked with close relatives of three different Mexican presidents in the past, and in allusions to his university years in which he proudly referred to being 'a founder of the University City ... a member of the very first class to study in the University City' (Hector, Interview 1).

With regard to his present life, Hector explained that since his retirement from the public sector, he has endeavored to remain productive by maintaining his private practice, doing occasional consulting, and studying English. He emphasized how important it is to keep up-to-date on changes in the world, to be flexible and willing to try new things. For him, learning English has been a therapy of sorts 'because you need to feel you are progressing in life' (Hector, Interview 1). Certainly, such pursuits appear to be a recipe for successful aging and psychological well-being. Yet at the same time they are indicative of the burden that is placed on older adults to preserve their health, active lifestyle and independence indefinitely by a society that puts a premium on production and deplores decay and dependency. In other words, older people are expected to conserve their youthful qualities and to remain forever 'healthy, sexually active, engaged, productive, and self-reliant' (Cole, 1992: 229).

Engagement and Disengagement

Although he talked about seeking new challenges, Hector also stated that he finds himself more alone and less attached to his friends and family, a situation he considers typical at this time of life. According to disengagement theory, decreased interaction between the older individual and others belonging to the same social system results in mutual distancing (Gubrium *et al.*, 1994). Hector described it this way:

Extract 8

1 You begin losing contact with others because from the
2 psychological point of view there occurs a flattening of affect.... In...
3 the French say, *'la belle indifférence'* and in Mexico they say, 'I
4 don't give a damn (*me importa madre*).' (Hector, Interview 4)

The loss of affect (line 2) is particularly evident in several remarks Hector made about his relationship with his wife during the course of the interviews. In Extract 9, he stressed how they now have different interests and lead fairly independent lives.

Extract 9

1 Well, it's a question of interests ... even in young people. You need to
2 be a newlywed like Fox[2] to go around holding hands with your wife.
3 ... So, with a married couple that is one way ... and that is the way I
4 experience it ... no, no, no ... whether it's right or not ... it is my
5 situation. It is ... I call it ... recovering the individuality of the person.
6 My wife is very religious ... and I'm not. She believes ... she has her
7 beliefs ... and I have mine. (Hector, Interview 3)

Hector provided further confirmation of his own disengagement or withdrawal from a social world in which he had formerly enjoyed an active role when he observed that the social aspect of his life began to decline once his children finished their schooling. He remarked, 'I think it's no longer mine [my moment]' (Hector, Interview 3).

Dependence and Independence

Hector acknowledged a change in his status that has come about over the years. He spoke with humor about his role reversal, from being a teacher to being a student in the classroom. In Extract 10, he recounted an incident which illustrates how his position in relation to his former medical students has reversed itself.

Extract 10

1 I was head of the teaching program at the Centro Medico ... and, well,
2 my [former] students logically, and because of their connections, were
3 moving up professionally. So when I retired, many of them were in
4 important positions.... So you ... you ... you keep on ... and later we
5 would go out for lunch ... with my former students ... especially the
6 female students ... and it seemed very funny to me because at the
7 corner of Doctor Marquez and Cuauhtemoc Avenue, when we were

8   about to cross the street ... they would take my hand like a little boy
9   ... and I thought, right, because they are going to look really bad if the
10   old man is left there in the street because they didn't take good care of
11   him. So now ... things have changed. It used to be me that would take
12   them by the arm in other times. Times have changed and now they
13   take me ... but by the hand like a little boy ... so that ... they say, 'At
14   least I am pulling him along, right?' So, no, all this has made me
15   come to accept my ... my age ... and the jokes I make ... I myself
16   make them at the expense of age. (Hector, Interview 5)

In this narration, Hector described how his former students have come to occupy the positions of stature he and his colleagues had formerly held, in a kind of changing of the guard (lines 1–3). Moreover, he recounted how they have traded places in social situations as well, giving the example of how his students took charge and looked after him as if he were a child (lines 7 and 8). His remark that 'it seemed very funny to me' (line 6) and the references to himself in the third person, in 'they are going to look really bad if the old man is left there in the street because they didn't take good care of him' (lines 9–11), suggest that the situation was both humorous and odd for him, in the sense that he seemed to feel he should expect to be regarded as an older person and yet is not quite comfortable with this change of identity. He again made the comparison of his treatment to that appropriate for 'a little boy' (line 13). The recurrent image of age as a second childhood in contemporary Western culture, or the inverted-U model, is part of ageist discourses because of the implications of declining competence and increased dependency. As Coupland *et al.* explain:

> A more elaborate conceptualisation of decrement in later life is the *inverted-U* model, which implies that elderly linguistic and other behaviours are in some specific respects not only moving towards lower levels of competence but moving *back* to the levels and types of behaviour associated with the early years of life. The model feeds off the more general mythological association of the old with children in our society – old age as a 'second childhood'. (Coupland *et al.*, 1991: 12, emphasis as in original)

In lines 14–16, Hector voiced his increasing acceptance of his age in a jocular tone, as here and elsewhere he made himself the target of his own humor. Yet humor can have both an upside and a downside, and making self-deprecating jokes is a common ageist practice among older people themselves. As such, it reveals 'the "buy-in" by older people themselves about the intrinsic devaluation of old age by society at large' (Cohen, 2001: 576). According to Levy, 'after a lifetime of exposure to a culture's age stereotypes, older individuals direct these age stereotypes inward' (Levy, 2001: 579). Perhaps this also explains why Hector shared the story with me, an older person like himself, whereas he might not have done so with a younger interviewer.

Age and Other Identities

Hector's age identity is intertwined with other subject positions, the prime one being his professional identity. The interviews are permeated with repeated allusions to his academic background and, more importantly, to his continued status as a professional. He remarked, 'I boast about it ... I am up-to-date ... and I have taken courses and everything' (Hector, Interview 2). Over the course of the interviews, a strong connection emerged between Hector's lifelong preoccupation with productivity as a professional and his gendered identity. He positioned himself as what is popularly considered to be a 'prototypical Mexican male', the breadwinner and head of the household, heterosexual and viewing with disdain his wife's religious beliefs and political aspirations. His enactment of a heteronormative gender identity was further manifested in the following commentary about the life cycle, in which he voiced intolerance for other sexual practices.

Extract 11

H = Hector; P = Patricia

1　H:　That's why I said to you 'the classic model': birth, growth,
2　　　reproduction and death ... and right now reproduction is in ... in
3　　　quotes. Young people don't want to reproduce.
4　P:　Not necessarily, right?
5　H:　Homosexuality, transvestism, and the whole list of things
6　　　people talk about ... and ... and ... even though it is more
7　　　elegant to call it ... yet it amounts to the same thing ... sexual
8　　　preference ... but, what it means is that ... homosexuals are
9　　　never ever going to have children.
10　P:　Uh huh.
11　H:　So then they adopt them ... and that is a very thorny subject.
12　　　What do they want to adopt them for? Because maybe what they
13　　　want is someone to live with them, right? Who knows? That can
14　　　lead to another ... another issue. (Hector, Interview 4)

A further link can be made with Hector's ethnic identity, about which he displayed negative feelings throughout the interviews. While Hector was able to achieve professional and economic success and the corresponding social status, the question of his ethnicity[3] raised an obstacle he felt was not entirely possible to overcome through academic merit. Short of stature, moderately dark-skinned and possessing many of the facial features characteristic of the precolonial indigenous populations, Hector's *mestizo*[4] appearance is one that is not highly valued in Mexico. Hector manifested a disparaging attitude toward his ethnicity in self-deprecating humorous remarks about being 'an Indian' (Hector, Interviews 1 and 3). In postcolonial Mexico, the term 'Indian' is an extremely offensive one, blending 'the diverse cultures of the natives into one deprecating name that became a symbol for vanquished, uneducated, and stupid' (Fortes de Leff, 2002: 620). Concern about his ethnicity carried great weight for Hector throughout his life, as can be appreciated in the following extract:

Extract 12

1   I married a pretty woman because I wanted my children to have
2   another ... another biotype ... because that, yes, can count a lot, even
3   though ... even though people don't say it. ... But ... but that ... those
4   matters are ... and in Mexico, yes, they are very ... very much to be
5   taken into account. That ... that perhaps, yes, has been one of the
6   [main] issues ... how can I say it? ... of social impact for me ...
7   because, well, for other people ... because some people maybe didn't
8   think I would achieve anything. I see it that way ... and when I did get
9   ahead they outdid themselves trying to do the same thing. 'If this guy
10 can, then why shouldn't I?' But, that was ... that was like saying that I
11 had fewer ... fewer resources, something that ... that no ... definitely
12 is not the case, OK ... because if ... if they had had the resources, they
13 would ... they would have achieved something on their own ... but if
14 ... or ... [they]wanted to take away what ... what I had gotten. They
15 never ... never took away what I had. (Hector, Interview 4)

In lines 1 and 2, Hector openly disclosed to me that he made a conscious decision to marry a pretty woman so that his children would look different. The word 'pretty' (*bonita*) in Spanish is clearly understood to mean 'fair-skinned' (*güera*) in this context. He himself pointed out that, while not normally acknowledged, prejudice exists in Mexico against people of darker skin color (lines 2–5). This is confirmed by Fortes de Leff:

Skin color remains important in social and political relationships today. It has been a principal symbolic organizer and identity model since the Conquest. Being 'white' or 'blonde,' as Mexicans call white-skinned people, is associated with the people in power, belonging to a higher social class, deserving privileges. Being 'dark' relates to an Indian origin, denoting an inferior social class and implying submission. (Fortes de Leff, 2002: 620–621)

Fanon has written how the visible signs of racial difference exert a powerful psychological force on the construction of the self, saying: 'I am overdetermined from without. I am the slave not of the "idea" that others have of me but of my own appearance' (Fanon, 1995: 325). Hector admitted that his physical appearance has given rise to a lifelong struggle on his part to succeed (lines 5–8). His perception that other people viewed him as less capable and less worthy is made forceful by his use of their voices to claim, 'If this guy can, then why shouldn't I?' (lines 9 and 10). Although this extract shows that Hector derived satisfaction in having gotten ahead while his detractors did not, it also suggests that he felt his triumph was earned despite his ethnicity.

Of all the participants in the study, Hector seemed the most concerned with his social identity. In his interactions with the teacher, his classmates and with me as the researcher, he took advantage of every opportunity to position himself as a success, a man of learning, professional stature and affluence. Access to the English language and to Anglophone culture have played an important part in the construction of his identity, for he attaches great prestige to British and 'Bostonian' English, and to European and American cultures. He explained that he learned to speak 'Bostonian' English, 'the English spoken by cultured people in the United States' (Hector, Interview 1), and believes that he is treated better than most Mexicans in the United States precisely because he speaks a 'cultured' variety of English.

Connecting the Pieces

While Hector's is largely a tale of progress, his story is a complex one. Decline discourses form an undercurrent that is never far from the surface, competing with positive aging discourses. Hector's narrative traces the unbroken upward movement of his life from his early academic accomplishments through a series of professional and economic triumphs that secured him a highly prized social position. Now that he is retired, he has both the satisfaction of having achieved many of his life goals and the self-imposed challenge of keeping his level of productivity up so that the progress narrative will be sustained.

Learning English is one way Hector has found to remain active and to continue to advance professionally. Being able to speak English is also an added bonus on his frequent trips to the United States. More importantly, it is a major source of prestige for him in view of all that English signifies in terms of cultural capital (Bourdieu, 1977). This constitutes his primary incentive for taking up the study of English again at this moment of his life. While he enjoys the academic challenge of learning, this undertaking has much more to do with his life in the world beyond the classroom. Thus, it is an integral part of the ongoing construction of his identity and of his life story.

Hector does not consider learning a language as an older adult to be a simple task. He espouses the popular belief that younger people have 'natural' advantages that enable them to learn more easily than older ones. Nevertheless, he feels that older learners can compensate for this by being more motivated and more dedicated to the task. The notion that 'younger is better' carries over into Hector's beliefs about age and aging in general. In general terms, he appears to be working under the assumption that aging is inherently a process of progressive mental and physical decrement. Yet there were various instances in the course of the fieldwork where he challenged the dominant age discourse of decline.

These beliefs and attitudes were played out in the classroom, where age was frequently a salient factor in Hector's relations with the other students and particularly with the teacher. He positioned himself, and perceived himself as being positioned by others, as an outsider because of his age, often choosing to self-segregate in the class activities. This suggests that perhaps he felt less entitled than the younger students, for example, to make demands in the class or complain about the way the lessons were conducted directly to the teacher. It may also explain in part his tendency to accommodate or collude with the teacher's overt ageism and to resort to self-deprecating humor. Such beliefs and attitudes were also evident during the interviews, where his narrations of incidents involving his life outside the classroom brought a wide repertoire of ageist discourses into play. Although Hector described the life course as taking a downward turn at around 60, he was adamant that this did not apply to him. His satisfaction in passing as younger and in having as yet no signs of the physical or mental deterioration he associates with old age, suggests that he resists aging. Such an 'anti-aging' discourse is in reality an ageist one, for little value is placed on growing old. This 'internalized ageism' (Cruikshank, 2003: 153) was reinforced by his frequently expressed admiration of youth culture and his desire to maintain a connection with it.

At the same time, Hector also displayed a positive aging attitude in different ways. He expressed an overall life satisfaction and a favorable view of the place where he now finds himself in the life course. The internal tension between an idolization of youth culture and satisfaction with his position as an older adult is palpable. The same contrasting discourses appear throughout Hector's story, where the sense of living in the present seems to collide at different moments with that of living in the past, as does that of being engaged with being disengaged, and being dependent with being independent. The interplay between decline discourses and positive aging discourses underscores the inconsistent and often contradictory ways in which Hector enacted age.

Hector's age identity is tightly interwoven with his professional, academic and social identities, for together they enable him to position himself as person who has been successful on many fronts over his lifetime. Moreover, they explain his continued endeavors to remain economically, professionally and academically active at this time of his life. In turn, Hector's lifelong concern with productivity seems to be closely tied to his gendered identity as a 'traditional Mexican male', while his perception of having once occupied an inferior social position, along with the persistent devaluation of his ethnicity, may account for the need to achieve that has characterized his life story. As a story of the construction of later adulthood, it offers an interesting example of a tale of progress, yet a highly complex and nuanced one.

Felix's Story: A Tale of Discontent

The story Felix tells is laced with disappointment and frustration. His life right now is not what he would have chosen. Forced to retire at the age of 56, he is overcome at times by a sense of powerlessness that has colored his present outlook on the world. His resentment about the current circumstances of his life is at times shrouded in self-pity, and at others manifests itself as barely contained anger. It seems that he was not prepared for the changes that have occurred at this moment of his life.

A Thumbnail Sketch of Felix's Life

Felix began his first audio-taped narrative account with this very formal third-person introduction:

Extract 13

1   Felix Rodriguez, retired, with 43 years of work experience, and at
2   present 68 years old, considers it necessary, as occupational therapy,
3   to continue acquiring knowledge that will allow him to keep mentally
4   and physically active, by undertaking something he has always wanted
5   to do: learn English. (Felix, Narrative account 1)

It is no coincidence that the first thing Felix mentions, after giving his name, is that he is retired (line 1). Felix worked his entire professional life as a public accountant in different government agencies, until he was compelled to retire because of his age, an event that precipitated a major downturn in his life. Up to that point, the years had elapsed under generally favorable circumstances for Felix. He was born in Sinaloa, in northern Mexico, where his grandparents had owned large extensions of land before losing most of their property during the *Cristero* and agrarian uprisings of the 1920s and 1930s.⁵ Felix's family then settled in a rural part of nearby Sonora where he spent most of his childhood. Subsequently, his parents took his nine brothers and sisters to California to work as *braceros*.⁶ Felix stayed behind because his godmother offered to send him to school; he became the only member of his family to receive a university education. After graduating, he was awarded a scholarship by the American Friends Service Committee and spent nearly a year in Europe before embarking on his long career in the public sector.

Much as in Hector's case, education provided Felix with the means to move from the limited conditions of his childhood, with its unpromising future prospects, to a more privileged socioeconomic position and professional solidity. Felix is married and has three adult children, university educated, all of whom he has sent abroad to learn English. At the present moment, Felix's greatest desire is to keep working, but he has been frustrated in his attempt to do so because he cannot find employment.

The Goal of Learning English

Like Hector, Felix has no pressing need to learn English. At this point in his life, he is taking English classes because he wants to keep active now that he is retired (lines 2–4 of Extract 13). He stated that he would like to recover the skills in English he formerly had when he learned the language as a university student. He also travels frequently to visit his relatives in California, where he has the opportunity to speak English.

The Construction of Age: In the Classroom

Felix declared that childhood is the ideal time to learn a foreign language because a child's capacity for absorption is at its peak at around seven years old. He went on to say:

Extract 14

F = Felix; P = Patricia

1 **F:** It's just that ... I regret not having begun to study a long time
2 ago.
3 **P:** Why?
4 **F:** Well, because of that ... eh? Because I think that ... now ... it is
5 more difficult to learn ... because to make progress at my age ...
6 well, I am losing my faculties, OK?
7 **P:** Such as?
8 **F:** Well, maybe to ... to ... grasp things ... to ... eh? But, if you

9	bring enthusiasm [to the task]... you can overcome this kind of
10	quote unquote disability. (Felix, Interview 1)

In this extract, it is clear that Felix sees age as a major impediment to learning a foreign language. His assumption that age brings with it the loss of mental abilities is expressed, in lines 4–6, in much stronger terms than Hector chose to use. He then tempered this assertion by conceding that enthusiasm can offset the loss of mental agility (lines 8–10).

Felix identified his principal problem with English as listening comprehension. Although he tries to understand what is going on through the context, he has a hearing problem which complicates things. He also has difficulties with pronunciation that he attributes to the fact that he wears dentures, which 'hinder the mobility of my tongue' (Felix, Interview 3). In extract 15, he linked these deficiencies to the aging process.

Extract 15

F = Felix; P = Patricia

1	**F:**	Well... but also when you are old you lose capacities.
2	**P:**	Which ones?
3	**F:**	Well, all kinds... auditory and motor... and whatever else you
4		can think of, eh? Yeah?
5	**P:**	OK.
6	**F:**	I... personally I feel... I... that is... I remember when I was
7		'less old'... I... that is, I was... I was... very energetic.
8	**P:**	Right. Aside from motor capacity and... what was the other one
9		you mentioned?... auditory [functions], ... with respect to
10		reasoning capacity, do you feel any difference?
11	**F:**	Yes... yes, I do.
12	**P:**	In what sense?
13	**F:**	Look... that is, of course, when I was working and when I was
15		studying, well, I had to reason... Now that I am retired... OK... it's
16		always... it's like it is harder for me to reason.
17	**P:**	Uh huh.
18	**F:**	But I try... to make the effort, OK? (Felix, Interview 3)

After stating plainly in that old age brings generalized deficits (lines 1, 3 and 4), Felix recalled that things were different when he was, as he put it rather jokingly, 'less old' (line 7). He admitted that it has been more difficult for him to reason since his retirement (lines 11 and 13–16). Again, his belief that age has a direct impact on language learning seems straightforward and unequivocal when compared to Hector's more tenuous view.

The classroom dynamics, in Felix's case, proved to be significantly different from Hector's experience, in that two practice teachers were assigned to work with the regular teacher for the duration of the course. This meant that the person who gave explanations and directed the activities changed frequently. From the beginning of the course it was clear that Felix's preconceived ideas of how a language class should be conducted clashed with the way things actually transpired. From his remarks in the audio-taped narrative accounts and interviews, it was evident that his expectations involved a traditional, teacher-fronted language lesson. In elaborating on his ideas, he spoke almost exclusively in terms of the teacher as the 'authority', 'expositor' and 'presenter', 'responsible for the exposition of the topics ... particularly for attaining uniformity in the exposition ... and an orderly and logical sequence'. He extended the teacher's obligations to the 'application of the corresponding dynamics ... covering the program ... and maintaining discipline and control'. He also indicated that the teacher's performance and productivity should be 'tracked' and 'evaluated' by the appropriate authorities (Felix, Narrative accounts 2–12). Interestingly, he never referred to the role of the students or of the materials. He expressed considerable dissatisfaction regarding the presence of the practice teachers, finding that it 'confuses us more than what we already are. Changing from one expositor to another I think distracts and interrupts our attention more than it already is' (Felix, Narrative account 7). From his point of view, the participation of three teachers, rather than providing a variety of complementary resources, simply disrupted the order of the lessons.

Perhaps Felix's choice of profession as a public accountant can offer some insight into his penchant for a highly structured, systematic and predictable world, both inside and outside the classroom, an idea which is considered again as it comes up in other parts of his story. This and his conviction that age inevitably brings losses that affect language learning are the principal beliefs and attitudes which had a bearing on his enactment of age.

Enactment of Age: Examining Classroom Activities

The second half of the textbook *American Headway 1* (Soars & Soars, 2001a)[7] formed the basis of the course, although small-group and pair work were routine features of the lessons and more supplementary material was used than in Hector's class. Felix was an active participant in the class and the teachers called on him frequently. In my observations, he had more difficulties in understanding and responding than most of his classmates. In fact, he was repeating the second-level course, and had passed the first-level course only after failing it the first time.[8]

Like Hector, Felix was assigned or took up the position of an older person in the group. The following are two examples of occurrences in which this was evident:

CLASS 11, MARCH 29, 2004

Time	Activity	Felix
10'	Comparison of adjectives Simon [S] claims that women use certain adjectives more than men and make more comparisons.	Volunteers (4×)
	S calls some students to front of classroom to make comparisons. He calls Felix [F] to the front and says: S: 'I'm younger than he is.' Then he turns to Felix and asks: S: 'How old are you?' F: '69.'	F participates willingly in this activity and states his age plainly.

CLASS 12, MARCH 31, 2004

Time	Activity	Felix
10'	S gives explanation about how superlatives are formed.	Volunteers (2×)
	S asks students to give examples.	F: 'I am the oldest in the class.' S: 'Felix is the wisest classmate in the class.'

As my classroom observation notes indicate, Felix readily revealed his age and adopted the position of an older person. Two things are particularly interesting in these exchanges. First, in Class 11, the teacher appeared to have no qualms about asking Felix how old he was. While disclosure of chronological age is frequent among older people, Coupland *et al.* (1991) found that it is customarily older people themselves who initially introduce it into the conversation. In fact, complex norms of etiquette determine when it is acceptable to ask a person's age in Anglophone cultures. These norms are virtually identical in Mexico. It would seem then, in this case, that Simon considered the particular topic of the lesson, comparative adjectives, to be sufficient grounds for waiving the rules normally prohibiting younger persons from asking older ones their age and, moreover, for doing so in a public setting.

The second incident took place in Class 12, in which Felix volunteered, 'I am the oldest in the class,' as an example of a superlative adjective. Simon responded by saying, 'Felix is the wisest classmate in the class,' recurring to a conventional positive stereotype about old people. This would hardly have been necessary were the subject of old age not surrounded by negative overtones. The case in point illustrates what Featherstone and Hepworth refer to as 'sanitised one-dimensional benign stereotypes' (Featherstone & Hepworth, 1991: 382).

Enactment of Age: In Relations with Fellow Students

Felix claimed that he liked finding himself 'surrounded by young people who are pursuing the same goal as I' (Felix, Narrative account 1). He commented that having people of mixed ages in language classes works well, that he enjoys being with young people and is happy to take his place as the old person in the group, where 'I've always been accepted as the "old fellow" there' (Felix, Interview 1). He also took on the responsibility for establishing relations with his classmates, much as Hector did. For instance, when it was time for small-group work, he invariably selected his partners. Moreover, while he frequently took part in friendly conversations with other members of the group, it was he who generally sought them out and not the other way around. However, unlike Hector, he did not appear to feel that his age put him in a disadvantaged or lesser position in relation to his classmates. On the contrary, I observed occasional manifestations of a strong urge to be in control, perhaps attributable to a belief that greater age entitled him to assume a position of authority, by virtue of the traditional role of the adult male in a patriarchal society.

The following incident lends credence to that interpretation. For the oral production section of the midterm examination, the students were asked to work in groups of three to prepare a script for a role-play exercise, either in a restaurant or in a store, and to present it in the next lesson. Felix first commented on the outcome in his weekly audio-taped narrative, in which he explained that he had made up a dialogue himself and his two partners refused to pay attention to him. What was intriguing here is that, on the one hand, Felix attempted to orchestrate the situation himself, and on the other, his teammates, for all intents and purposes, ignored him. In a subsequent interview, I asked Felix to expand on his version of this episode. Extract 16 includes part of this conversation.

Extract 16

    F = Felix; P = Patricia

1	F:	Well, the teacher told us to make up a conversation in groups of
2		three so she could grade our oral work.
3	P:	Right.

4	F:	Now, I had prepared something ... but my teammates wouldn't
5		pay attention to me.
6	P:	What did they say ... when ... ¿
7	F:	No, they said ... they did ... there was ... one of them, a heavy-
8		set girl ... she is very stubborn ... well, 'No, we're going to do it
9		the way I said last time.' So, OK, well ... there were two of them
10		... Elsa and her ... against me. We didn't sit down to study, no,
11		no, no. No ... they didn't want ... what do I say¿ ... what I had
12		done ... the ... the dialogue that I had made up ... how the waiter
13		greets you, how he takes you ... *Please, this way* ... he takes you
14		over there to your table, and things like that. I had done it that
15		way, OK¿
16	P:	But you made it up together¿
17	F:	No ... well, I had done it and I was going to propose it to them.
18	P:	Oh, I see. And they didn't like it.
19	F:	They didn't like it. She said, 'No, we're going to do it the way I
20		... the way I say.' OK¿ Well, I gave in and went along with what
21		they wanted, see¿ So, well ... it was very ... no ... no ... there
22		wasn't any dialogue ... and I felt really frustrated. (Felix, Interview 4)

In this extract, Felix's annoyance and frustration with his teammates, both of whom refused to go along with his ideas, are palpable. Moreover, his comment that 'there were two of them ... Elsa and her ... against me' (lines 9 and 10) suggests that he felt victimized. Felix's reference to one of the girls as 'heavy-set', in lines 7 and 8, points up a flaw she has (in the eyes of modern-day society) that has nothing to do with the power struggle taking place, but which may constitute a kind of retaliation for his not being taken into account, evening the playing field in his telling of the incident. Although the assignment had been to make up a conversation in teams of three, Felix took it upon himself to work alone, apparently expecting that his teammates would agree to perform the role-play script he had written (line 17). When one of the partners defied him directly, saying that they were going to do things her way, he conceded defeat and stopped trying to impose his own plan on them (lines 19–22). Nevertheless, he was unhappy with the results and clearly felt that things would have been more satisfactory had he been in control.

This episode, as Felix described it, turned into one of confrontation in which his authority as the senior member of the group was undermined. It illustrates the change that is taking place in contemporary Mexican society, where men have traditionally been considered to exercise undisputed power within the context of a patriarchal culture. According to some scholars, as the family structure has moved toward greater individualization and personal autonomy, relations between the younger and older generations are increasingly based on more democratic and less authoritarian dynamics

(Ariza & Oliveira, 2001; Salguero Velásquez, 2006). The belief that 'men have the last word' (Salles & Tuirán, 1996: 127–128) is now being challenged and reshaped, as the incident with Felix and his teammates demonstrates.

Other instances arose in which Felix attempted to exercise control over the group. From his comments to me, I surmised that he tried to persuade several of his classmates to support his point of view regarding the deleterious effect the involvement of practice teachers was having on their learning. This can be perceived in the following extract in which he described the upshot of informal conversations he had with some of his classmates before and after the lessons.

Extract 17

1   Reflection of March 10, 2004. I have talked to my classmates about
2   this [SOUND OF PAPERS RUSTLING].[9] 'What do you think about
3   the way the course is being given?' Answer. They tell me that they are
4   not happy with things. That the teacher does not teach the class. And
5   that at times they don't understand and are confused by the way the
6   practice teachers work. We decided that four or five of us would talk to
7   the teacher in order to express our concerns because we feel that we
8   are not learning or making progress in the course as we should be, and
9   the midterm exam is coming up soon. (Felix, Narrative account 2)

Here, Felix initiated the conversation with his classmates by calling attention to the 'problem' of the practice teachers, directly asking them how they felt about the class (lines 2 and 3). The responses, as Felix reported them (lines 3–6), enumerate the very complaints that he listed in his audio-taped narratives, leading me to believe that Felix may have aired his grievances to his classmates and then sought endorsement from them. In lines 6–8, his repeated use of the plural 'we' gives the impression that a general feeling of dissatisfaction was shared by others in the group, as was the decision to take up the issue with the teacher. While I never directly observed any signs of discontent in other members of the group, it is possible that they felt it to some degree.

In order to pursue the matter, I took the opportunity to sound out the situation with Elsa, another participant in this study, and a member of the group. In contrast to Felix, she commented that she found the teachers very dynamic and the lessons never boring. When I asked her specifically about the participation of the practice teachers, she said that both were very knowledgeable and that Simon's explanations helped her a great deal. She also indicated that she would like to have practice teachers in future courses if they were like Simon.

I also found support for my construal of Felix's relationship with his classmates in an interview with Simon, the practice teacher to whom Elsa referred in the conversation mentioned above, at the end of the course. He had this to say about Felix:

Extract 18

    S = Simon; P = Patricia

1   **S:** When he worked in a group, Felix made the team work his way.
2   **P:** Uh huh.
3   **S:** His... with his... with his... maybe his method. I don't know.
4   While the other teams, yes, had some very... unusual ideas, not
5   Felix. His way was... he followed very traditional steps.
       (Simon, Interview)

My sense, then, is that very likely Felix put pressure on his companions to see and do things his way. His relationship with them seems to be based on the patriarchal or gerontocratic notion of authority that is thought to have held sway for generations in traditional Mexican society and that only now is giving way to alternate patterns of social control (Salles & Tuirán, 1996). Salguero Velásquez observes:

> Authority continues to play a central role in the subjectivity of many men, although some changes can be noted that contemplate relations which are more egalitarian, closer and more affective. (Salguero Velásquez, 2006: 171)

Such changes, where they exist, signify more democratic relations among the generations and a greater participation of both young and old in decision-making processes.

Enactment of Age: In Relations with the Teachers

Felix devoted virtually all of the 12 audio-taped narrative accounts to giving vent to his escalating feelings of resentment toward Nidia, the assigned teacher. As lines 1–3 in the following extract show, it piqued him that she generally arrived late, rarely intervened in the lessons and only stayed for a short while, leaving the brunt of the teaching responsibilities to the two practice teachers.

Extract 19

1   Pat, as you could see in the class on Monday March 22, the teacher
2   arrives late, she leaves early, she doesn't intervene at all. The practice
3   teachers begin and end the class. I ask myself, 'Is that by chance the
4   behavior and attitude that the designated teacher of a subject should
5   take with her students? Don't we deserve that... a little of her
6   attention? Or is it that the school administration demands or orders her
7   to allow... [SOUND OF PAPERS RUSTLING] to allow the practice

8   teachers to give the class the entire time?' Who could answer this for
9   us? (Felix, Narrative account 3)

Felix believed that Nidia should give some personal attention to the group, and that by not doing so she was shirking her responsibilities as the assigned teacher (lines 1–3). His question 'Don't we deserve that ... a little of her attention?' (lines 5 and 6) reflects his perception of being slighted. He went on to ask whether it was the school's policy to let practice teachers take over the classes entirely (lines 6–8). Although these questions seem to be rhetorical, they were likely directed to me in the hope that, as a senior member of the English department, I would take some action to remedy the situation.

On the few occasions when Nidia took a more active part in the class, Felix claimed that it was because she felt guilty. This seems to be entirely his interpretation, as nothing of the kind was mentioned in my interview with Nidia at the end of the course. Moreover, when Felix confronted her, saying that a lot of people wanted her to give the class, she responded that 'you have to give the practice teachers ... the new teachers ... an opportunity' (Felix, Interview 2).

I asked Felix at several points in the interviews to reflect on the specific ways in which having practice teachers was affecting his learning. His comments were vague at best and centered on his feelings of not being given his due. When I repeated the question in the second interview, Felix once again redirected his response to the matter of Nidia's lack of dedication and sense of responsibility. He remarked that 'she already has a lot of experience' (Felix, Interview 2). This is important because it pinpoints the core issue for Felix, namely, that the practice teachers are inexperienced. After further insistence that he describe the way in which he felt this situation was impeding his learning, he responded, 'No ... it's not obstructing me. ... I'm growing accustomed to having the practice teachers give the class' (Felix, Interview 2). However, this does not seem to be the case for Felix continued to protest about having practice teachers to the very end of the course.

The question of experience is essentially an age issue. While Felix recognized that Simon was dynamic and dedicated, saying that he 'gives the class well', 'has more spark [than Tomas]' and 'is concerned, because he tries to teach us and to explain things well' (Felix, Interview 2), all qualities that he had hoped to find in Nidia, he never overcame his sense of being defrauded by having what he perceived as two inexperienced and unproven teachers for this course. He spoke of Nidia as 'a good teacher, with some ups and downs in her teaching technique, but definitely an experienced teacher' (Felix, Narrative account 9). His unrelenting opposition to the presence of the novice practice teachers shows Felix practicing a kind of ageism called 'adultism', which targets young people and discriminates against them for their lack of experience (Horsch *et al.*, 2002). It is based on paternalistic suppositions that 'adults are more knowledgeable, rational, responsible, experienced, selfless, and intelligent' (Neustadter, 2002: 724) than children or young people. When such stereotypes are reinforced, young people are disenfranchised and often left out of decision-making processes. Their positive input is easily overlooked, as happened in this case. Felix either willingly or inadvertently disregarded any constructive contributions made by the two young teachers.

The Construction of Age: Beyond the Classroom

As with Hector, Felix's enactment of age as a language learner overlaps with his other identities and fits into the broader context of his life. This is particularly evident in his patriarchal assumption of authority and desire to be in control of those younger than he. Even so, his story is also interspersed with moments of confusion and doubt about his position as an older adult in a world that is changing.

Competing Discourses of Age

Felix, too, vacillates between accepting and resisting discourses of decline. Yet the issues that surfaced in the course of the fieldwork are distinct from those in Hector's case. Felix did not manifest any tendencies to yearn for the past, disengage socially or acknowledge a growing dependence on others. He did, however, struggle with concerns about the loss of his physical and mental capacities.

Competence and Incompetence

Felix and I had an extensive discussion about the question of age and loss of competence. Because of the length of this part of the interview, it has been divided into the four extracts which follow (Extracts 20–23).

Extract 20

F = Felix; P = Patricia

```
1   F:   No matter what, age ... is going to win out, I think, no? ...
2        because just the fact that you are an older person means that it is
3        inevitable that you will lose your capacities.
4   P:   In everything?
5   F:   In everything. In every area.
6   P:   Really?
7   F:   Yes. And it's a constant battle. You have to go to the doctor so
8        he can give you something, OK. But ... but the doctor ... the
9        doctor charges you money, and you can do a lot of things for
10       yourself without having to go to the doctor. You can use ... how
11       to say it? ... psychological therapy on yourself. I look for
```

12		whatever... whatever it is that I have to do... so that... I won't
13		die. (Felix, Interview 3)

In this part of the interview, Felix stated categorically that growing old and the associated loss of capacities are, in the final analysis, unavoidable (lines 1–3). He reinforced this standard discourse of decline in line 5, and then went on to say that he is doing his best to stave off the inevitable, using whatever means he can, so that he 'won't die' (lines 7–13). His directness in referring to the taboo subject of dying is surprising, yet his orientation to it reflects Western culture's current preoccupation with averting death. As pointed out in Chapter 3, trying to escape mortality rather than seeking meaning and value in the present moment of one's life is a manifestation of an anti-aging discourse that arises from the deficit model of aging.

I then asked Felix to be more specific about his own loss of competence. Extract 21 contains his account of the process he experienced.

Extract 21

F = Felix; P = Patricia

1	P:	So... when exactly did that process of losing your capacities
2		begin?
3	F:	Well, see... ever since I was 56.
4	P:	Really? Just in your case... or do you think that's a general rule?
5	F:	No... in my case.
6	P:	Uh huh.
7	F:	Because we are all different.....
8	P:	But you were already feeling the effects of... ?
9	F:	I was already feeling the effects of age. What's more... the
10		company I worked for... made me retire because of my age.
11	P:	Uh huh... uh huh.
12	F:	Not because of years of service.
13	P:	Uh huh. But you said that you were feeling something from the
14		time you were 56?
15	F:	Well... I felt that my capacity was decreasing. I worried a lot
16		about it. I worried a lot... and when the company retired me
17		because of my age, I went into a depression.
18	P:	Well, of course.
19	F:	You have no idea.
20	P:	I can imagine.
21	F:	Because it was like... and I have looked for a job.
22	P:	OK.
23	F:	I'm still looking for a job.
24	P:	Right.
25	F:	But since I am very old, even though I have 43 years of
26		experience in my field... but because of my age, they...

27	P:	You mean they don't value experience?
28	F:	No, they don't value experience.
29	P:	Why not, do you think?
30	F:	I think ... maybe because ... perhaps the company has certain
31		parameters for measuring your capacity. Maybe they apply some
32		parameter ... some psychological test ... or that type of thing ... I
33		don't know. But for people who are old .... (Felix, Interview 3)

In this extract, Felix pinpointed the beginning of his own downturn at age 56 (line 3). His perception that his 'capacity was decreasing' brought him considerable distress (lines 15 and 16). This was compounded when he was forced to retire because of his age, an event which precipitated a severe depression (lines 9, 10, 16 and 17). No longer permitted to have a productive role in society because of formal retirement policies based on institutionalized age restrictions, Felix also seemed to doubt whether he still measured up to the criteria of the current labor market (lines 30–33). Thus, despite his long years of experience, he found himself summarily relegated to the sidelines, in consequence of the fact that 'it has been occupational activity and "productivity" that has come to define a boundary between the core and periphery of society' (Coupland, 2001: 192). Felix resisted being positioned as a marginalized and nonproductive member of the community by seeking employment (lines 21 and 23). However, he has had little success in this endeavor because of societal attitudes toward age (lines 25–28).

In the next part of the interview, Felix described his experience working for a short time in a low-status position at Home Mart, a local building supply store.

Extract 22

F = Felix; P = Patricia

1	F:	I'm 68 now ... OK. Look ... I tried. I found a job ... I ... I ...
2		they hired me there at Home Mart.
3	P:	Oh, yes, you told me.
4	F:	They hired me at Home Mart. The guy said, 'Well, what you are
5		going to do here is ... you are ... you are going to keep records
6		of the merchandise that comes in and goes out, and of the stock
7		in the warehouse.
8	P:	Uh huh ... OK ... OK.
9	F:	So ... records of incoming and outgoing merchandise ... and a
10		control of that sort of thing. I know how to do that because I am a
11		public accountant, OK.
12	P:	Right.
13	F:	So, I started to work ... but there in the warehouse, I also had to
14		lift things ... and I had to sweep and mop and operate machines
15		and ... and ... keep their records and ... and take the rubbish
16		from the warehouse out to the trash container and then ...

17		compact the cardboard in a machine they had there ... and I ...
18		and I didn't mind doing all that. The only thing that was difficult
19		for me ... you know what it was? That I had to lift things.
20	P:	Well, yeah.
21	F:	And they were heavy things.
22	P:	Uh huh ... well, yes.
23	F:	So I said to my boss, 'Hey!' And I asked myself 'Why are you
24		... ?' They had me ... I was doing everything. I swept, I mopped,
25		I cleaned the bathroom ... because they had me doing that. I put
26		everything in ... in the trash containers and I carried everything
27		back XXX. So, he said, 'Don't quit.' 'No,' I told him, 'because
28		I've found another job more in line with my age.' But he didn't
29		want me to leave. Why? Well, because I was ...
30	P:	You were doing everything.
31	F:	I was doing everything ... everything. Everything they asked me
32		to ... I did. Of course ... lifting and moving things, especially ...
33		that was my problem.
34	P:	Sure ... sure ... right.
35	F:	My biggest problem. Everything else was easy for me.
36	P:	So, you hadn't lost ... that kind of capacity.
37	F:	Exactly. Everything else ... believe me ... I got to work and got
38		everything done quickly.
39	P:	Good.
40	F:	But, well ... and that was just a short time ago, OK. It was last
41		year ... and I lasted three months working there ... but my
42		children said, 'That's enough, Papa. Leave that place. You don't
43		need to work.' But, I tell you, the only thing I lost the capacity
44		for was lifting things. In other words, I showed myself that I
45		could do it. I can do anything. (Felix, Interview 3)

In this job, Felix had to perform a number of menial tasks in the warehouse, including cleaning and emptying the trash as well as keeping records of the merchandise (lines 4–19). Even though this was a far cry from his former, more prestigious position as a public accountant, Felix declared that he willingly did whatever he was told to do (lines 17, 18, 31 and 32). In lines 37 and 38, he expressed pride in being able to get everything done quickly and easily. In this respect, he shows himself to be less concerned than Hector about maintaining a high social profile, and more interested in simply remaining active. The principal problem he encountered was his difficulty in lifting heavy objects (lines 18–21, 32 and 33). In the end, this prompted his decision to leave after only three months on the job (lines 23–29). His children also urged him to quit, arguing that he has no financial need to work, but perhaps missing the point that their father needs to feel useful (lines 41–45). However, the fact that Felix mentioned their viewpoint suggests that it may have been a factor in his decision as well. On the other hand, it could have been that he was demonstrating to them that he is still capable of working and of being a productive member of society. By far, the most interesting occurrence in this segment of the interview takes place in lines 35–45 when Felix made a complete turnabout from his earlier insistence that he was losing all his capacities (extract 21) and asserted that, aside from the physical task of moving heavy merchandise, 'I showed myself that I could do it. I can do anything' (lines 44 and 45).

I used this affirmation to turn back to the issue of studying English, and asked Felix if that same outlook fit into the question of his language-learning competence. Here, in Extract 23, is what he responded:

Extract 23

1   Yes ... yes. ... I always wanted to learn English. ... Another language.
2   It's important. That was it ... by taking that job ... I'm glad you
3   reminded me ... I was able to demonstrate to myself that I could do
4   things ... to get out of my depression. (Felix, Interview 3)

The abrupt reversal of Felix's earlier bleak outlook on his capacities and his 'rediscovery' of the possibilities still open to him give an indication of how opposing discourses of aging compete with each other in his case. Moreover, his remark 'I'm glad you reminded me' (lines 2 and 3) is particularly noteworthy in that it demonstrates how, when the researcher and those researched interact closely and the agenda is set more flexibly by both parties, the research process itself can be empowering (Cameron *et al.*, 1993).

The fluctuations in Felix's self-appraisal were also evident when he was asked to sketch the life course. He first thought that a straight line would best represent his own life course. However, as he began to talk about the ups and downs of his life, he decided that a better picture would be a line which showed the high and low points (see Figure 4.2).

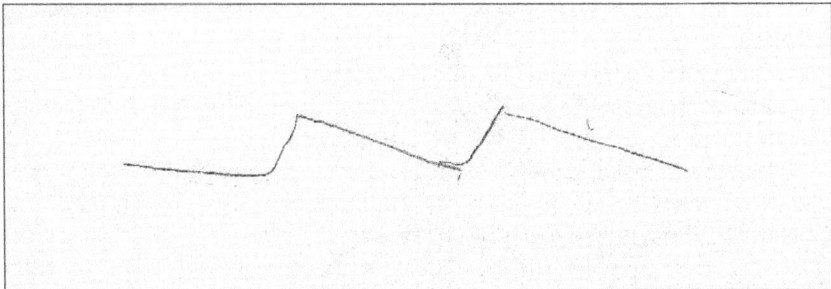

Figure 4.2 Felix's sketch of the life course

Age and Other Identities

Felix's age identity is closely interlocked with his professional identity and with his subject position in his family. Like Hector, being identified as a productive member of society, primarily through professional activity, was uppermost in his mind at this particular moment of his life. Unlike Hector, however, he spoke only once about his professional accomplishments, expressing less ambition and more satisfaction in simply having carried out his work well over the years. As he described it, his professional life seems to have been smooth, free of conflict and overall a rewarding experience. The gratification he received from carrying out the functions of his profession, working with accounting, taxes and audits, suggests that perhaps he is most comfortable in a world that is predictable, consistent and exact. The crisis came, as has been noted, when he was asked to retire very abruptly because of his age. He clearly was not prepared for such an eventuality. The following extract reveals the depth of his unhappiness:

Extract 24

1   When you are working ... when you are developing professionally ...
2   and they say to you, 'Look, well, you are very old now. Just leave,
3   OK.' ... even though you are a productive person and you have ideas
4   and ... and you can still make important decisions in life. I mean, it
5   cuts you short. But why does that happen, I say ... why is it that those
6   of us who can continue to be productive ... these very same people
7   bring ... our career, OK ... your life ... to a standstill at a given
8   moment? So, you, as a human being ... at least in my case, for
9   example, they cut me short. 'You are no longer of any use to us. We
10 are going to retire you. We are going to pension you off' ... and things
11 like that. It is really horrible, OK ... really horrible ... really horrible.
12 It is terrible. It demoralizes you. You ... I ... when they told me that
13 ... you can't imagine. (Felix, Interview 4)

This commentary is all the more poignant because of the way Felix used voicing in a constructed dialogue to show how other people no longer considered him to be of value professionally (lines 2, 3, 9 and 10). So important is his professional identity to him that this occurrence left him feeling that his very life 'as a human being' (line 8) had been 'cut short' (line 9).

While the role of sole wage earner is central to the position of the 'archetypal Mexican male', of equal importance is that of head of the family (Salles & Tuirán, 1996). Both Hector and Felix took up these subject positions. However, Felix gave the impression of being more family oriented than Hector. For example, when asked to identify the best moment of his life, he responded without hesitation that it was the birth of his first child. He remarked that he has worked to give his own children opportunities, saying that they are the 'beginning and end' of his life (Felix, Interviews 3 and 4). He has also positioned himself as a kind of patriarch in his extended family network, where he is the oldest surviving member. He referred to his two sisters and more than 40 nieces, nephews, great-nieces and great nephews as *mi gente* (my people), and expressed regret that he has not had the means to help them out in times of difficulty, a role he clearly would have enjoyed. However, when I asked how his family and friends see him, he responded that they consider him to be an old man now because he is retired. He added that it does not matter what they think because he is 'young inside' (Felix, Interview 4). Once again, a contradiction can be perceived in the way Felix positions himself and the way he is positioned by others.

The subject position of head of the family is strongly coupled with Felix's gendered identity. He claimed that the life cycle is different for women because 'they have another kind of mission in life ... to have children ... and ours [men's] to make them' (Felix, Interview 4). When asked what his wife did, he replied that she makes the meals and takes care of the house. He added that she has lately become very religious, and has a group of friends who 'are active in the church, read the Bible, do social work and that kind of thing' (Felix, Interview 1). The similarity with Hector's wife is striking, as is the position of the traditional Mexican male adopted by both Hector and Felix.

Connecting the Pieces

Felix's story is characterized by the dissatisfaction he feels with his present life position. Up to the point of his compulsory retirement, his life as he described it had been generally rewarding, both personally and professionally. However, he is currently undergoing a period of frustration, disappointment, and frequently futile efforts to recover the sense of fulfillment he formerly had. He defines this primarily in terms of the socially prized value of productivity.

His tale is, like Hector's, a complex one for there is a wide divergence between the way he is positioned by society, family and friends as old and less capable, and the way he often positions himself as still fully competent. Yet at other times he, too, accepts prevalent decremental narratives and claims to be losing his physical and mental faculties. An additional age discourse he espouses is adultism, whereby he positions himself as entitled to exercise authority over and to receive deference from those younger than he. The resulting interplay of the adultist discourse with the decline discourses he alternately embraces and rejects makes his enactment of age a compelling, yet difficult phenomenon to understand.

For Felix, studying English has provided a way to remain active and to keep mental decline at bay. He is also cognizant of the fact that there are added advantages to knowing English, yet learning the language is an interim measure for him. While he is filling up his life with this and other similar activities, his real desire is to be working again. In the meantime, studying English is a challenge that is largely about proving himself.

Felix, like Hector, maintains that 'younger is better' when it comes to learning a foreign language. However, in explaining this, he focuses on the deleterious effects of aging on mental abilities rather than on the superior qualities children purportedly possess. Even so, he believes that enthusiasm and dedication can allow older people to be successful in this enterprise. On a personal level, Felix experienced serious difficulties with English during the months I observed him. Perhaps for this reason, he was seldom willing to talk about his own progress with the language and preferred instead to concentrate on the deficiencies he found in the teachers' methods.

His beliefs about language learning, along with his manifest need for a highly structured and systematic environment, underscored the way in which he experienced the English course at this moment of his life. He expressed dissatisfaction throughout the term with what he judged to be the disorganized and faulty manner in which the lessons were given. He was particularly adamant about the adverse effects of the participation of the two practice teachers and the lack of involvement of the regularly assigned teacher. His repeated criticism of the practice teachers centered on his perception that they were too young and inexperienced to perform their job adequately.

In his relations with his fellow students, he positioned himself and was positioned by them as an older person, yet this clearly meant different things in each case. The behavior of the students suggests that, for them, Felix was simply an old man, no longer a presence to be reckoned with, an outsider in the group, and someone they could disregard for the most part. On the other hand, Felix believed that being an older adult in the group entitled him to assume a position of authority and to exercise a certain control over the younger students in his interactions with them. He expected them to defer to his decisions, yet this did not happen and caused him considerable frustration.

Such a paternalistic attitude on Felix's part carried over into his life beyond the classroom, where he continues to position himself as the 'traditional patriarch' in both his immediate and extended families. The self-confidence deriving from this subject position had always been linked to his strong gendered and professional identities. However, the forced retirement that edged him out of the work force occasioned a crisis in his sense of self-worth, which he calculates primarily in terms of productivity and accumulated experience. As a consequence of his retirement, his family and friends now consider him an old man. At times, Felix rejects being so positioned and adopts a more positive age identity, constructing himself as young, still interested in life and fully competent.

As in Hector's case, competing discourses of aging vie with one another and make the ongoing task of reconstructing his multiple identities a complex one. This is further complicated by the fact that Felix is loath to accept change, a circumstance which may be closely related to his choice of a profession that is systematic and predictable. Given that the very meaning of aging is change, it follows that Felix's enactment of age is necessarily fraught with discord.

Conclusion

The tales that Hector and Felix tell are two compelling examples of the construction of age in later adulthood. Their stories attest to the fact that age is an integral part of the identity of language learners and show how the experience of learning a language is closely intertwined with a world that extends far beyond the classroom. The close examination of Hector's and Felix's stories undertaken in this chapter highlights some of the specific ways in which age is enacted by older adults and contributes to our overall understanding of the impact of age on adult language learners of different ages. Among the most noteworthy findings to emerge are the following:

The impact of age on the language-learning experience varies according to where each person positions her/himself in the lifespan.

In the case of Hector and Felix, taking up the study of English in later adulthood has responded principally to a need to remain active after retirement. Although they are not oblivious to the utilitarian benefits to be found in knowing the language, its chief attraction for them has been that it constitutes a challenging, socially acceptable and prestigious leisure-time activity.

The beliefs and attitudes EFL learners have about age and SLA have an effect on their language-learning experience.

Both Hector and Felix contended that, as older adults, they are disadvantaged in relation to the younger university students in their efforts to learn English. However, they believe that dedication and discipline can make up for their age-related cognitive deficits. While it is not possible to determine, on the basis of this study, the extent to which such ageist beliefs had a direct impact on the linguistic outcomes of the course, they evinced themselves in different respects in the enactment of age in the classroom.

The coconstruction of age in the classroom context is rooted in the prevailing cultural discourses of age.

The language-learning experience proved to be different in significant ways for Hector and Felix in the months during which the study was undertaken. Both Hector and Felix positioned themselves, and accepted being positioned by their fellow students and teachers, as older adults. In Hector's case, this meant not only being an outsider in the group but also the target of ageist remarks by the teacher. For the most part, he chose to accommodate to or collude with the ageist attitudes he found in the class. At the end of the course, he declared that he was quite satisfied with the experience. Felix, on the other hand, resisted the construal of old age that put him in a subordinate position and struggled to establish himself as an authority figure in the group by reason of his age. He expressed considerable resentment about the participation of the young and inexperienced practice teachers, demonstrating his own ageist attitudes. His overall assessment of the course was unfavorable. In evaluating their experience, neither Hector nor Felix gave more than minimal attention to their personal progress, leading me to conclude that studying English at this moment of their lives meant much more than mastering the language.

Both present and prior life circumstances have an impact on the language-learning experience.

The single most defining event that has shaped Hector's and Felix's construction of later adulthood is retirement from the workforce. As pointed out in Chapter 3, retirement generally brings about the end of a person's economic activity and often, with it, social disengagement, marginalization and a diminished status in many productivity-oriented Western cultures. In addition, because most older people become recipients of institutional services rather than contributors to the economy, later life may be viewed as an economic, political and social problem. To a certain extent, both Hector and Felix have internalized this powerful ageist discourse. However, major differences can be found in their experience of retirement. Whereas Hector opted to retire from his main job in a hospital but to remain economically active in his private practice and as a consultant, Felix was compelled to retire and has been unable to find comparable work ever since. It is important to mention that in neither case have the economic constraints, often resulting from retirement, constituted an issue for them.

The construction of the age identity of language learners occurs both within the classroom and in the world beyond it, moving back and forth between the two.

Far more onerous have been the social consequences of retirement, for Hector and Felix have had to contend with having a series of negative traits associated with old age attributed to them by an ageist society. Hector has resisted such negative positioning by drawing attention to his past achievements in order to establish himself as a person of stature, whereas Felix has chosen to adopt the traditional position of 'patriarch' or elder in his social world. Yet, along with such demonstrations of resistance, we find other instances in which acceptance of ageist discourses plays an important role in the construction of their identities. Felix's diagnosis of his own presumed age-related cognitive deficits is a telling example of the internalization of ageist discourses, in which 'the myth of mental decline becomes a self-fulfilling prophecy—and one that brings active harm to the aged' (Combe & Schmader, 1999: 97).

Age as a subject position is interlinked with other subject positions in adult language learners.

Hector's and Felix's enactment of age as language learners is not separable from their professional, social and gendered identities, either in or out of the classroom. For both of them, professional success and social prestige interact with the strong gendered position of the traditional Mexican male in the ongoing construction of their complex new identities as older adults. These new identities constitute a crucial nonlinguistic outcome of their language-learning experience.

All told, a remarkable number of similarities can be found in Hector's and Felix's life stories. Their early life experiences, professional achievements, socioeconomic status and family situations run parallel to one another over the years. This has taken place against the backdrop of an era in Mexican history which has witnessed the emergence and consolidation of a significant middle class (Schettino Yáñez, 2002; Selby & Browning, 1992; Zúniga Herrera, 2005). Now, in later adulthood, competing discourses of aging vie with one another in the construction of their identities. Yet, significant differences in their present experience of age can be appreciated in Hector's overall satisfaction and Felix's considerable dissatisfaction with their respective life positions. As Coupland aptly points out:

> [A]ge-identities ... are the products of the evaluative component of our own life narratives ... the cumulative assessment of where we stand, developmentally – as individuals and in relation to our social environments. ... [I]dentity in ageing ultimately connects to morale and wellbeing. (Coupland, 2001: 203)

Life-position appraisal may offer the most important key to understanding Hector's and Felix's stories and their construction of later adulthood. In the next chapter, the combined stories of four women furnish helpful insights into the construction of the middle years.

Notes

(1) The lines of the extracts appearing in Chapters 4 through 6 are numbered for easy reference.
(2) Hector is referring to Vicente Fox, who at that time was President of Mexico and who had recently remarried.
(3) Ethnicity is a highly complex concept and has been defined in a variety of ways. In the context of Mexico, it would certainly include racial or physical traits along with cultural criteria, such as ancestry, tradition and language, among others.
(4) *Mestizo* refers here to the racial and cultural mix of Spanish and indigenous peoples (Ashcroft *et al.*, 1998: 136–137). The Indian part of that identity became 'the symbol of the uncultured, the savage, the "other"' (Fortes de Leff, 2002: 620).
(5) The *Cristeros* were pro-Catholic peasants rebelling against the anticlerical measures of the Mexican Constitution of 1917. The *agraristas*, on the other hand, were landless peasants and supporters of agrarian reform, many of whom struggled to obtain land by forcibly seizing it.
(6) The term *braceros*, as used in this context, refers to the unskilled laborers allowed to work in the United States as part of a temporary contract labor program begun in 1942.
(7) This textbook is part of the same series used in Hector's course.
(8) The general English program at the university language center consists of six semester-long courses or levels.
(9) In several of his narrative accounts, papers could be heard rustling. Felix evidently prepared his narrative accounts in writing before audio-taping them. Moreover, he used a formal register, quite different from the conversational tone of our interviews.

5 Constructing Age in 'Middle' Adulthood

Introduction

In this chapter, I interweave the stories of four women whose ages fluctuate between 34 and 59 years. In Mexico, people in this age range, between young adulthood and old age, are rather loosely designated as 'adults'. No named category exists in Spanish equivalent to the English term 'middle-aged'.[1] This difference constitutes an important contrast between contemporary Mexican and Anglophone cultures, one that is central to understanding the construction of age identity by these participants. This chapter is organized along similar lines to the previous one, beginning with brief biographical sketches of the four women, followed by a discussion of their reasons for studying English. After that comes a description of their enactment of age both in and out of the classroom. The chapter concludes with some reflections on the construction of 'middle' adulthood and how what has been learned in the course of the fieldwork addresses the issues of interest in this book.

The Women Tell Their Stories

Introducing the Participants

Elsa, Gilda, Adela and Berta, the 'midlife' participants in the study, work in distinct professions and have different family situations, competence levels in English and chronological ages. Table 5.1 gives some basic information about each of them. Elsa, 34, is the youngest of the group of participants who identified themselves as 'adults'. She has worked for several years as a clerk in the silver department of a large and prestigious department store in Mexico City. At the time of the fieldwork, her daughter was 17 and her son seven years old. She never mentioned a husband or partner, even when given express opportunities to do so in the interviews. In fact, she shared little information about her own childhood or personal life. When I asked directly

TABLE 5.1 The 'midlife' adult participants

Elsa	Gilda	Adela	Berta
• English level 2	• English level 6	• English level 6	• English level 3
• 34 years old	• 36 years old	• 48 years old	• 59 years old
• Marital status not specified	• Engaged	• Married	• Married
• Two children	• No children	• Two children	• Three children
• Sales clerk – department store	• Actuary – insurance company	• Spanish teacher – *secundaria* (equivalent to US middle school)	• Physician – public health clinic

about her leisure-time activities, she indicated that she occasionally has lunch with women friends, but that she is normally too busy working, studying and caring for her family to be involved in other pursuits. She had begun doing her undergraduate studies a short time before through a distance education program offered to the department store employees. She had only been studying English for a year at the time I initiated contact with her, and was repeating the second-level course.

Although only two years older than Elsa, Gilda finds herself in a very different place in her life. Whereas Elsa has been a mother since the age of 17, Gilda, 36 at the time of the fieldwork, was only then planning for marriage and possible motherhood. She has worked as an actuary in various insurance companies ever since her graduation from university. She was still living with her parents, as is the custom in Mexico, and she described her relationship with her family as a close one. She has traveled extensively and, in general, enjoyed a privileged lifestyle. Gilda began studying English in primary school and her level of mastery was notably better than that of the other students in the sixth-level course. That course, the final one in the general English program, leads to a certificate of proficiency necessary for registering in the special advanced courses that Gilda hopes to take in the future. Prior to enrollment in the course, she had completed one semester of a year-long English teacher training course at another campus of the university.

Adela, 48, also a student in the sixth-level course of general English, teaches Spanish language and literature in a public *secundaria* (equivalent to US middle school). She had studied English in *preparatoria* (equivalent to US high school) and then later at a private language institute when she was in her early twenties. At the time of this study, her son was living at home and studying at a local university. Her daughter was attending a university in a nearby city and came home only on weekends. Adela reads for enjoyment and signs up for many of the short courses that are offered to teachers by the Ministry of Education. She began to take English classes at the university the semester before she was asked to participate in this study and, despite not having studied the language for over 20 years, placed in the fifth-level course. She is also studying Italian.

Berta has worked for many years as a physician in a public health clinic. She was 59 at the time of the fieldwork and planned to retire within the year. She has three adult daughters, two of whom were still living at home. In the afternoons, Berta spends her free time doing a variety of crafts. She had never studied English before and began with the basic courses three years previously. She has had to repeat some of the courses and, in fact, was repeating the third-level course at the time I initiated contact with her.

The Goal of Learning English

All of the women were employed at the time of the study except Gilda, who was planning her August wedding.[2] In addition, they had obligations at home, such as preparing meals, running the household, spending time with both immediate and extended family members and providing for their affective needs, in line with prevailing norms for women in Mexico (Salguero Velásquez, 2006; Sandoval Ávila, 2002). Thus, taking English classes implied forfeiting part of their free time. For that reason, both motivation and expectations regarding the courses were high. Elsa and Berta indicated that they wanted to learn English because they had not had the opportunity to do so in their student years, whereas Adela had studied the language with some reluctance as a young student, but is now interested in becoming a fluent speaker of English at this point in her life. Gilda, already proficient in the language, was taking the course as a way of maintaining her fluency.

All harbor some vague notions of using English in the future. For example, Elsa hopes to move up from her job as a clerk to that of a buyer in the department store where she is employed. The store sends buyers to other countries, but they must speak English. She also mused about the possibility of giving private English classes at some future date, once she has mastered the language herself. Adela is also considering becoming an English teacher after she retires.[3] Now that her children are older and more independent, she finds herself with the freedom to study. Much as in the case of Hector and Felix, learning English would seem to signify the acquisition of cultural capital (Bourdieu, 1977) for these women rather than serving an immediate pragmatic need.

The Construction of Age: In the Classroom

When asked, the four 'midlife' participants concurred with the widely held belief that childhood is the best time to learn a language, and the younger the better. Elsa maintained that this is so because children 'do not have everyday worries or the responsibilities of a job ... they retain things more quickly' (Elsa, Interview 1). Similarly, Gilda pointed out that young people still have their minds uncluttered whereas older ones have theirs saturated, in a sense. She also mentioned that adults experience difficulty learning anything new, not just languages. Adela emphasized that children do not have to concern themselves with rules, that they simply absorb the language like sponges. Berta also likened young learners to sponges, an image that appears frequently in the interviews. Even so, the four women were hopeful of succeeding in the task of learning English, by spending time outside of class studying, by reading books and magazines and by bringing greater effort and dedication to the task. In addition, Elsa and Adela both stressed the importance of liking the language in achieving success.

Enactment of Age: Examining Classroom Activities

Student Books 1 (2001a), 2 (2001b) and 3 (2003) of the *American Headway* series were used in the courses in which the four women were enrolled. As pointed out previously, this series targets the adult and young adult market. Hence, the situations, topics, characters and exercises in these textbooks are likely to have been more suited to the interests of the group of 'midlifers' than to those of the more mature students. The global perspective of the materials would also have resonated more with these participants, as moderately well-traveled and experienced professionals, than with the younger students. Nevertheless, the related class activities devised by the teachers in the lessons that I observed were generally geared to the younger university-age students and often involved sharing personal information.

The latter practice made Elsa particularly uncomfortable. Two occasions on which this was evident are recorded in my classroom observation notes.

CLASS 9, MARCH 22, 2004

Time	Activity	Elsa
10'	Tomas [T] gives an explanation of 'how much' and 'how many'.	T asks Elsa [E] how much money she spends on the weekend with her boyfriend. E is ill at ease and does not respond.

CLASS 20, MAY 5, 2004

Time	Activity	Elsa
35′	Simon [S] checks workbook exercises – present continuous used for near future.	S asks E where she is going with her boyfriend tonight. She does not answer.
	Some confusion arises. Nidia [N] clarifies how the structure is used.	Then S gets distracted and he does not return to E.

Earlier in the term, I had asked Elsa about an activity in which the students talked in small groups about how they had met their first girlfriend/boyfriend, how long the relationship had lasted and why it had ended. She remarked that the students seemed enthusiastic about the exercise but that she herself prefers not to talk about personal matters. She went on to say:

Extract 25

1   At times I even ... at times I make up things, OK ... in other words ...
2   so ... they ask me something and I make something up, OK. ... It's
3   not ... it's not necessary to say what really was or what. ... it's only to
4   practice. (Elsa, Interview 2)

Here, Elsa presents the view that the class activities are designed for practice and do not constitute genuine communication. This contrasts strikingly with the interaction she reported having in English with a Pakistani colleague at work who does not speak any Spanish. She said that he would sometimes go and talk to her 'like he wanted to make friends ... because he didn't ... like he didn't know anybody' (Elsa, Interview 1). In the next interview, when I asked her how talking to him was different from talking to her classmates, she responded:

Extract 26

1   Well, what happens is that with this man I can talk about any topic,
2   OK, about what countries he has been to ... where he works ... or
3   sometimes I ask him if what I am saying is correct ... or how to say
4   something. ... It isn't difficult for me. Well, at least what we have
5   talked about ... the topics we have talked about ... anything from, for
6   example, his family ... where he lives ... why he came to Mexico ...
7   things that I know a little about. (Elsa, Interview 2)

In fact, the topics of conversation she mentioned in this extract are substantially the same as those that typically come up in English classroom activities. However, her remarks suggest that, because her Pakistani interlocutor knows no Spanish, this is an authentic communicative situation, a 'real' conversation and one that necessarily has to take place in English. For her, it is apparently distinct from contrived conversations among Spanish-speaking students in an English classroom. In this, her appreciation diverges from Breen's (1985, 2001a) notion of the classroom as an authentic learning community. Nor is she likely to agree with the contention that 'classroom language is a real use of language, and we cannot just dismiss the classroom setting and all that takes place in it as being by definition "artificial"' (Taylor, 1994: 6). Taylor explains that learners generally understand and accept the conventions of classroom discourse and create their own authenticity. However, as in the case of Elsa, this does not always happen.

Enactment of Age: In Relations with Fellow Students

All four women positioned themselves as distinct from both the young students and those they identified as old. When referring to the younger members of the group, they used terms like 'children' or 'adolescents' and very often punctuated their remarks with 'we' and 'they', thereby constructing a clear partition between the inside (university) and outside communities. Elsa claimed that the essential difference is that the younger students' motivation is related to the language requirements in their fields of study whereas hers is more directly involved with her present job. Berta also cited the students' motivation, or rather the lack of it, lamenting the fact that they do not appreciate the language courses, which are cost-free for them, with schedules compatible with their studies, and classes conveniently located on the same campus.

When I asked Adela how she perceived her relations with the other students, she maintained that they all work well together. Nevertheless, she recounted how at first she felt out of place in the group because of her age, particularly when she failed to understand some of the comments and jokes of the younger students. As she explained it:

Extract 27

1   Personally, I feel fine. I feel quite fine. At first, well, you have already
2   been through adolescence, right? ... so ... like I said ... it's like I feel
3   that you miss ... some comments, some jokes ... but now I fit in. Now
4   I feel fine with the young people. (Adela, Interview 1)

The interplay between the first person 'I' (lines 1–3), which Adela used to express her current positive feelings about her relationship with the younger students, and the impersonal, generalized 'you' (lines 1 and 3), which serves to mark a distance from the initial problems she encountered, is perhaps indicative of a situation not fully resolved.

The extract also reinforces what was noted in Hector's and Felix's stories, namely, that it is the older members of the group who take on the responsibility for initiating and maintaining relations with the younger students. As Gilda observed, adolescents 'don't see anything beyond their own world', being, by definition, rather self-absorbed; consequently, it is older people who adapt to younger ones because they 'have already been there [through adolescence]' (Gilda, Interview 1).

While it is evident that the women participants do not consider themselves to be young adults, neither do they position themselves as older ones. For example, Gilda made a definite distinction between herself and one of the older adults, calculating that she was 'exactly in the middle' in the group, between 'Claudio who is in his 60s' and the 'very young adolescents who are around 18 or 19' (Gilda, Interview 1). Again, it is important to note that in Mexico people in the vast age range between adolescence, or young adulthood, and old age are incorporated into the broad undetermined category of 'adults' (see Chapter 3 for a discussion of this point).

Enactment of Age: In Relations with the Teachers

As with Hector's group, ageist humor surfaced in the group where Adela and Gilda were students. For example, on one occasion, Ramon, the teacher, pointedly asked Adela if she knew how to use a computer, to which she responded that although she uses one for work, she is 'old' and prefers to write her letters by hand. In another group, the same teacher made a comment to Berta about the 'older generation's' inability to use the internet. This was one of a number of instances in which ageist and other humorous remarks were directed at Berta by this teacher, causing her visible embarrassment. Easily flustered, she also reported having considerable difficulty understanding the teacher's fast-paced speech as well as the lyrics to the songs he often used in the lessons. She commented:

Extract 28

1 He [the teacher] puts on a song in English ... and I say, 'My God, who is
2 that?' I mean ... to begin with I also feel out of date ... out of place ...
3 because there are youngsters who are in ... like that with the music ... with
4 the singers and everything. (Berta, Interview 2)

This extract also brings to light Berta's perception of belonging to a world very different from that of young people. By disqualifying herself as 'out of date' and 'out of place' (line 2), she echoes the rhetoric that glorifies youth culture. In addition, the teacher's propensity to target her for humorous remarks and his somewhat derisive attitude toward her when she asked questions or responded in class confused and upset her. Although she admitted having a slight hearing deficiency, she claimed that this did not account for the whole problem. She told me she felt so discouraged that she had stayed home and missed a class. In particular, she talked about her fear of being ridiculed, saying, 'I am very self-conscious ... and I get embarrassed when I make a mistake and am afraid that everyone will laugh at me' (Berta, Interview 1). At times she expressed the desire to drop out of the course and at others she believed she should persevere. Finally, after six weeks she stopped attending the class altogether.

Gilda, on the other hand, was not in the least abashed by Ramon's ageist and sexist remarks. When he made allusions of questionable taste to her upcoming wedding and honeymoon plans, she counterattacked with humorous rejoinders and found other occasions to make fun of him. Like the other three women in the study, she positioned herself as an adult, distinct from both the younger and the older persons in the group.

Elsa's interaction with her teacher, Nidia, and the two practice teachers, Simon and Tomas, was impersonal, largely limited to responding when called on during the lessons. Occasionally, she volunteered a response and only twice did she ask the teachers a question during the course. In my classroom observations, I noted that her participation was minimal in comparison with her classmates. When the teachers were interviewed later, they described her as shy, quiet and seldom participative. Tomas believed that Elsa suffered from a lack of confidence and needed the teacher's approval whenever she participated. Simon remarked that Elsa was accepted by the group, but rather neutrally or indifferently. The picture that emerges, then, is of a highly reserved person who remained guarded and aloof in her relationship with the teachers and fellow students. This coincides with my own perception of Elsa, formed in the course of our work together.

Adela went through important changes in her feelings about the two teachers in charge of her group, Martin and Ramon, who gave lessons on alternate days. Early in the term, she commented that Ramon made her nervous and that she became blocked when he called on her in class, whereas she felt less anxiety in Martin's class. She remarked, 'I feel more at ease ... I come [to class] more relaxed, OK, and with ... with Ramon I feel a bit tenser' (Adela, Interview 2). In her next narrative account she again mentioned that she felt less fearful and discomfited in Martin's class, although she thought it was interesting to have two teachers. She went on to say that Martin reinforced her knowledge of grammar, but that with Ramon she had more opportunity to speak. By the middle of the term she began commenting how much she liked Ramon's lessons, especially the kind of literary analysis he made of the reading texts. She approached him after class one day to ask if he had studied literature and after they had talked, he suggested she take an advanced reading and writing course he gives on Saturdays. In our final interview, Adela made the point that Ramon challenged her and made her wish she had more vocabulary at her command so she could participate actively in the class. She commented, 'There came a moment in which ... I was eager to express myself and ... and ... I had so many ideas that I couldn't communicate' (Adela, Interview 5). It seems that once Adela overcame her initial fears and acquired some self-confidence, she preferred Ramon's more demanding teaching style.

The question of age did not appear significant in any obvious way in the relations of any of the four women participants with their teachers. Perhaps this can be explained by the fact that, with the exception of the two young practice teachers in Elsa's group, the teachers all fell into the same broad age-range category of 'adults' as these women, putting them on par, so to speak.

The Construction of Age: Beyond the Classroom

As noted in Hector's and Felix's stories, a consideration of the age identity of language learners cannot be limited to the language classroom, for age is a part of every aspect of a person's life. It links up with other identities and gives special meaning to the language-learning experience, just as learning English at a certain moment in a person's life course becomes significant for them in the world they inhabit outside the classroom.

The interview setting provided the principal window from which I could contemplate the larger world of the participants. Their tales were coconstructions, a cooperative venture, to the extent that I tended to direct the course of the interview, although not rigidly, and the women decided what they wanted to share and how they would tell their stories. In this, our relative positions became crucial, and some notable differences arose in the way this took form with each of the women. Most striking was their choice of either the familiar or the formal 'you' in Spanish (*tú* or *usted*) when speaking to me. Whereas both Hector and Felix had easily addressed me using the familiar form, among the women participants only Berta and Gilda did so without prompting. I had suggested to Adela at the beginning of the course that we use the familiar '*tú*' with each other, yet it was not until the final interview that she switched from the formal '*usted*' to '*tú*'. Interestingly, Elsa never addressed me directly in any of the five interviews. Her participation was limited to cautious and concise responses to the questions I put to her. Although it is impossible to state categorically which combination of personal and social factors governed each participants' election of a form of address, it seems probable that my position as an older woman had some bearing on their decision.

The most significant discovery I made with this group of participants came to light when they were asked to describe the life course. All the women unhesitatingly identified childhood and adolescence as life stages, and some spoke of young adulthood as following adolescence. They also pinpointed old age as a life stage beginning around 60 or 65. They simply denominated the period in between adolescence or young adulthood and old age as 'adulthood', where they all positioned themselves. No one made any distinctions within the 'adult' category. When I asked Elsa directly if adulthood were subdivided, the exchange went as follows:

Extract 29

    E = Elsa; P = Patricia

1   **P:** OK ... then from 20, more or less, which you say is where
2   adulthood begins ... until the 60s, you don't distinguish any ...
3   any other stages?
4   **E:** Not that I recall, no. (Elsa, Interview 3)

To verify her response, I asked her again in the following interview.

Extract 30

    E = Elsa; P = Patricia

1   **P:** OK. Then between what is adulthood, for example, where you
2   are right now in your life ... and old age, you don't distinguish
3   any transitional stage?
4   **E:** Between adult[hood] and old age? Well, what would it be? Well,
5   maybe because I still haven't gotten there yet. (Elsa, Interview 4)

When Adela described the life course, she indicated that adulthood has different moments, depending on what is happening in a person's life and how this changes them. However, she clarified that these stages do not have any special names in Mexico except for old age, which has now become part of the lexicon. According to her, old age begins at 60 but is not separated into other subdivisions. I then asked her specifically about middle age. Extract 31 contains that part of the conversation.

Extract 31

    A = Adela; P = Patricia

1   **P:** So, there is nothing in Spanish that refers to that point between
2   adulthood and old age?
3   **A:** No, no ... no, not that I know of ... no.

4	**P:**	OK. When a woman begins menopause, for example, that is a ...
5		like a sign that a kind of change is going on, right?
6	**A:**	Of course, but that would belong to ... I don't know ... there is
7		no stage like that ... or a specific name ...
8	**P:**	... especially for that?
9	**A:**	There is nothing like that. (Adela, Interview 4)

The fact that none of the participants distinguishes any subdivisions within the adult category confirms my own findings that the concept of 'middle age' is not part of the view of the life course in Mexico. As suggested previously, named age categories come into a language when social issues make it necessary to differentiate one age group from another (Hareven, 1995). In the case of the term 'midlife', the problems of forced early retirement and the empty-nest syndrome, which gave rise to its adoption into the English language, seem to be either incipient or missing entirely in Mexican culture (see Chapter 3 for a more detailed discussion of this point).

Competing Discourses of Age

The construction of age plays out differently with the four women who position themselves as 'adults' from they way it does with the two older adults, Hector and Felix. The discourses the women draw upon are more subtly contested in their case. In this section, I look at two features of their enactment of age which are particularly noteworthy, the decline and progress narratives they tell and the presence of an unwritten, yet powerful, timetable that regulates their lives as adults.

Decline Narratives and Progress Narratives

The interplay between decline and progress narratives, while very much a part of the construction of later adulthood, and in Gullette's (2004) view also of middle adulthood in the United States, is much more attenuated in the case of the four Mexican women participants in the study. Certainly, decline discourses are palpable in their comments about the difficulty of learning a new language at this point in their lives. To a person, they voiced the opinion that childhood would be the best moment for such an undertaking and that, among adults of different ages, the university students have the advantage of youth in their favor. A clear illustration of this is Adela's assertion in an interview that she enjoys being in class with the younger students because she believes they are in close contact with English on a daily basis, whereas she has the impression that her own vocabulary contains many words that are no longer in use.

Outside the question of language learning, ageist remarks and humor on the part of the 'midlifers' surfaced only occasionally in the lessons and in their conversations with me. The following typical example, taken from my classroom observation notes, involves Gilda:

CLASS 17, APRIL 26, 2004

Time	Activity	Gilda
30'	Reading text: 'Finally He Passes!' (*American Headway 3*, Unit 10, 74) discussion of learning how to drive	Gilda [G] participates in discussion
	R reads text out loud	(It starts to rain hard at this point and G makes a comment that she does not want to get wet because she is 'old' and needs to take care of her health.)

Two things are happening here. First, Gilda interjects a humorous comment based on conventionally accepted ideas about old age that render it a frequent source of amusement. In this, there is nothing especially notable in her quip other than that it reflects the society-wide decremental view of aging. Second, her joke may well have been a subtle rebuke aimed at Ramon, the teacher who regularly made ageist and sexist remarks. Gilda's participation in the lessons often included humorous remarks directly or indirectly targeting the teacher. What is important is that the incidence of explicitly ageist comments in this group of participants proved to be considerably less than in that of the older adults.

This can be attributed to the fact that the women's construction of 'middle' adulthood differs fundamentally from Hector's and Felix's construction of later adulthood. In the interviews, the four women enacted an age firmly rooted in the present moment. Although they spoke about the past and acknowledged that there have been high and low moments in their lives, the meaning the past has for them is derived principally from its connection to the present, a point in their lives where they all find themselves satisfactorily situated. At the same time, they shared their short-term and long-term plans with me as they look optimistically toward the future. In other words, their vision of the life course is based on a progress narrative.

This is also evident in the drawings each participant made of the life course, invariably depicted as linear and ascendant. Gilda described her life as 'always moving upwards', saying 'I have always been interested in ... continuing to grow' (Gilda, Interview 3) (see Figure 5.1).

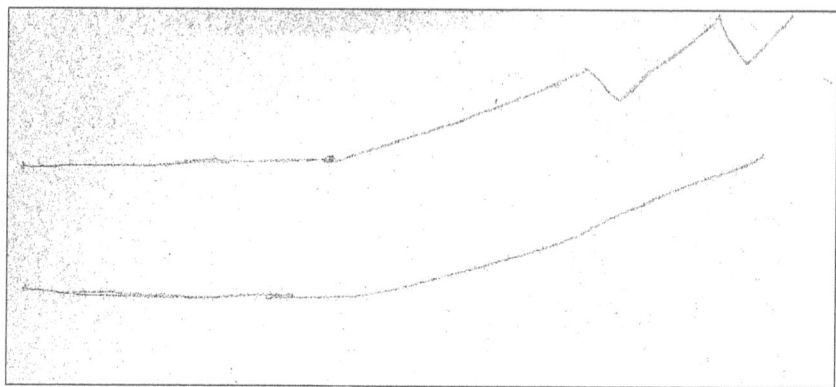

Figure 5.1 Gilda's sketch of the life course

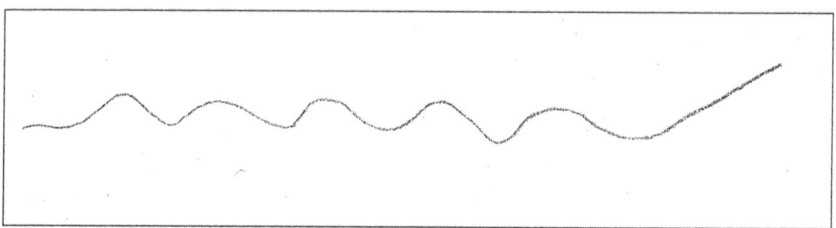

Figure 5.2 Adela's sketch of the life course

Adela stated that her life is getting better because now her children are grown and she has more free time and fewer economic pressures. This has allowed her to take on new projects and finish old ones (see Figure 5.2).

Elsa remarked, 'ever since I began to work in *preparatoria* (equivalent to US high school) ... and now that I have had the opportunity to study a profession as well as English ... well ... I have been going up a little' (Elsa, Interview 3) (see Figure 5.3).

When the women were asked what they envision happening after retirement, the signpost separating adulthood from old age for them, they spoke in terms of continued progress, of new activities and careers, of grandchildren and of travel. Only Gilda addressed the issue of decline, although largely in terms of something she hopes to avoid. Extract 32 contains her remarks on the subject:

Extract 32

    G = Gilda; P = Patricia

1 **P:**   And how do you picture your old age?
2 **G:**   Together [with her future husband] ... But not so very old.

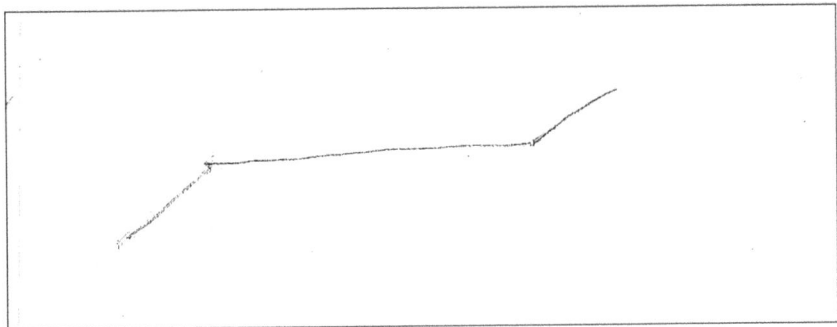

Figure 5.3 Elsa's life course

```
3   P:   What do you mean?
4   G:   I mean ... the truth is ... well, I, yes, I'd like to get to be ... to be
5        old, a little old lady ... but only if I can take care of myself. ...
6        not have health problems or not be able to move or need to depend
7        on someone ... and, I mean, the truth is ... I'd like to be together with
8        him but not like that ... but rather ... that is ... that you have to deal
9        with someone in that sense and someone also old like you ... I mean,
10       it's difficult. Yes, I want to grow old ... old together with him ... but
11       always in good health ... or always where we can take care of ... first,
12       our own selves and then take care of each other. (Gilda, Interview 3)
```

In this extract, Gilda conveys her abhorrence of the physical deterioration and loss of independence associated with old age in the prevalent discourses of contemporary Western society. As I pointed out in Chapter 3, such discourses can be misleading for three reasons: (1) not everyone experiences aging into old age in the same way; (2) the meanings and values given to physical change are social constructions; and (3) the exclusive focus on decremental biological processes disregards other equally significant aspects of aging that do not necessarily involve decline.

Unlike Hector and Felix, none of the women expressed an immediate concern with anything but their progress narrative. The reason for this is very likely that none of them has yet retired and, with the exception of Berta, they still see retirement as a remote event in their lives. At 59, Berta had plans to retire within the year, yet her construction of age differs markedly from that of Hector and Felix in that she does not manifest any conflict about questions of productivity, social status or marginalization up to now. This reinforces the observation I made previously that retirement defines the crucial moment dividing the construction of later adulthood from earlier stages in the lives of the participants.

Keeping to the Schedule

Although the narratives of these participants are not overtly ageist in the usual sense of devaluing age, they reflect an evident concern with age-appropriacy. In reality, this too is a manifestation of ageism for, as discussed earlier, prevailing discourses of aging have a direct impact on norms of behavior. In essence, tacit rules determine what is considered suitable or appropriate behavior for persons of a given age in each society. The question of age-appropriacy cropped up again and again in the interviews with the women participants, where I observed that a major preoccupation for them was whether they were 'on schedule' or not. An unwritten, but very definite, timetable that guides one through the adult years, indeed through the entire life course, appears to have governed their assessment of their own accomplishments. Not keeping to the schedule would seem to require an explanation, as both Gilda's and Berta's stories illustrate in the following extracts.

At the time the course began in the winter, Gilda had stopped working in order to plan her August wedding. She commented on the fact that she and her fiancé, at 37 and 39 respectively, are both older than is customary in Mexican society to begin married life and start a family. She told me:

Extract 33

```
1   So, I think that ... I mean ... [our] age ... maybe it's not the best ...
2   because we are old ... especially when you think about having
3   children. ... That is if I can ... because the truth is, I mean, at this
4   point my age doesn't help me very much to ... to wait for too long ...
5   to get pregnant. (Gilda, Interview 3).
```

Gilda's concerns about having passed the appropriate time to get married and have children were among those Berta also shared. Berta related some of her experiences, tracing the long route she took to becoming a physician.

Extract 34

B = Berta; P = Patricia

```
1   B:  Well, my ... my luck is like ... like very funny because I am one
2       of the oldest ones ... and well, in those times, in a family of
3       twelve ... there were twelve of us ... I, as the oldest of the girls,
4       had to work. So, after leaving secundaria ...
5   P:  ... off to work.
6   B:  Nobody asked me, 'Do you want to work or not?' Off to work. I
7       was ready for it. So I stopped studying ... just imagine, it was
8       like ... it took me nine years to return to school to start
```

9		*preparatoria* ... because I told myself ... well, all my brothers
10		and sisters are studying ... and what about me?
11	**P:**	In other words, you didn't go to *preparatoria* until nine years
12		later?
13	**B:**	Nine years later.
14	**P:**	You worked during that period?
15	**B:**	Yes ... and after that I went to *preparatoria* ... I met my
16		husband there ... but, at the same time I worked. I got married
17		after finishing *preparatoria* ... I was already 28 by then. I said
18		to myself, no, well I am going to study a profession. So that's
19		how I started studying medicine and my husband law.
20	**P:**	Where?
21	**B:**	In the National University.
22	**P:**	Good.
23	**B:**	Yes, ... and then, well ... we finished our university studies
24		when we were rather old ... and, well, I never had the chance to
25		study English.
26	**P:**	Right. (Berta, Interview 1)

In lines 1–4 of this extract, Berta narrated how she had to leave school at a young age to begin working to help support the large family of which she was a member. The fact that all her brothers and sisters obtained a university education suggests that academic achievement had a certain importance for her family. So, although not entirely unheard of in urban Mexican society, the case of a young woman beginning her work life at the age of 14 would seem to constitute being 'ahead of schedule' rather than 'behind schedule'. However, because of her determination to study both *preparatoria* (equivalent to US high school) and then university (lines 6–10 and 15–19), Berta found herself spending the subsequent years trailing behind her contemporaries in terms of the 'proper' or accepted age for accomplishing such undertakings. Her awareness that she was not adhering to the timetable of age-appropriate behavior manifests itself throughout her narration. For instance, she mentioned that she was 'already 28' when she and her husband got married (line 17), and that they were 'rather old' (*grandecitos*) by the time they graduated from university (line 24).

Berta went on to comment in the same interview that perhaps she did not learn things as easily as the younger students studying medicine because of her age, but also because she was busy with a job, a husband and a young family. Because she felt that she was getting old and it might be too late if she waited, she decided to have children immediately, giving birth to her three daughters while still in medical school. Thus, Berta's accomplishments occurred at ages not typical of the general population at that time, a fact that appears to have troubled her to some extent throughout her life. Nevertheless, she is now set on learning English, despite her belief that it is no longer the best moment to do so. She said, 'I am going to keep on persisting here and see what happens' (Berta, Interview 1).

Age and Other Identities

As with the older adults, age identity is intertwined with various other subject positions in the case of the 'midlife' adult participants in the study. Professional identity is particularly salient, for all of the women have careers that provide them with considerable satisfaction. Except for Berta, whose retirement was imminent, the women spoke of their hopes of advancing in their careers. An important connection between their subject positions as professionals and their gendered identities was evident throughout the interviews. When Gilda talked about her professional aspirations, she made it very clear that a 'glass ceiling' exists in the corporate world in Mexico. Extract 35 contains her description of the possibilities she feels are open to her.

Extract 35

```
 1  P:  And what are your hopes in regard to your professional life?
 2  G:  Actually what I am looking for is a position at ... at ... at a high
 3      level ... which here in Mexico, be it good or bad ... although
 4      they say there is no discrimination ... that everything is
 5      equitable ... the same for men and for women ... it isn't true.
 6  P:  Uh huh.
 7  G:  So, as a woman, I mean, well ... it is difficult ... to reach certain
 8      levels. So, at least as far as I am concerned ... that is ... I am
 9      looking for something like that. To show that just because you
10      are a woman doesn't mean that you are worth less ... I mean ...
11      more stupid ... but that you have the skills and the capability of
12      doing it [the job].
13  P:  And when would this happen ... if everything goes well for you?
14  G:  I hope it would be within a short to medium term.
15  P:  OK. Talk to me in years.
16  G:  In years? I don't know ... about four ... five years at the most.
17  P:  You would only be forty.
18  G:  Uh huh.
19  P:  And then what? What happens after that ... in your professional
20      life?
21  G:  I think, well, you reach a certain point and you can't advance
22      any further. I mean, and more so as a woman. I mean, to strive
23      for a position as general director ... I mean, only if I had my
24      own company ... and I were the general director of my own
25      company. But in the job market ... that is ... as an employee ...
```

26   I think it can't happen. I think that only up to a certain level . . .
27   as an assistant director or director of an area . . . that's as far as . . .
28 **P:** And that is where you stay?
29 **G:** That is where I would stay. (Gilda, Interview 3)

In this extract, Gilda makes no secret of her ambition to reach the top of the corporate ladder in her field. At the same time, she is completely realistic about the unlikelihood of this ever occurring in present-day Mexico. Despite claims to the contrary, that 'there is no discrimination . . . that everything is equitable . . . the same for men and for women,' Gilda contends that it is simply not true (lines 3–5). She explained that, at a certain point, women are simply not promoted to higher-level positions in the private sector (lines 7, 8, 21 and 22). It is not a matter of their relative merits. In fact, Gilda herself wants to demonstrate 'that just because you are a woman doesn't mean that you are worth less' or even 'more stupid' but that women 'have the skills and the capability' of performing the job well (lines 9–12). The only way she sees that a woman can aspire to be a chief executive is to be the owner of her own company (lines 23–26). Her plans are to go as far as she can in the next few years and then to remain in that position until she retires (line 29). The dissatisfied tone of the extract conveys the sense that Gilda's identity as a successful professional is irrevocably bound to, and in conflict with her gendered identity. In line with Baxter's (2003) thinking, it would seem that being assigned the less powerful subject position of a woman in Mexican society generates a clash between discourses that explains in part Gilda's discontent.

A similar conflict is played out on a more personal level in the case of Adela. Extract 36 describes how she struggled to have a teaching career.

Extract 36

A = Adela; P = Patricia

1   **P:** And . . . and your whole life . . . let's say . . . when you are . . . you
2   were raising your children, you've worked?
3   **A:** Yes.
4   **P:** And that was your decision?
5   **A:** It was a question of battling against several things. Maybe also
6   against the idea that they have of women in Mexico . . . a little
7   difficult . . . for me. When I got married my husband didn't want
8   me to work and . . .
9   **P:** Oh, that was the . . . the mentality, right?
10 **A:** Yes, yes . . . yes, despite the fact that my husband . . . that is . . . is
11   a graduate of the National University . . . he has a doctorate . . .
12   yes, he didn't want me to [work]. So, I told myself . . . this just

13		can't be. Did I study all these years just to be here? It's not
14		possible. So I engineered things ... yes ... I arranged my
15		schedule ... yes ... so that when he went to work, I left for work.
16		When he got back ... I was there at home.
17	**P:**	Right.
18	**A:**	So, it was ... it was a [constant] struggle. After my children were
19		born, well ... 'All the more reason,' said my husband, 'No,
20		well, you have to be here.' [Adela:] 'No, no, but I can do it.'
		(Adela, Interview 2)

Adela narrated, in this extract, the difficulties involved in standing her ground against her husband after she made the decision to work. It became a persistent source of conflict, first arising after she got married, and then again after her children were born (lines 10–16 and 18–20). Even though by the 1980s it had become more common for women in Mexico to work outside the home, particularly after the economic downturns brought on by a series of currency devaluations, many people resisted the change of customs (Oliveira & Ariza, 1999). In lines 10 and 11, Adela pointed out that her husband is a well-educated man, suggesting that she believes he should have understood her own professional aspirations. Nonetheless, patriarchal traditions in Mexico are deep-rooted and cross all social classes. Adela's solution was to devise ways to comply with her husband's expectations regarding the behavior of a stay-at-home wife, such as being at home when he left for or returned from work, preparing meals and so on, while assuming the responsibilities of a job in her own time, a practice adopted by many working women in Mexico (Blanco, 2001). This functioned well until she gave birth to her first child, when her husband again voiced strong objections to her working outside the home, based this time on the 'incontestable' obligations of motherhood (lines 19 and 20) (Blanco, 2001; López Hernández, 2007).

Not giving up, Adela sought support from her mother-in-law who offered to care for her infant daughter. As she explained, 'My husband realized that my mother-in-law ... his [own] mother ... was supporting me ... and so I ... I got to work' (Adela, Interview 2). One further crisis arose when her school-aged son went through a period of asthma attacks and her husband told her she should stop working to take care of him. However, Adela decided that it would be worse if she were at home because she might actually cause her son to be sick by worrying excessively about him. This time, the vice principal of the school came to her support by giving Adela a schedule that allowed her to spend more time with her children when she needed to. After that, the situation seems to have ended in an undeclared truce. Adela's experience is typical of that of many professional women in Mexico where, to this day, the subject positions of wife and mother are expected to take precedence over all others (Blanco, 2001; López Hernández, 2007).

The association of adulthood with responsibility is another recurring theme, and one that is very closely connected with both age and gendered identities. If retirement marks the onset of later adulthood, then I suggest that responsibility separates young adulthood from 'middle' adulthood for these participants. Elsa described it this way:

Extract 37

1   I think that from ... from adolescence until you reach the stage of ...
2   of adulthood, is the most enjoyable [time]. After that ... when you
3   become an adult is when responsibilities begin. (Elsa, Interview 4)

Elsa claimed that she is happy as an adult, even though adulthood has brought many more responsibilities with it. Adela also spoke of the responsibilities that come with adulthood, particularly obligations that women have as mothers. She referred to 'certain burdens that Mexican society itself makes us feel', adding that 'as a mother you have to be there at every moment' (Adela, Interview 3). In the traditional breakdown of gender roles in Mexico, such as we saw in the cases of Hector and Felix, men are thought to have the obligation to provide for the family economically and women the responsibility for running the household, raising the children and waiting on their husbands (Blanco, 2001; López Hernández, 2007). However, since many women have become economically active in order to contribute to the family economy or for motives of personal growth, they can no longer attend to all the needs of every member of the family in the multiple activities they had formerly undertaken (Sandoval Ávila, 2002). And, in view of the fact that men seem to have largely remained reluctant to share household chores and childcare, it is the grandmothers who often step in to offer support to their daughters in carrying out these responsibilities (Guijarro Morales, 2001; Partida, 2004; Zermeño, 2005).

Connecting the Pieces

The four 'midlife' women, Elsa, Gilda, Adela and Berta, all convey a sense of satisfaction with their present life positions, seeming neither to yearn for the past nor to be more than usually preoccupied about the future. Their stories are tales of progress, in which they envision their lives as moving steadily in an upward direction.

They are studying English for similar reasons, either finishing a task begun earlier in their lives, in the case of Gilda and Adela, or initiating one they had hoped to accomplish before now, in the case of Elsa and Berta. While they each cite the obvious advantages of being able to speak English, such benefits tend to be removed from the practicalities of their present-day lives. From my perspective, it seems that learning English constitutes a means for them to acquire cultural capital (Bourdieu, 1977) and, as such, is part of their enactment of age and the construction of their identity as 'midlife' adults.

The women share the belief that languages are best learned early on in life because younger people are better able to absorb new knowledge and their lives are less complicated. Nevertheless, they point out that adults are often more focused, more motivated and more serious than adolescents or young adults when it comes to the task of studying a foreign language. Such 'adultist' attitudes may well have contributed to a sense of separateness from the younger students. This division is also evident in the use of 'we' and 'they' in their descriptions of classroom relations. At the same time, the 'midlife' women positioned themselves as different from the older adults in their groups. In general, decline discourses appeared less often among this group of participants, whose focus is primarily on the present and for whom the future is largely a promising one.

In the larger worlds in which they live, the 'midlife' adult women have taken up or been assigned a number of subject positions. Foremost among them are their professional and gendered identities, which frequently compete with each other in a society where, until recently, tradition has tended to discourage Mexican women from assuming these dual positions (Zermeño, 2005). When women have insisted on doing so, they have been compelled to demonstrate both in the workplace and at home that they can fulfill all the corresponding obligations. This has engendered different kinds of conflict.

In addition to accepting the responsibility they equate with adulthood, the 'midlife' women displayed a concern with keeping to the tacit timetable that indicates what conduct is appropriate at different moments in the life course. This often occasioned a measure of anxiety, for the timetable is still more rigid in Mexico than in the United States or the United Kingdom, despite changes that are recently taking place.

The participants all constructed an age identity as 'midlife' adults that was clearly distinct from that of both younger and older adults, despite the fact that, in chronological terms, the age range among them spanned 25 years. Based on what has been learned from the fieldwork, I am led to reaffirm my contention that it is the assumption of responsibility that constitutes the onset, and retirement the end, of what these participants call 'adulthood'. Of particular interest is the fact that the women do not recognize any division within the adult category that corresponds to 'middle age'.

Conclusion

The overall findings to emerge in the stories Elsa, Gilda, Adela and Berta tell coincide with those that came to light in the stories of the older adults, in the sense that they address the same basic issues. Nevertheless, the specific ways in which the construction of age plays out for the 'midlifers' distinguish them from both the older and younger adults. Their tales reveal how they enact their age identity and enhance our understanding of the bearing age has on adult language learners. The following observations focus on the particularities relevant to 'middle' adulthood.

The impact of age on the language-learning experience varies according to where each person positions her/himself in the lifespan.
For the 'midlife' women, learning English at this moment of their lives satisfies the desire to accomplish something that is particularly meaningful to each of them. They are not, like the older adults in this study, looking for leisure-time activities for, with the exception of Gilda, they are busy working and caring for their families. However, they have decided to use whatever extra time they have at the moment either to work toward a new goal or one they have had since childhood. While they suggest that career opportunities might open up for them in the future if they know English, the 'here-and-now' benefits appear to be tied more closely to the prestige associated with the language and to the identities they wish to construct for themselves as 'adults'. Again, the key concern is the acquisition of cultural capital (Bourdieu, 1977).

The beliefs and attitudes EFL learners have about age and SLA have an effect on their language-learning experience.
The 'midlife' participants, like the older adults, are convinced that the younger university students possess a greater ability to learn new languages. Nonetheless, they contend that their own motivation, resolution and dedication to the task can offset any cognitive advantages the students may have. Although the design of this study does not allow for conclusions to be drawn regarding the effects of such factors on the linguistic outcomes of the course, certainly the more serious attitude to language learning of the 'midlife' adults was in evidence in their enactment of age in the classroom, distinguishing them from their young adult companions.

The coconstruction of age in the classroom context is rooted in the prevailing cultural discourses of age.
Elsa, Gilda, Adela and Berta all positioned themselves and were positioned by their classmates and teachers as 'adults', a vague, rather imprecise category that hovers between 'young adulthood' and 'old age'. Gullette remarked, 'Once those in the years between young and old had no name because they were the most powerful and unclassifiable; the norm, unseen' (Gullette, 2004: 95–96). This still describes the situation in Mexico, where 'middle' adulthood has only recently begun to take on the ageist tint of present-day Anglophone cultural discourses. While occasional signs of decline ideology surfaced in the behavior of the women participants, it was their

manifestation of adultism that provided a clearer indication of the presence of ageist attitudes in the classroom.

Like the other participants in the study, the issue of age-appropriacy weighed heavily on the 'midlifers'. Yet, part of what has been learned in this study is that what comprises age-appropriacy varies for each age group. In the case of the 'midlife' women, it manifested itself as a concern with accomplishing particular things or reaching certain goals within a determined time frame. Such reliance on chronological age as the sole reference for judging proper behavior can lead to the generation of ageist stereotypes (Hazan, 1994).

Both present and prior life circumstances have an impact on the language-learning experience.

Learning English is part of the identity construction of the 'midlife' women and of their ongoing progress narratives. As such, its significance goes beyond acquiring expertise in the language. Having overcome obstacles in the past in order to reach the place where they currently find themselves, they are perhaps the most comfortable of all the participants in the study with their present life circumstances.

The construction of the age identity of language learners occurs both within the classroom and in the world beyond it, moving back and forth between the two.

Part of the enactment of their 'midlife' age identity is evident in the way the women demonstrated a sense of responsibility both in and out of the classroom. They approached the language-learning experience much as they approach the other obligations they have taken on in their personal and professional lives, with the maturity and seriousness that for them constitutes being an adult, as opposed to being a young person. It also distinguishes them from older adults, whom they perceive as having shed the burden of professional activities and some, but not all (as we have seen), of their family responsibilities.

Age as a subject position is interlinked with other subject positions in adult language learners.

As the women have aged into 'middle' adulthood, their professional and gendered identities have come increasingly into conflict. The roles of family members in Mexico follow strict gender lines. Because the father is responsible for providing economically for his family, his professional and gendered identities do not normally clash. He exercises the power and his position is supreme. The mother, on the other hand, is expected to provide absolute love and willingly sacrifice herself for her family. Herein lie the seeds of conflict, for any needs and desires of her own are necessarily subordinate to those of other family members. In the case of the women in this study, learning English fell under the category of a personal desire or ambition and hence had to be carefully juggled with their 'primary' responsibilities to their families.

To the extent that this was successfully done, the language-learning experience furnished them with a sense of satisfaction and contributed to their construction of new identities.

The four women each positioned themselves as an adult, an amorphous category that is basically defined by what it is not, that is, neither 'young' nor 'old'. Perhaps because of the broad and somewhat nebulous character of 'middle' adulthood in Mexico, the stories of these participants contain more similarities than differences with respect to their experience of age. For each of them, it is the assumption of responsibility that signaled the beginning of their adulthood and it will be retirement that denotes its end. Despite finding themselves at different points along the trajectory toward old age, their assessment of where they currently are coincided in an overall satisfaction with their present life positions. In the following chapter, the construction of young adulthood comes to life in the story of a university student. His narrative leads to some final reflections about later, 'middle' and young adulthood.

Notes

(1) To emphasize this point, single quotation marks are used to refer to 'middle' adulthood or 'midlife' adults throughout the chapter.
(2) Gilda accepted a job one month before the course ended and was unable to attend after that. She was allowed to present the final exam, which she passed easily, and to receive her certificate of proficiency.
(3) As a public school teacher, Adela is a federal employee and therefore entitled to retire after 28 years of service and to receive a small pension. Because the salary scale is low, most teachers retire as soon as they are eligible, collect their monthly pension and supplement it with other types of remunerative activity if their wages are vital to the family economy.

6 Constructing Age in Young Adulthood

Introduction

This chapter is about David. As the only young person to participate in the study, his story provides a single, but telling, example of the construction of young adulthood in Mexico. After first giving a short biographical sketch of David's life, I turn to focal points in his audio-taped narrative accounts, our interviews and my classroom observation notes to illustrate his enactment of age both in and out of the classroom setting. I end with reflections on David's construction of his identity as a young adult, and then connect his story to those of the 'middle' and older adults as a way of drawing the three data chapters to a close.

David's Story

Sketch of David's Life

At the time of the study, David was a 23-year-old university student majoring in applied mathematics and computer science. Although he had completed the regular course of studies, he still had to pass the final examinations in two subjects he had failed, fulfill the language requirement and write a thesis in order to graduate. Thus, he was slightly older than the other university students in the sixth-level English class where I observed him. He lives with his mother, who has been widowed since David was four years old. An older sister is married and lives nearby. His mother acquired a new partner four years after being widowed but, although this person lives with them, he did not assume the role of stepfather and, in fact, has always had a strained relationship with David, according to David's own account. David's mother has worked hard over the years to provide her children with a home and to satisfy their basic needs. She was employed in a low-level administrative job in a public school from the age of 16 until her retirement at 49. She now supplements her small pension by selling candy and sweets at a nearby school and by selling sweaters and baby clothes that she knits. The straitened circumstances of David's home life are reminiscent of Hector's and Felix's own early years.

David's mother obtained a scholarship for him to study in a private primary school through her connections in the Ministry of Education. He then attended public schools for both *secundaria* (equivalent to US middle school) and *preparatoria* (equivalent to US high school). Starting the university proved to be a watershed moment in his life. David put it this way: 'Actually, I feel that it was like a big leap to go to the university . . . not just in the academic sense but also from a personal standpoint' (David, Interview 3). He spoke often in the interviews of the close friends he has made in his years at the university.

David's plans for the future are rather nebulous. Although he talked about getting a job after completing his undergraduate degree, he does not seem to have any specific professional goals. He also mentioned the possibility of going abroad for graduate school, yet it is not clear that he has the required academic standing or the means to finance such a venture, for he has never worked. Considering his mother's limited economic resources, it is unlikely that she can continue to support him unless he lives at home.

The Goal of Learning English

David claimed to be taking English classes because he hopes to study or work abroad after graduation. He also talked about wanting to read a novel in English some time. Yet when asked whether he consulted the literature in the field of computer science in English, he said that, having finished the course of studies, he no longer has any need to read. What proved most interesting in the conversation is what David did not mention, namely, that he must pass the final examination of the sixth-level course in order to receive a certificate of proficiency in English that is a requirement for graduation for computer science majors. Thus, David appears to value English for its worth as symbolic or cultural capital (Bourdieu, 1977) rather than for its immediate utility to him in obtaining his college degree. This omission was intriguing, for it gave David's story a certain quixotic tenor that I encountered subsequently in other parts of his narrative.

The Construction of Age: In the Classroom

Although he claimed it is never too late to learn a new language, David considers early childhood to be the best time to begin learning one. He remarked that if very young children are exposed to two languages, they may mix them up for a time but will eventually sort them out. He added that once they get to primary school, children in Mexico will necessarily become more proficient in Spanish, but will have a head start in acquiring the L2.

Referring to his own case, he stated that because he started studying English in primary school, he has had an advantage over those classmates who only began to learn the language in the university. He also commented that, in his view, the older members of the group from the neighboring community probably have even greater difficulties learning a language 'because they may have stopped studying for a long time' and 'it's like starting to use something again that you haven't used in a long while' (David, Interview 1).

While David considered his English to be above average in the group, he acknowledged that he has a problem with speaking. He said that he thinks he just needs more practice. Nevertheless, he chose to participate minimally in the lessons, thus missing many opportunities to practice speaking. When he did respond in class, he made frequent mistakes, and I judged his proficiency to be slightly lower than that of the other students in the group.[1] David insisted that when the time comes and he needs to speak English, for example in a job interview, he is sure that he will be able to because he 'won't have any choice' (David, Interview 2). Again, this comment suggests that David's appraisal of his real-life situation perhaps borders on the fanciful.

Enactment of Age: Examining Classroom Activities

David was a student in the same sixth-level course as Adela and Gilda (see Chapter 5). Two teachers, Martin and Ramon, gave lessons on alternate days, using Student Book 3 (Soars & Soars, 2003) of the *American Headway* series. As mentioned previously, this textbook series attempts to capture the interest of the adult and young adult market. However, the content and activities of *American Headway* are only marginally successful in appealing to university-age students such as David, for the global focus of the series targets persons with a wider experience of the world than that generally found in the student population of this public Mexican university. David, for example, has never traveled out of the country nor has he ever held a job. The following incident was recorded in my classroom observation notes:

CLASS 21, MAY 12, 2004

Time	Activity	David
10'	Exercise 1: 'The First Day of Vacation' (*American Headway* 3, Unit 11, 82) discussion of hotels	David [D] says that he has never stayed in a hotel. He either camps out or stays with relatives when he goes on vacation.

According to the publishers of *American Headway*, this type of content is intended to touch on the aspirations, rather than the experience, of young adults in developing countries like Mexico (Gray, 2002). On the other hand, the classroom activities developed by the teachers, in particular Ramon, were as a rule directed specifically to university-age students in the lessons I observed.

Although David attended the English course regularly, he participated very little in the ongoing activities in comparison with his classmates. In the lessons taught by Ramon, he responded when called on but only occasionally volunteered to answer. Because Martin generally had the students self-select when he asked questions, David's participation was even more limited in those lessons. He seldom took part in role-play or singing activities. In our interviews, David explained to me that he prefers to observe rather than call attention to himself and that he tries not to stand out in a group. In the following extract from one of his narrative accounts, he expanded on this idea:

Extract 38

```
1   And it's also kind of funny ... or interesting ... to observe how all of
2   us sit way in the back right up against the wall. Sometimes we students
3   have the idea that only show-offs or nerds sit up front ... that is, those
4   who participate and raise their hand all the time and are always talking
5   ... and the 'brains' ... and, I don't know, we put them down, OK ...
6   we label them ... and in a way we even treat them badly because it's
7   like they want to stand out a lot ... or ... I don't know, but it's typical
8   of 'good little children' that they sit up front and ... and everybody
9   else, well, [they sit] wherever they want, OK? Personally, I mean, I sit
10  in the back because I like to observe. ... I don't ... I don't like to feel
11  that someone is behind me ... or ... I don't know, it's like you have a
12  different perspective ... broader ... from my point of view, in the back.
13  So, it's just because of that I almost always sit way in the back and in a
14  corner right next to the window. (David, Narrative account 9)
```

In lines 1–8 of this extract, David gave voice to a deeply entrenched norm of student culture, namely, that it is not socially acceptable to show off in class. The corollary of this is that it is not 'cool' to perform well academically, at least not publicly, for that is tantamount to being a nerd (Bishop *et al.*, 2004). This coincides with Benwell and Stokoe's (2002, 2005) findings in a study of students in a postcompulsory university setting in the United Kingdom. They noted a resistance to or distancing from academic identity, that is, 'students co-construct the discursive limits in which being "too clever" is problematic: being a student seems to necessitate being "average" and not standing out' (Benwell & Stokoe, 2005: 138).

Challenging the teacher, joking and doing the minimum amount of work are connected with popularity. Preece (2009) encountered similar identity constructions in multilingual university students from working-class black and minority ethnic backgrounds in London. While these students also resisted identification with the academic community, she observed that gender accounted for some interesting differences in the enactment of 'laddish' masculinities and 'ladette' femininities. Thus, it is perhaps no surprise to find that this norm, generally associated with high-school adolescents, still has currency among young university students in Mexico. It helps shed light on David's stated preference for sitting unobtrusively in the back of the classroom, and observing rather than taking an active part in the activities (lines 9–14).

The significance of peer culture and its corresponding peer pressure is a theme that runs throughout David's narrative and is a determining factor in his enactment of age. He revealed that he is afraid of making mistakes in front of other people, commenting, 'I don't know ... it's hard for me to speak, and "God, I messed up." In other words ... "Why did I bother to open my mouth?"' (David, Interview 2). He also stressed that the fact that some students participate more in the lessons does not necessarily mean they are better.

Enactment of Age: In Relations with Fellow Students

David invariably sat with students of his own age group. He remarked that he was acquainted with many of them from previous English courses. When asked to work in pairs or small groups, he always chose teammates sitting nearby. Although there were only about 12 students in the class, David never interacted with any of the older members of the group. He made the following comments in one of our interviews:

Extract 39

D = David; P = Patricia

1   **P:**   OK, I wanted to ask you about your classmates.
2   **D:**   Uh huh.
3   **P:**   Because I see that there are several who are very young ...
4   around 18 ...
5   **D:**   Yeah ... most of them.
6   **P:**   And then there are older people.
7   **D:**   Uh huh.
8   **P:**   What about you? How ... where do you fit ... in ... in ... among
9   them?
10 **D:**   Well, I feel I ... I hang out more with the young people.
11 **P:**   Uh huh.
12 **D:**   Because maybe ... I don't know ... with Adela ... well, I do say

13		hello to her ... but, I mean ... I don't ... I don't know ... I don't
14		talk to her ... I don't ... I don't get together [with her].
15	**P:**	Right. And what about Gilda ... Gilda, for example?
16	**D:**	Yes, she strikes me as interesting ... for example, because she
17		has traveled ... because of her comments in class ... she is a
18		person ... I don't know ... the way she is ... catches my
19		attention ... but, no, I haven't had the opportunity to ... to talk
20		... to go up to her [to talk]. But, well, I mean, yes, I ... I hang
21		out more with the young people. (David, Interview 3)

In this extract, David positioned himself unequivocally as a young person, even though he is slightly older than the majority of the university students in the group (lines 10, 20, and 21). There is a clear division for him between the younger and older English students, although he made no distinction between the 'midlife' adults and older adults. From his remarks it would seem that he has no particular interest in talking to Adela (lines 12–14). However, he indicated that he is intrigued by Gilda, although he has not made any overtures to strike up a conversation with her (lines 16–20). His comments tend to confirm the 'midlife' and older adults' appreciation that they must take the initiative in establishing relations with the younger students (see Chapters 4 and 5).

In another interview, David speculated on what it might be like to be a mature student in an English class.

Extract 40

1	I feel that within the atmosphere of the classroom, yes, they probably
2	feel like 'My gosh, here I am and everyone else is young. I am the old
3	person ... the oldest here, right?' So, I feel that it can work two ways,
4	OK. It either motivates them ... or it gets to them ... or when they slip
5	up ... well, they feel worse, OK. Well 'My gosh, I messed up badly ...
6	and here I am the old person. What am I doing here? I should be
7	resting, right ... I don't know ... I shouldn't be here.' But the other
8	way, OK, is that it pushes them ... yes, no, that is, 'I can do it and I
9	know I can do it.' Let's say that I've found both things here [in the
10	university]. (David, Interview 1)

In David's view, being older in a classroom of young people can have two possible effects, either motivating them or discouraging them (lines 3–5). He imagined what the older students might say and used their voices to express either the embarrassment they experience at making mistakes (lines 5–7) or the impetus they feel to succeed (lines 8 and 9). The picture he gave of mature students would seem to be the product of his own reflections rather than of personal contact with these people.

Both extracts (39 and 40) demonstrate the kind of insularity that the older participants in the study perceived in their younger classmates (see Chapters 4 and 5). This may be attributed to what some authors have observed to be the increasing tendency in contemporary society for young people to spend less time interacting with adults and more time interacting with their peers (Dayrell, 2005; Eckert, 1997a; Feixa, 2003; Reguillo, 2001). In fact, avoidance has been identified as one of the signal characteristics of younger-to-older adult communication in many parts of the world.

> There is an underlying ambivalence or tension among young people when interacting with older interlocutors in that they are prone to keep their distance and also avoid such interactions. (McCann *et al.*, 2005: 304)

Enactment of Age: In Relations with the Teachers

Of all the participants in the study, David had the least amount of personal interaction with his teachers. This is likely a consequence of his limited participation in classroom activities as well as his desire to remain inconspicuous. Nevertheless, his audio-taped narrative accounts contained extensive comments on the two teachers, their styles and their strengths and weaknesses. His opinion of them oscillated from good to bad and back again as the course progressed. At times he praised one teacher and found fault with the other. A few weeks later he would recognize new qualities in the teacher he had criticized and find defects in the other. Although his comments were often incisive, they never referred to any personal contact with either teacher.

When the teachers were asked to give their appraisal of David at the end of the course, they coincided in their view of him as quiet and reserved. Martin complained about David's apathy and lack of interest in the class. Ramon took a more tolerant view, finding David responsible and interested in his own progress in English. However, he mentioned that he was often distant, not always joining the group in the classroom activities.

David's reluctance to connect with either of the teachers on a personal level likely reflects the same tendency to avoid involvement with the mature students in the group. In his case, it is a clearly identifiable facet of his enactment of age as a young adult.

The Construction of Age: Beyond the Classroom

To understand how David constructed his age as a language learner, and what meaning learning English had for him at the time of this study, it is valuable to explore the broader context of his life. What follows are some characteristic displays of David's construction of his age identity that occurred during the course of the interviews and that focus on the interconnections between David's subject position as a young adult and his other identities.

Competing Discourses of Age

In his enactment of age, David appears to hover between his new-found autonomy as a young adult and his continuing dependence on his mother for economic support. His present contentment with the life of a university student is occasionally at variance with his desire to press forward to a future in which he expects to achieve full independence. These competing discourses are set against David's view of the life course as a progress–decline narrative, making that a good place to begin this section.

Decline Narratives and Progress Narratives

David first sketched the life course horizontally as a series of curves reflecting the ups and downs of his life. He then decided that the drawing needed to be rotated so that the spiral moved vertically in an upward direction starting with his birth, suggesting that he sees his life as having followed a path of continued progress to date (see Figure 6.1). Like the 'midlife' women in this study, David did not extend his representation of the life course beyond the moment in which we had our interviews. However, when asked, he identified different life stages, beginning with childhood, from birth to 10 or 12, followed by adolescence, ending at around 18 or 20. He classified a relatively long period lasting from the age of 20 to 35 as young adulthood. The next stage he called adulthood or maturity, from 35 to 45, followed by old age, from 45 to 60. David referred to those over 60 as *ancianos* ('aged persons').

David's perception of the life course differed in significant ways from the division of the life stages made by the older and 'middle' adult participants. Not only does he envisage young adulthood as spanning a lengthy 15-year period, but he also situates the onset of old age at a much earlier moment in the lifespan, at 45. In the following brief extracts, David talked about how he imagines himself at the age of 45 or 50.

Extract 41

1   So, well ... I suppose that, like everything, right, you need to know ...
2   when to retire ... in time. So, I imagine that after ... between 40 and
3   50 ... I ... well ... I'd better go ... if I've been working such a long
4   time. (David, Interview 3)

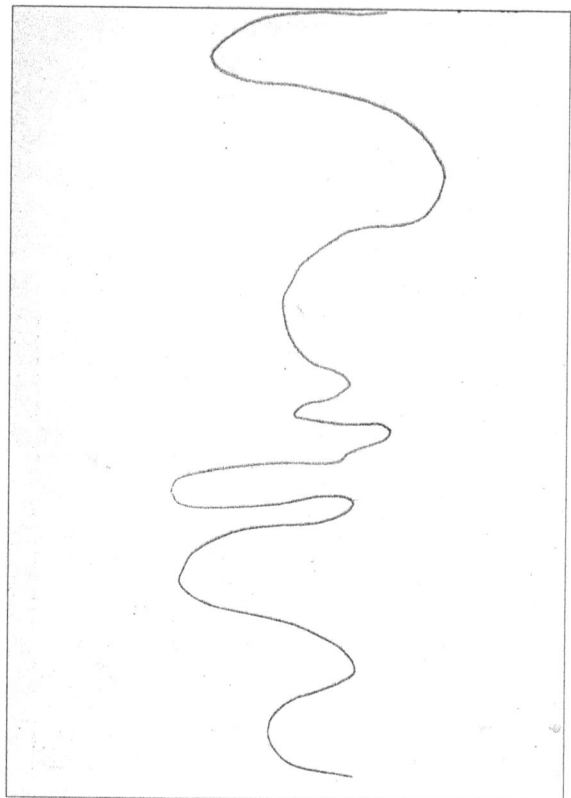

Figure 6.1 David's sketch of the life course

Extract 42

D = David; P = Patricia

1 **D:** Maybe when I'm 50, I won't be able to work. So ...
2 **P:** Why wouldn't you be able to work?
3 **D:** Because, well, maybe I'll be tired. (David, Interview 4)

David envisions young adulthood as a period of personal and professional progress. He spoke of it as the time in his life when he expects to get married, have children, embark on his career and achieve economic stability. Perhaps that is why he sees it as such a prolonged period of time, for the progress narrative ends here for him. In effect, for David, life declines early on. At the moment, however, his life has been one of unbroken progress. The only decline he mentioned is the ability to learn a foreign language, which he believes diminishes after childhood.

Dependence and Independence

Bourdieu (2003) remarked that it is erroneous to speak of young people as if they formed a single social unit or group in view of the fact that major differences exist among them. To illustrate this, he called attention to same-age young adult workers and students, emphasizing that these two subgroups have few interests or characteristics in common. He claimed that students, for example, are characterized by a kind of provisional irresponsibility; for some things they are adults and for others they are children. This apparent contradiction is reflected in the way adult society positions students and the way students position themselves. Bourdieu noted that, even among the working classes in France, young people are given a 'margin' as long as they are studying, after which time they are expected to assume full adult responsibilities. The same holds true in contemporary Latin America where young urban workers, peasants and members of indigenous communities move almost seamlessly from childhood to adulthood. For students, however, this transition is delayed as long as possible. Even in homes with less than favorable economic conditions, young adult students in Mexico often expect their parents to provide them not only with basic necessities but also with leisure time goods and luxuries, and the parents comply as a matter of course. At the same time, these students typically turn down part-time jobs, considering them too poorly paid to be worth their while.

David's situation fits this pattern to a large extent for he is entirely dependent on his mother for economic support. Interestingly, while he never mentioned feeling any concern about the burden this might represent, he criticized his sister for continuing to receive help from their mother after her marriage and the completion of her university education. In this, he is acknowledging what Flores (2002) has indicated, namely, that at the end of their student years, young people are expected to assume their responsibilities as adults. That David envisions achieving his own financial independence after graduation is made clear in his description of the life course, as was seen in the previous section.

While still economically dependent on his mother, David exercises a great deal of autonomy in his personal life. He is no longer accountable to his family for his conduct or decisions, and instead looks to his circle of friends for guidance and approval. Like most of his contemporaries, David's subject position as a university student is characterized by the rather curious interplay of emotional independence and economic dependence.

Living in the Present and Living in the Future

David lives very much in the present moment, as is typical of most young adults. According to García Canclini (2004), young people have little or no sense of history or connection with the past. The sensation that everyone is living in the same moment and that everything is occurring in real time is fortified by the technological advances of the day. Television, telephones, videoconferences and chats, along with video and virtual reality games, simulators and other digital pastimes, create a digital experience of (artificially) simultaneous times in which there is no past or future (Feixa, 2003). Moreover, the experience of constant social change has contributed to the difficulty young people have in visualizing where they come from, what they bring with them from the past and at the same time of projecting future horizons and imagining alternative lives (Lechner, 2004). As a consequence, young people are firmly anchored in the present.

This would seem to apply to David, for whom being a university student largely defines the moment he is living and how he constructs his identity as a young adult. He spoke at some length in our interviews of his group of friends, of their interests and solidarity and of how these years in the university have signified personal as well as academic growth for him. At the same time, David had little to say about his childhood, with the exception of remarking on the impact of his father's death when he was four years old. And with regard to the future, David painted a positive, although still remote, scenario for himself.

Extract 43

1   I'd like to see myself married ... well ... that is, I don't know, right
2   now I am 23. By 33 I'd like to be ... already married ... and to have at
3   least one child ... probably have a ... a stable job ... let's say, have
4   experience by then ... and ... small children ... I don't know ...
5   maybe two, three, four years old. In fact my ... my idea is to get
6   married ... at 28 ... more or less ... after having traveled, after have
7   worked in different places ... after having known ... I don't know ...
8   people, places. That is, getting married right now is not my priority ...
9   and within ten years, for example, I don't know, to have a house and
10 be paying it off ... to have, I don't know, the possibility of having a
11 car ... and maybe it won't be mine either ... but to be paying for it ...
12 to be seeing to my children's education ... to my family's needs, in
13 other words, to be making a home and family. (David, Interview 3)

The aspirations David has are common to the group of young men Salguero Velásquez (2006) interviewed in the metropolitan area of Mexico City. He found that they all harbor hopes of achieving a better life, both economically and socially, for themselves and for their children, despite the economic realities of a country where such expectations are met with ever-increasing difficulty. He commented that the style of life they aspire to includes owning their own home, sending their children to private schools and other visible signs that they are 'successful', even when the tradeoff is often a life of constant tension, sacrifices and frequent confrontation with the impossibility of meeting many of their goals. Salguero Velásquez called theirs a world of mystification, illusions and dreams.

Although David mentioned needing to complete the requirements for graduation, he never pinpointed a time when he expected this to occur. He still was not clear on whether he would look for a job or go to graduate school after finishing his studies. Both options appealed to him in a vague way, but he had no concrete plans for his immediate future at the time of our interviews, confirming the impression that his connection to the future is at best a tenuous one.

Age and Other Identities

As with the other participants in the study, David's age identity as a language learner is interlinked with his other identities and tied to the larger world in which he lives. This is particularly evident in the way David's position as a young adult overlaps in nearly every aspect with his subject position as a university student. He belongs to a kind of school subculture and shares a 'student style' (Bourdieu, 2003: 148) with a select group of friends. They have similar attitudes and behavior and a need to establish some distance from their families at this moment of their lives, all characteristics typically found in student peer groups in many parts of the world (Bishop et al., 2004). For David, the friendships he has made during his years at the university comprise the most important and gratifying part of his present life. He said this about his group of friends:

Extract 44

D = David; P = Patricia

1	D:	We all started hanging around together and we have become
2		very ... very close, very tight. In fact, now almost everybody in
3		our class[2] at the university knows our group ... well, everybody
4		knows that we are always together, the same people ... that we
5		get along and that, in a certain way ... the group is made [so
6		that] ... when an outsider comes along ... it's very difficult for
7		him to fit in. Maybe he'll be there for a while, but just as likely
8		he ... we ourselves will make him feel uncomfortable and he'll
9		end up leaving.
10	P:	So you are all in the same major?
11	D:	Yes, we're from the same class. Obviously we each have our
12		different beliefs ... different points of view, but, I mean, we get
13		along quite well. ...
14	P:	And when you think about the future, do you imagine that you
15		are going to stay in touch?
16	D:	I will try to ... that is ... we are so ... I feel ... so close in a way.

| 17 | ... yes, we would remain in contact. ... So, that is what I value |
| 18 | right now. (David, Interview 4) |

The importance of social connections in David's life as a university student is made clear in this description of his peer group. 'Hanging around together' (line 1) is the way David and his friends, and young people in general, respond to their need for communication, solidarity, autonomy, affective relations and above all, identity. Close friendships make up a fundamental part of the social life of young adults, and are nurtured by a kind of communication whose function is 'not primarily to exchange information, but to establish or maintain social identity by sharing experiences and negotiating or affirming the values and norms of the group' (Corbett, 2003: 119). In the case of David's group, this also involves closing ranks and excluding outsiders, as is seen in lines 5–9. So important to him are these friendships that David feels certain they will stand the test of time (lines 16 and 17). In an earlier interview he commented, 'The fact is that I wouldn't allow [myself] to lose track of my friends' (David, Interview 3).

Although David's subject position as a student was the primary one at the time of this study, it did not carry over into the academic world that provided the setting for the enactment of this identity. During the course of our interviews and in his narrative accounts, David talked about his formal studies only in the most general terms. He did not evince much enthusiasm for his career choice other than mentioning that it should lead to his obtaining a job after graduation. This impassiveness extended to his English classes as well, where his participation, as noted earlier, was minimal. According to Lechner (2004), it is outside the classroom where young people most often acquire the knowledge, skills and emotional resources they need to get along well in the world of today. This would certainly appear to be true in David's case, for the construction of his identity as a student was achieved primarily through interaction with his peer group whereas the opportunities afforded by the university as an academic institution did not seem to hold much interest for him.

Despite his desire to exercise his new-found autonomy as a young adult, David's subject position in his family remains a deeply rooted, if discordant part of his identity. The preeminence of the family in Mexican life, alluded to in Chapters 4 and 5, does not preclude the presence of internal strife. David spoke of experiencing friction with every member of his immediate family except his mother. He related a long history of difficulties with his mother's partner, notwithstanding the 15 years he has lived in their home. When talking about him, David did not refer to him by name or as his stepfather, but instead said 'he' or 'my mother's new partner' (David, Interview 3). Although it seems unlikely that David could remember much about his own father, he stressed that his mother's partner 'is nothing like my father' (David, Interview 3), making it clear that he has never entertained the notion that this person could occupy a role in the family. After years of conflict, David has now opted to keep his distance, a solution consistent with the desire of young adults for freedom from family ties.

Establishing distance has also been the pattern for dealing with his strained relations with his sister and her husband. David commented that his brother-in-law 'comes from a different background' (David, Interview 4), tantamount, in this context, to saying that he is socially inferior. Moreover, he added that his brother-in-law is 'dark-skinned' (*prieto*), a term that, for Mexicans, encompasses more than mere physical appearance (David, Interview 4). It is an oblique reference to a series of associated, and negatively viewed, ethnic and cultural characteristics whose importance as a dimension of social identity in Mexico came to light very vividly in Hector's story (see Chapter 4). The remark is also a rather circuitous way of pointing out that David himself is fair-skinned, and thereby positioned as socially advantaged in a culture where the question of ethnicity remains a deeply ingrained and complex phenomenon. The undertones in David's allusion to ethnicity become evident when considered in the context of present-day Mexico and against the larger backdrop of the social history of the country.

With regard to his gender identity, David is grooming himself to take up of the position of head of the household in the future. Salguero Velásquez (2006) points out that for the young generation of Mexican men, 'being a man' means taking the initiative, setting goals, solving problems and assuming responsibility for the family, even when the role of economic provider is shared with one's partner. David's comments in all our conversations adhered to this updated version of traditional masculinity. For example, he displayed a greater awareness than either Hector or Felix of the dilemma faced by women of whether to start a career or a family because it is often difficult to do both. He also said that, although 'machismo' has supposedly been eradicated in Mexico, the fact is that women are still subject to physical and psychological abuse in the home, sexual harassment in the workplace and, when applying for a job, often refused access to certain positions and still commonly asked for a pregnancy test. He remarked that although the situation of inequality used to be 'more pronounced', there is 'still a long way for us to go' (David, Interview 4).

Connecting the Pieces

David positioned himself and was positioned by others as a young adult, a category quite separate from childhood and adulthood. He expressed great satisfaction with his life at this stage and, although he expected that he would continue to find fulfillment in the future, he seemed in no hurry to move on. This was also evident in the lack of urgency he manifested with respect to finishing his university studies.

At the time of the study, David's principal interests were his social involvement with his group of friends at the university and, to a lesser extent, completing the coursework in his major needed for graduation. Learning English did not seem to be high on his list of priorities, despite the fact that he must fulfill a language requirement in order to graduate. Taking language classes is, for many university students like David, simply one of several activities they engage in on campus. Although he mentioned the possibility of doing graduate work abroad in the future, for which he would need English, and clearly saw the value of knowing the language as an entrée into the job market, he acknowledged that English was of little practical use for him at the present time. Thus, learning the language for David seems to signify the acquisition of cultural capital (Bourdieu, 1977), a resource to be called upon in the future. Studying English is a part of his construction of young adulthood only to the extent that it is an activity associated with his identity as a university student and a means of participating in student culture.

David believes early childhood to be the ideal time to learn a new language, but he also emphasized the value of continued practice in developing language skills. In this, he feels advantaged because he began to study English in primary school whereas many of his classmates were studying it for the first time as university students. He is also of the opinion that having been in school virtually all his life puts him in a privileged position with respect to the older members of the class, who may have lost the discipline of study once they stopped going to school. In general, he sees the trajectory of the life course as progressing upward from infancy through adulthood and then heading into decline around the age of 45.

David's age identity is interlinked with other subject positions, most obviously with that of a student, and more subtly with his gendered and ethnic identities. In the classroom David preferred to be surrounded by other university students, purposely segregating himself from the adults in the group. To a large extent, this was also true of his life beyond the classroom, where his social involvement is primarily with his friends and interaction with family members is often troubled and so kept to a minimum. Still, his desire to be independent of his family is at variance with his current economic dependence on them.

As with the constructions of age as an 'adult' or an 'older adult' that have been explored in this study, young adulthood is a category that must be attenuated, for young people construct particular ways of being young. The temptation that exists to speak of 'young people' as if they constituted a single, unvarying group needs to be resisted, for what it means to be young varies according to the particular sociocultural and historical context, and indeed even within the subgroups sharing that context (Lechner, 2004; Reguillo, 2001). Moreover, Dayrell (2005) points out that young adulthood should not be understood as a stage having a predetermined end and much less as a period of preparation which will be surmounted when adult life begins. It is a particular moment in the life course having a value in its own right.

Conclusion

In this section, I take another look at David's tale, as an instance of the enactment of young adulthood, and link it where applicable to the stories of the 'middle' and older adult participants in an endeavor to formulate a single, comprehensive account of how the age identity of language learners is constructed and what bearing it has on their life experience both in the classroom and beyond it. In this way, the findings of the three data chapters are drawn together, bringing this part of the book to a close.

The impact of age on the language-learning experience varies according to where each person positions herself/himself in the lifespan.

David positions himself and is positioned by others as a young adult. While he believes that knowing English may be of potential help to him at some point in the future, taking language classes at this moment of his life is basically a part of the way he enacts his identity as a university student. It is what students do. Therefore, his main motivation for studying English is that of acquiring cultural capital (Bourdieu, 1977), as is true in a broad sense for every participant in the study. They all showed themselves to be fully cognizant of the prestige that comes with knowing English in Mexico. Yet, as has been seen, this wide-ranging designation plays out differently for each of the age groups.

The beliefs and attitudes EFL learners have about age and SLA have an effect on their language-learning experience.

Not surprisingly, David agreed with all the other participants that childhood is the best time to learn a language. With respect to differences among adult learners, he also shared their opinion that the older one becomes, the more difficult it is to acquire a new language. Nevertheless, like the other participants, David recognized that other factors come into play, such as motivation, discipline and dedication, which may cancel out what are perceived to be the detrimental effects of aging.

The coconstruction of age in the classroom context is rooted in the prevailing cultural discourses of age.

David positioned himself and was positioned by his teachers and fellow classmates as a 'young adult', just as the women participants positioned themselves and were positioned by others as 'adults', and the two other men as 'older adults'. These three constructed age categories, with their variations, emerged unequivocally during the course of the study out of the cultural discourses surrounding age that are currently prevalent in Mexico. The basic and most widespread age discourse is that of decline. David, like the other participants, described the life course in terms of a progress–decline narrative, yet compared to the older and 'middle' adults, ageist narratives were almost imperceptible in his case.

Competing discourses of dependence and independence characterize young adulthood in Mexico, particularly as it is constructed by university students like David. Although students struggle to be emotionally independent of their families, they nevertheless expect to be supported financially by them. Both strong family traditions and the precarious economic climate of the country have impeded the development of the kind of autonomy enjoyed by many young adults in the United States and Europe.

Both present and prior life circumstances have an impact on the language-learning experience.

David's experience as a young adult learning English is colored by the fact that he is presently a student. Studying languages is part of university student culture yet, because it is seen as an extra activity having no immediate utility; most students do not bring the same drive to the task that they do to their regular courses. David's earlier contact with English in primary school gave him self-confidence and the sense that he had an edge over classmates who were initiating their language studies at a later age.

The construction of the age identity of language learners occurs both within the classroom and in the world beyond it, moving back and forth between the two.

David's enactment of young adulthood revolves almost entirely around his identity as a student. His social interaction with the particular group of friends he has made at the university constitutes the single most important facet of his life at present. Through shared attitudes, interests and values, David and his friends have constructed an identity as a group that distinguishes them from other groups at the university. At the same time, they participate in the broader student culture that connects them with the community of university students. The norms of peer culture exercise pressure on David, who found it difficult to take part in the English lessons for fear of standing out or of making a mistake in front of others. His relationship with older people both in and out of the classroom was also affected by his identity as a young adult, for he tended to amplify the differences and to distance himself.

Age as a subject position is interlinked with other subject positions in adult language learners.

David's position as a young adult is tightly interwoven with his identity as a university student. These two subject positions impact his gendered identity, and we see a different kind of masculinity being enacted in David's case from either Hector or Felix's performance of gender. As pointed out earlier, the traditional 'patriarchal model of masculinity' in Mexico is giving way to a more egalitarian one in the young university-educated generation.

'Maleness', in this modified version of the Mexican family structure, still entails assuming the primary responsibility for the well-being of one's family, but now incorporates the possibility of sharing the economic and domestic burdens with a partner. David envisions taking up this position in the future.

In what follows, I discuss the findings of the empirical work presented here in light of the conceptual framework of the book and reflect on the significance of what has been learned.

Notes

(1) This assessment proved to be a valid one, as David did not pass the sixth-level course.
(2) The term 'class' (*generación*), as used in this extract, refers to the entire group of students entering a particular school of the university in the same year.

Final Reflections

Introduction

The aim of this book has been to explore the ways in which age as socially constructed is experienced by adult EFL learners in Mexico. As an exploratory study, the purpose was not so much to arrive at definitive conclusions about the construction of age in adult language learners as to determine what the issues were, to question basic assumptions, to ponder the significance of what emerged and to point to further directions that might be taken in the search for answers.

I began with a review of the literature on the CPH in order to find out what has been learned about age in SLA to date that could be useful to me in my study of adult students. I discovered that CPH and other research on the age factor does not take into consideration distinctions among adults of different ages nor does it address the social or experiential side of language learning as contemplated in a sociocultural approach to SLA, both of which were precisely the points I wanted to learn about. I then turned to the identity work of discourse-oriented sociolinguists, as informed by social constructionism, to guide me in the study of the enactment of age in social interaction.

Because of its focus on the collaborative construction of reality, social constructionism proved to be an excellent framework for understanding more clearly how people give meaning to age and make sense of their experience through discourse and in their relationships with others. It also made it possible to move away from essentialist notions of age and to view it as constructed through discursive interaction in a specific cultural context and a particular historical moment. This is consonant with work carried out by contemporary discourse-oriented sociolinguists which has brought greater depth to our understanding of other social dimensions, such as ethnicity and gender. In a similar way, a socially constructed view of age can enhance our comprehension and appreciation of its many complexities.

People construct age in discursive interaction, drawing on the cultural discourses available to them to position themselves and to position others. In the case of urban Mexico, the prevalent age discourse is that of decline, as it is elsewhere in contemporary Western society. This translates into ageist discourses in many forms that provide the principal framework people utilize to interpret the experience of aging and to enact their age identity. This was confirmed by the narratives and stories the participants in the study told. It also became evident in their enactment of age that age identity cannot easily be separated from their other identities; age is often interwoven with gender, ethnicity and social class.

Age and Second Language Acquisition: What We Have Learned

I now return to the research questions that provided the initial impulse for this study and discuss what was learned.

- How is age coconstructed in the EFL classroom context and in the personal narratives of adult language learners?

The data generated by interviews, classroom observations and the audiotaped narrative accounts of the participants in the study contributed to a better understanding of how age is constructed by English language learners in Mexico. It became clear in their narratives and in their interaction with the teacher and classmates that these language students positioned themselves and were positioned by others in the three general categories of older, 'middle' (or merely 'adult') and young adults. This is noteworthy because there were no disputed cases, suggesting that many tacit cultural discourses are at play. Not surprisingly, these three age categories bear only a tenuous relationship to chronological age. Other factors were seen to carry more weight. Although the selection of participants included someone from each 'decade', the way they positioned themselves in the three general categories fell, coincidentally, along gender lines. The older participants were both men and the midlife adults were all women. The only young adult was male.

It was also interesting to note that Berta, for instance, is closer in chronological age to both Hector and Felix than to any of the 'middle' adult participants, yet she is unequivocally positioned as a 'middle' adult. This is likely to change once she stops working, for what emerged in the study is that one of the significant factors in determining the boundary between 'middle' and later adulthood among these participants is retirement from the work force. At the other end of the spectrum, the divide between young and 'middle' adulthood seems to revolve around the issue of responsibility. Young adults, specifically university students such as David, are perceived as being largely free of the economic and emotional responsibilities that family and work entail.

An unexpected finding was the discovery that 'middle' adulthood is at present an undefined category in Mexico, distinguishable only by the frontiers that separate it at one end from young adulthood and at the other from later adulthood. In other words, 'midlife' adults are positioned simply as 'not old' and 'not young'. In this, they do not share the decline discourses associated with 'middle age' in Anglophone cultures (Gullette, 2004; Shweder, 1998). The four women participants in the study, as 'midlifers' in Mexico, have assumed the responsibilities of jobs and families, and are chiefly concerned with issues of age-appropriacy that are closely linked to a tacit timetable which shapes their progress narratives. Because of the sense of urgency this engenders, they approached their English classes with a seriousness they found wanting in their classmates. This brought about occasional manifestations of 'adultist' attitudes toward the younger students and ageist, dismissive attitudes toward the more mature ones.

Ageism in its various guises, including adultism, ageist humor and age segregation, surfaced in the classroom context in the manner in which the older and younger participants positioned others and were positioned by them as well. David's membership in a peer group of other young students was the most salient identity he enacted during the course of the fieldwork. As a young adult, he distanced himself physically and avoided interaction with the 'middle' and older adults, including the teachers. By his own account, David's self-segregation extends to the world outside the classroom as well.

The older adults' construction of their age identity also reflected the societal ageism that is deeply ingrained in Mexican culture. While at times Hector and Felix displayed a vigorous resistance to ageist discourses, at others they appeared to have internalized them by accepting the negative construals of later adulthood. In their English classes, they positioned themselves and were positioned as 'outsiders'. This carried over into their lives beyond the classroom, where as older adults they were often marginalized, no longer considered to be major players in mainstream society.

- What beliefs and attitudes do adult language learners have about age and about language learning, and how do these beliefs and attitudes intersect with the way age is enacted?

The participants in all age categories share similar beliefs about the difficulties involved in learning a language in adulthood. They indicated that as adult learners they are disadvantaged when compared to children. Moreover, they maintained that the ability to learn a language diminishes with age, moving in a downward spiral throughout adulthood. Despite this, they all believed that any age-related cognitive shortcomings could be counterbalanced by dedication, motivation and hard work. That they are convinced they can succeed is evidenced by the fact that they are enrolled in English classes.

Although the particular motivation of each of the participants for studying English at this moment of their lives was largely contingent on the age group in which they positioned themselves, and generally linked to their prior life experiences, in the final analysis it came down to a question of acquiring cultural capital (Bourdieu, 1977). The experience of learning English, in every case, meant more than mastering the language for them, for being language students was part of the construction of their complex identities both in the classroom and beyond it. The way in which the language-learning experience carried over into other facets of their lives varied according to where each person positioned herself/himself in the lifespan and was colored by their prior life circumstances. This was one of the outcomes of the empirical phase of the study.

Having said that, it is important to clarify that, while determining the degree to which prevalent ageist ideas and attitudes directly affect the linguistic outcomes of a language course was beyond the scope of this particular study, the issue of success in language learning is one that should not be entirely discounted. Further research correlating course results and the constructed age of the students would be a valuable complement to the study reported in this book.

- How is age as a subject position interlinked with other subject positions in adult language learners?

Teasing out the age identity of the people who took part in the study from their other identities proved to be a challenge. Gender, for example, played a decisive role in shaping the construction of later, 'middle' and young adulthood of the participants. Cultural discourses surrounding masculinity and femininity exert considerable power over people of all ages in Mexico, dictating acceptable behavior both in the family and in the work place. By the same token, professional identity turned out to be a key factor for the 'middle' and older adults in this study, and identity as a university student a comparable one for David. Ethnicity and social status were also important considerations in some of the cases. The interplay of these multiple subject positions with that of language learner provided the basis for the ongoing construction of the participants' age identities.

As older adult men, Hector and Felix provide good examples of traditional Mexican masculinity. Their professional and gendered identities afforded them the social prestige they enjoyed up until their retirement from the work force. However, since that time they have experienced difficulty commanding recognition from others, often finding themselves positioned on the periphery of mainstream society. Their enactment of age reflects the conflict that this situation has generated both in the language classroom and beyond it.

As women, the 'midlife' participants have not benefited from recent changes in the family structure in Mexico for they have all had to struggle against entrenched male-oriented traditions in order to combine their professional lives with their subject positions as women. The difficulties escalated in the cases where the women were expected to subordinate their positions as professionals to those of wife and mother. This extended to their desire to satisfy personal ambitions by taking English classes.

Out of the interplay of these various subject positions emerges a more intricate and nuanced picture of age as it intersects with language learning. The narratives reveal an image of the language learner as a complex individual with multiple interests and identities that extend well beyond the classroom context. These facets of the learner, as Pavlenko (2001a) has pointed out, are seldom explored in SLA research and yet are central to understanding her/him as a social being whose learning depends on social interaction with others.

Implications of the Findings

What has been learned by looking at age as socially constructed has ramifications for foreign language teaching and learning, for SLA research and for the field of age studies.

Implications for Teaching Foreign Languages

The pedagogical implications of taking a social constructionist position on age only make sense when SLA is viewed from a sociocultural perspective. This is because the cognitive tradition in SLA gives scant attention to the social aspects of language learning and places more emphasis on psycholinguistic factors, whereas the sociocultural orientation to SLA addresses the social dimensions of the language-learning experience. Consequently, the following observations presuppose a sociocultural approach to language teaching and learning, considered as a complex social practice.

- People age in a variety of ways and at different moments in the lifespan. This means that adult learners cannot be treated as a single undifferentiated population. There are age-related differences that distinguish students from one another. However, chronological age is not a reliable indicator of where a person is in the life course. For this reason, adult students should not be 'classified' by age-in-years. This is especially pertinent in the case of foreign language classes, where the students are assigned by level of proficiency, with the result that a teacher will typically encounter a mixed-age group of adults.

What has come to light in this study is that age, as socially constructed, is a complex and nuanced identity. It is enacted in interaction and is dynamic rather than fixed or static. Age cannot be isolated from other factors, such as gender, ethnicity and social class. Adult students may adopt or be assigned a number of subject positions as part of their age identity, depending on the particular situation in which they find themselves and the cultural discourses available to them. These discourses of age will potentially intersect with other discourses in the language classroom, so that teaching methods, learning styles, student–student relations and teacher–student interactions may color the particular way age is enacted. Both differences and affinities will surface among the language learners. The challenge for the teacher, then, is to face a group of students whose age is an important part of a complexity of identities and to establish a course of action for treating them that takes this variability into account.

- The extent to which biological limitations have an impact on adult L2 learners is not fully understood. If anything, maturational constraints operate in conjunction with a number of other affective, psychological and social factors. Therefore, the teaching of foreign languages should not be based on preconceptions about possible shortcomings in adult learners.

Aging can affect certain physiological and cognitive components, yet not others. For example, older learners may be more inclined to suffer hearing impairments than younger learners. This could have an effect on L2 listening and speaking skills. However, such deficits are often compensated for by the judicious use of other strategies, such as giving greater attention to facial gestures, body language and contextual clues.

- Age is socially constructed in our interaction with other people, and according to the culturally specific discourses and narratives that are available. The dominant age discourse in Western culture is that of decline. This has given rise to many manifestations of societal ageism. Textbooks, teaching materials and class activities often inadvertently reinforce ageist discourses by infantilizing young adults or demeaning older ones. Careful selection and planning on the part of the teacher can counteract this. Textbook authors and publishers also need to show a heightened sensitivity to potentially problematic age issues.

Ageist discourses operate both overtly and covertly, and the students may have internalized them. For instance, the more mature students often believe they are less capable language learners than younger ones. They may self-handicap or be marginalized by fellow students in the classroom. Teachers can work to demythologize some of the ageist beliefs that underscore this type of conduct.

The teacher's own attitudes and behavior may unwittingly reflect ageism. An increased awareness of what is said and done in the classroom can offset this tendency. For example, the use of ageist humor, while still socially acceptable in many sectors of society, is potentially offensive. In the same way, treating younger adult students as children or adopting a patronizing attitude toward mature students can be degrading.

- Learning a new language involves fundamental experiences of a social nature that shape this undertaking in significant ways. The formal language class can be seen more broadly as an experience that leads to both linguistic and nonlinguistic outcomes for adults of all ages. Thus, a teaching focus that is exclusively aimed at mastery of the language overlooks opportunities for the lessons to provide a rewarding and meaningful experience for the learner, seen as a complex person who lives in and participates in a world extending far beyond the classroom. What takes place in the classroom often spills over into the students' lives outside it and vice versa. Ideally, the language class satisfies the real-world concerns and aspirations of the learners, including, but not limited to, linguistic attainment. An awareness of this signifies taking a different pedagogic approach to the lessons, activities, classroom dynamics and relations with the students.

Implications for SLA Research

Looking at age as social also has repercussions for the field of SLA research, which has traditionally focused on age only as an isolated biological factor that could account for differential success in language learning. A social constructionist approach offers a more nuanced understanding of age, one that contemplates the experiential side of language learning and extends to both linguistic and nonlinguistic outcomes. While a growing body of SLA work in the sociocultural tradition has undertaken studies of socially constructed dimensions of identity, including gender, social class and ethnicity, age has not been included. This is a major oversight. Age, as I have argued, is an important part of the complex of a person's identities. Understanding the language learner as a whole person means taking into account their temporality – where they position themselves and are positioned by others at a specific moment in time, as well as where they have been. One of the purposes of this book has been to rectify this gap.

Another is to add a different perspective on age to what has been learned in psycholinguistically oriented SLA research. Because of the CPH debate, age has been a central topic in discussions surrounding language learning. The social constructionist focus on age taken in this book is intended to provide a complement to work carried out in the cognitive tradition of SLA.

Implications for Age Studies

Lastly, the research has relevance for the growing interdisciplinary field of age studies, whose 'founding proposition [is] the priority of culture in constructing age' (Gullette, 2004: 106). Age studies group together a number of different theoretical and methodological approaches that all point up the cultural, in contrast to the biological, aspects of age and aging. For that reason, the findings presented here can be added to the body of work available in this new field. Built on age research carried out in a variety of contexts, this book is novel in that it investigates age as socially constructed in the previously unexplored context of the foreign language classroom and in the uncharted territory of present-day urban Mexico.

Concluding Remarks

The stories the participants told and the enactment of their age identity augments what is known about the bearing age has on adult language learners. I maintain that people cannot understand each other without a sense of where they are in the life course relative to each other. Their temporality is always a part of their complex identity. Nor can we comprehend what language learning means in students' lives both inside and outside the classroom without taking into account the way they construct their age identity. While only one context has been explored, that of English as a foreign language in Mexico, what has come to light in this study may resonate with researchers looking at other related contexts. I hope to have added a very small piece to a very large picture.

Three main points stand out in my mind as I look back at the research I undertook to write this book. First, age is a core part of a person's identity, but it has greater salience in some moments than in others. Although I have tried to present some telling examples of the enactment of age both in the classroom and outside it, it is important to clarify that other subject positions, such as gender or professional identity, may be more prominent in a given moment.

The second point is that the experience of learning a language varies according to each person's position in the lifespan and involves both linguistic and nonlinguistic dimensions. This ratifies the notion that, although some commonalities exist, people age in very different ways. Caution, then, is required in making assumptions about age and language learning.

Lastly, the age identity of foreign language learners is closely interconnected with their other subject positions. This point cannot be emphasized too much for it is this interplay of positions that constitutes a person's complex identity. As I hope to have demonstrated, age identity is invariably nuanced by other social dimensions, such as gender and ethnicity. Moreover, a person's enactment of age changes in different contexts and over time. Hence, what can be said about age is best stated in terms of a specific sociocultural and historical context.

I end this book where I began – by reflecting on the significance of the research for my life. In the first place, what I have learned in the process of this investigation has indelibly changed the way I work as an EFL teacher and professional. I no longer see adults as predetermined by chronological age or age categories, but rather as individuals whose age identity is socially constructed in a variety of ways in interaction with others. I am conscious that the beliefs and attitudes many of my adult students have about age are based on prevailing decline discourses that can be a hindrance to their learning and negatively affect other aspects of the language-learning experience. When I am able, I try to counteract self-handicapping, self-marginalization and other manifestations of ageism in the classroom by raising awareness of the fallacies inherent in ageist discourses. I am more careful to avoid materials, activities and textbook content that reinforce ageist stereotypes. I now recognize that the language-learning experience touches the lives of the students as persons who inhabit a much larger world than the classroom and, for this reason, their interests and aspirations are of paramount importance.

As an added bonus, the way in which I understand my own aging process has also undergone fundamental changes as I have learned more about it during the course of writing this book. I find myself resisting being positioned in preestablished slots that society has designated based on a long-standing view of aging as decline. I am more comfortable with the ongoing changes I am experiencing and have a greater appreciation of the possibilities open to me at every point in the life course.

References

Abrahamsson, N. and Hyltenstam, K. (2008) The robustness of aptitude effects in near-native second language acquisition. *Studies in Second Language Acquisition* 30, 481–509.
Abu-Rabia, S. and Kehat, S. (2004) The critical period for second language pronunciation: Is there such a thing? Ten case studies of late starters who attained a native-like Hebrew accent. *Educational Psychology* 24, 77–98.
Adler Lomnitz, L. (1999) La gran familia como unidad de solidaridad en México. *Revista de Psiquiatría* 16, 203–207.
Ainlay, S.C. and Redfoot, D.L. (1982) Ageing and identity-in-the-world: A phenomenological analysis. *International Journal of Ageing and Human Development* 15, 1–15.
Andrews, M. (1999) The seductiveness of agelessness. *Ageing and Society* 19, 301–318.
Arber, S. and Ginn, J. (eds) (1995) *Connecting Gender and Ageing: A Sociological Approach*. Buckingham: Open University Press.
Ariès, P. (1962) *Centuries of Childhood: A Social History of Family Life* (R. Baldick, trans.). New York: Vintage Books.
Ariza, M. and Oliveira, O. (2001) Familias en transición y marcos conceptuales en redefinición. *Papeles de Población* 28, 9–39.
Ashcroft, B., Griffiths, G. and Tiffin, H. (1995) Introduction to Part VII: Ethnicity and indigeneity. In B. Ashcroft, G. Griffiths and H. Tiffin (eds) *The Post-Colonial Studies Reader* (pp. 213–214). London: Routledge.
Ashcroft, B., Griffiths, G. and Tiffin, H. (1998) *Key Concepts in Post-Colonial Studies*. London: Routledge.
Atkinson, D. (2002) Toward a sociocognitive approach to second language acquisition. *Modern Language Journal* 86, 525–545.
Atkinson, D., Churchill, E., Nishino, T. and Okada, H. (2007) Alignment and interaction in a sociocognitive approach to second language acquisition. *Modern Language Journal* 91, 169–188.
Austin, J.L. (1962) *How to Do Things with Words*. Oxford: Clarendon Press.
Bakhtin, M.M. (1981) *The Dialogic Imagination* (C. Emerson and M. Holquist, trans., M. Holquist, ed.). Austin, TX: University of Texas Press.
Bakhtin, M.M. (1986) *Speech Genres and Other Late Essays* (V.W. McGee, trans., C. Emerson and M. Holquist, eds). Austin, TX: University of Texas Press.
Baxter, J. (2003) *Positioning Gender in Discourse: A Feminist Methodology*. Basingstoke: Palgrave Macmillan.
Benwell, B. and Stokoe, E.H. (2002) Constructing discussion tasks in university tutorials: Shifting dynamics and identities. *Discourse Studies* 4, 429–453.
Benwell, B. and Stokoe, E.H. (2005) University students resisting academic identity. In K. Richards and P. Seedhouse (eds) *Applying Conversation Analysis* (pp. 124–139). Basingstoke: Palgrave Macmillan.
Bialystok, E. (1997) The structure of age: In search of barriers to second language acquisition. *Second Language Research* 13, 116–137.

Bialystok, E. and Hakuta, K. (1999) Confounded age: Linguistic and cognitive factors in age differences for second language acquisition. In D. Birdsong (ed.) *Second Language Acquisition and the Critical Period Hypothesis* (pp. 161–181). Mahwah, NJ: Lawrence Erlbaum.
Bijarro Hernández, F. and Mendiola Infante, S.V. (2009) *La vejez: una discriminación múltiple*. Edición electrónica gratuita, accessed 10 June 2011. www.eumed.net/libros/2009a/489/
Birdsong, D. (1992) Ultimate attainment in second language acquisition. *Language* 68, 706–755.
Birdsong, D. (ed.) (1999) *Second Language Acquisition and the Critical Period Hypothesis*. Mahwah, NJ: Lawrence Erlbaum.
Birdsong, D. (2005) Nativelikeness and non-nativelikeness in L2A research. *IRAL* 43, 319–328.
Birdsong, D. (2006) Age and second language acquisition and processing: A selective overview. *Language Learning* 56, 9–49.
Birdsong, D. and Molis, M. (2001) On the evidence for maturational constraints in second-language acquisition. *Journal of Memory and Language* 44, 235–249.
Bishop, J.H., Bishop, M., Bishop, M., Gelbwasser, L., Green, S., Peterson, E., Rubinsztaj, A. and Zuckerman, A. (2004) Why we harass nerds and freaks: A formal theory of student culture and norms. *Journal of School Health* 74, 235–251.
Blackledge, A. (2002) The discursive construction of national identity in multilingual Britain. *Journal of Language, Identity, and Education* 1, 67–87.
Blackledge, A. and Pavlenko, A. (2001) Negotiation of identities in multilingual contexts. *International Journal of Bilingualism* 5, 243–257.
Blanco, M. (2001) Trayectorias laborales y cambio generacional: Mujeres de sectores medios en la Ciudad de México. *Revista Mexicana de Sociología* 63, 91–111.
Bley-Vroman, R. (1989) What is the logical problem of foreign language learning? In S.M. Gass and J. Schacter (eds) *Linguistic Perspectives on Second Language Acquisition* (pp. 41–68). Cambridge: Cambridge University Press.
Block, D. (2003) *The Social Turn in Second Language Acquisition*. Washington: Georgetown University Press.
Block, D. (2007) The rise of identity in SLA research, post Firth and Wagner (1997). *Modern Language Journal* 91, 863–876.
Blommaert, J. (2005) *Discourse: A Critical Introduction*. Cambridge: Cambridge University Press.
Bongaerts, T. (1999) Ultimate attainment in L2 pronunciation: The case of very advanced late L2 learners. In D. Birdsong (ed.) *Second Language Acquisition and the Critical Period Hypothesis* (pp. 133–159). Mahwah, NJ: Lawrence Erlbaum.
Bongaerts, T. (2005) Introduction: Ultimate attainment and the critical period hypothesis for second language acquisition. *IRAL* 43, 259–267.
Bongaerts, T., van Summeren, C., Planken, B. and Schils, E. (1997) Age and ultimate attainment in pronunciation of a foreign language. *Studies in Second Language Acquisition* 19, 447–466.
Bourdieu, P. (1977) *Outline of a Theory of Practice* (R. Nice, trans.). Cambridge: Cambridge University Press.
Bourdieu, P. (2002) *La Distinción: Criterios y Bases Sociales del Gusto* (M.C. Ruiz de Elvira, trans.). Mexico: Taurus.
Bourdieu, P. (2003) La juventud es sólo una palabra. *Cuestiones de Sociología* (pp. 142–153). Madrid: Istmo.
Bourdieu, P. and Wacquant, L. (2005) *Una Invitación a la Sociología Reflexiva* (A. Dilon, trans.). Buenos Aires, Argentina: Siglo XXI Editores.
Breen, M.P. (1985) Authenticity in the language classroom. *Applied Linguistics* 6, 60–70.

Breen, M.P. (2001a) Postscript: New directions for research on learner contributions. In M.P. Breen (ed.) *Learner Contributions to Language Learning: New Directions in Research* (pp. 172–182). Harlow: Longman.
Breen, M.P. (ed.) (2001b) *Learner Contributions to Language Learning: New Directions in Research*. Harlow: Longman.
Brigeiro, M. (2005) 'Envejecimiento exitoso' y 'tercera edad': Problemas y retos para la promoción de la salud. *Investigación y Educación en Enfermería* 23, 102–109.
Bruner, J. (1990) *Acts of Meaning*. Cambridge, MA: Harvard University Press.
Burr, V. (1997) Social constructionism and psychology, online document, accessed 16 December 2002. http://carlisle.unn.ac.uk/CHP/Psychology/Year3/adult/BURR.htm
Burr, V. (2003) *Social Constructionism* (2nd edn). London: Routledge.
Butler, J. (1990) *Gender Trouble: Feminism and the Subversion of Identity*. New York: Routledge.
Butler, R.N. (1969) Age-ism: Another form of bigotry. *The Gerontologist* 9, 243–246.
Calasanti, T. (2005) Ageism, gravity, and gender: Experiences of aging bodies. *Generations* 29, 8–12.
Cameron, D. (1999) Performing gender identity: Young men's talk and the construction of heterosexual masculinity. In A. Jaworski and N. Coupland (eds) *The Discourse Reader* (pp. 442–458). London: Routledge.
Cameron, D. (2005) Language, gender, and sexuality: Current issues and new directions. *Applied Linguistics* 26, 482–502.
Cameron, D., Frazer, E., Harvey, P., Rampton, B. and Richardson, K. (1993) Ethics, advocacy and empowerment in researching language: Issues of method in researching language. *Language and Communication* 13, 81–94.
Candlin, C.N. (2001) General editor's preface. In M.P. Breen (ed.) *Learner Contributions to Language Learning: New Directions in Research* (pp. xvi–xxii). Harlow: Longman.
Cicirelli, V.G. (1993) Intergenerational communication in the mother-daughter dyad regarding caregiving decisions. In N. Coupland and J.F. Nussbaum (eds) *Discourse and Lifespan Identity* (pp. 215–236). Newbury Park, CA: Sage.
Cilliers, P. (1998) *Complexity and Postmodernism: Understanding Complex Systems*. London: Routledge.
Clay, R.A. (2003) Researchers replace midlife myths with facts, online document, accessed 14 October 2004. http://www.apa.org/monitor/apr03/researchers.html
Cohen, E.S. (2001) The complex nature of ageism: What is it? Who does it? Who perceives it? *The Gerontologist* 41, 576–577.
Cole, T.R. (1992) *The Journey of Life: A Cultural History of Aging in America*. Cambridge: Cambridge University Press.
Collins, J. and La Santa, A. (2006) *Analysing Class and Ethnicity as Communicative Practices: A Case Study of Migration-Based Multilingualism in Upstate New York*. Working Papers in Urban Language and Literacies. Paper 40. Albany, NY: University at Albany/SUNY.
Combe, K. and Schmader, K. (1999) Naturalizing myths of aging: Reading popular culture. *Journal of Aging and Identity* 4, 79–109.
Cook, V. (1995) Multi-competence and effects of age. In D. Singleton (ed.) *The Age Factor in Second Language Acquisition* (pp. 51–66). Clevedon: Multilingual Matters.
Corbett, J. (2003) *An Intercultural Approach to English Language Teaching*. Clevedon: Multilingual Matters.
Coupland, N. (1997) Language, ageing and ageism: A project for applied linguistics. *International Journal of Applied Linguistics* 7, 26–48.
Coupland, N. (2001) Age in social and sociolinguistic theory. In N. Coupland, S. Sarangi and C.N. Candlin (eds) *Sociolinguistics and Social Theory* (pp. 185–211). Harlow: Longman.

Coupland, N., Coupland, J. and Giles, H. (1991) *Language, Society and the Elderly*. Oxford: Basil Blackwell.

Coupland, N., Coupland, J. and Nussbaum, J.F. (1993a) Epilogue: Future prospects in lifespan sociolinguistics. In N. Coupland and J.F. Nussbaum (eds) *Discourse and Lifespan Identity* (pp. 284–293). Newbury Park, CA: Sage.

Coupland, N. and Nussbaum, J.F. (eds) (1993) *Discourse and Lifespan Identity*. Newbury Park, CA: Sage.

Coupland, N., Nussbaum, J. F. and Grossman, A. (1993b) Introduction: Discourse, selfhood, and the lifespan. In N. Coupland and J.F. Nussbaum (eds) *Discourse and Lifespan Identity* (pp. x–xxviii). Newbury Park, CA: Sage.

Cruikshank, M. (2003) *Learning to Be Old: Gender, Culture, and Aging*. Lanham, MD: Rowman and Littlefield.

Curtiss, S. (1977) *Genie: A Psycholinguistic Study of a Modern-Day 'Wild Child'*. London: Academic Press.

Curtiss, S. (1982) Developmental dissociations of language and cognition. In L.K. Obler and L. Menn (eds) *Exceptional Language and Linguistics* (pp. 285–312). New York: Academic Press.

Curtiss, S. (1988) The special talent of grammar acquisition. In L.K. Obler and D. Fein (eds) *The Exceptional Brain: Neuropsychology of Talent and Special Abilities* (pp. 364–386). New York: Guilford Press.

Chopra, D. (1993) *Ageless Body, Timeless Mind*. New York: Harmony Books.

Dayrell, J. (2005) Juventud, grupos culturales y sociabilidad. *Revista de Estudios sobre Juventud* 9, accessed 23 April 2008. http://ver2.imjuventud.gob.mx/pdf/rev_joven_es/22/Juarez%20Dayrell,%20Juventud,%20grupos%20culturales%20y%20sociabilidad.pdf

De Bot, K. (2008) Second language development as a dynamic process. *Modern Language Journal* 92, 166–178.

De Bot, K. and Makoni, S. (2005) *Language and Aging in Multilingual Contexts*. Clevedon: Multilingual Matters.

De Bot, K. and Schrauf, R.W. (eds) (2009) *Language Development Over the Lifespan*. New York: Routledge.

Deats, S.M. and Lenker, L.T. (1999) Introduction. In S.M. Deats and L.T. Lenker (eds) *Aging and Identity: A Humanities Perspective* (pp. 1–20). Westport, CT: Praeger.

DeKeyser, R.M. (2000) The robustness of critical effects in second language acquisition. *Studies in Second Language Acquisition* 22, 499–533.

Dörnyei, Z. (2005) *The Psychology of the Language Learner: Individual Differences in Second Language Acquisition*. Mahwah, NJ: Lawrence Erlbaum.

Dörnyei, Z. (2009) Individual differences: Interplay of learner characteristics and learning environment. *Language Learning* 59, 230–248.

Dumas, A., Laberge, S. and Straka, S.M. (2005) Older women's relations to bodily appearance: The embodiment of social and biological conditions of existence. *Ageing and Society* 25, 883–902.

Eckert, P. (1988) Sound change and adolescent social structure. *Language in Society* 17, 183–207.

Eckert, P. (1997a) Age as a sociolinguistic variable. In F. Coulmas (ed.) *The Handbook of Sociolinguistics* (pp. 151–167). Oxford: Blackwell.

Eckert, P. (1997b) The whole woman: Sex and gender differences in variation. In N. Coupland and A. Jaworski (eds) *Sociolinguistics: A Reader and Coursebook* (pp. 212–228). Basingstoke: Macmillan.

Eckert, P. and McConnell-Ginet, S. (1995) Constructing meaning, constructing styles. In K. Hall and M. Bucholtz (eds) *Gender-Articulated: Language and the Socially Constructed Self* (pp. 469–507). London: Routledge.

Ellis, N.C. (1998) Emergentism, connectionism and language learning. *Language Learning* 48, 631–664.
Eubank, L. and Gregg, K.R. (1999) Critical periods and (second) language acquisition: Divide et impera. In D. Birdsong (ed.) *Second Language Acquisition and the Critical Period Hypothesis* (pp. 65–99). Mahwah, NJ: Lawrence Erlbaum.
Fanon, F. (1995) The fact of blackness. In B. Ashcroft, G. Griffiths and H. Tiffin (eds) *The Post-Colonial Studies Reader* (pp. 323–326). London: Routledge.
Featherstone, M. and Hepworth, M. (1989) Ageing and old age: Reflections on the postmodern life course. In B. Bytheway, T. Keil, P. Allatt and A. Bryman (eds) *Becoming and Being Old: Sociological Approaches to Later Life* (pp. 133–157). London: Sage.
Featherstone, M. and Hepworth, M. (1991) The mask of aging and the postmodern life course. In M. Featherstone, M. Hepworth and B.S. Turner (eds) *Body: Social Process and Cultural Theory* (pp. 371–389). London: Sage.
Featherstone, M. and Hepworth, M. (1995) Images of positive aging: A case study of *Retirement Choice* magazine. In M. Featherstone and A. Wernick (eds) *Images of Aging: Cultural Representations of Later Life* (pp. 29–47). London: Routledge.
Featherstone, M. and Wernick, A. (1995) Introduction. In M. Featherstone and A. Wernick (eds) *Images of Aging: Cultural Representations of Later Life* (pp. 1–15). London: Routledge.
Feixa, C. (2003) Del reloj de arena al reloj digital. *Revista de Estudios sobre Juventud* 7, accessed 20 April 2008. http://cendoc.imjuventud.gob.mx/clr/docs/pdfre/019002.swf
Felix, S.W. (1985) More evidence on competing cognitive systems. *Second Language Research* 1, 47–72.
Firth, A. and Wagner, J. (1997) On discourse, communication and (some) fundamental concepts in SLA research. *Modern Language Journal* 81, 285–300.
Firth, A. and Wagner, J. (2007) Second/foreign language learning as a social accomplishment: Elaborations on a reconceptualized SLA. *Modern Language Journal* 91, 800–819.
Flege, J.E. (1999) Age of learning and second language speech. In D. Birdsong (ed.) *Second Language Acquisition and the Critical Period Hypothesis* (pp. 101–131). Mahwah, NJ: Lawrence Erlbaum.
Flege, J.E., Murray, J.M. and MacKay, I.R.A. (1995) Factors affecting strength of perceived foreign accent in a second language. *Journal of the Acoustical Society of America* 97, 3125–3134.
Flores, J.I. (2002) Tipos de identidad y generaciones en México. In R. Pozas Horcaditas (ed.) *La Modernidad Atrapada en su Horizonte* (pp. 73–99). Mexico: Porrúa.
Flynn, S. (1989) The role of the head-initial/head-final parameter in the acquisition of English relative clauses by adult Spanish and Japanese speakers. In S.M. Gass and J. Schacter (eds) *Linguistic Perspectives on Second Language Acquisition* (pp. 89–108). Cambridge: Cambridge University Press.
Flynn, S. and Manuel, S. (1991) Age-dependent effects in language acquisition: An evaluation of 'critical period' hypotheses. In L. Eubank (ed.) *Point Counterpoint: Universal Grammar in the Second Language* (pp. 117–145). Amsterdam: John Benjamins.
Fortes de Leff, J. (2002) Racism in Mexico: Cultural roots and clinical interventions. *Family Process* 41, 619–623.
Francis, N. and Ryan, P.M. (1998) English as an international language of prestige: Conflicting cultural perspectives and shifting ethnolinguistic loyalties. *Anthropology and Education Quarterly* 29, 25–43.
Franco Saldaña, M., Villarreal Ríos, E., Vargas Daza, E.R., Martínez González, L. and Galicia Rodríguez, L. (2010) Estereotipos negativos de la vejez en personal de salud

de un Hospital de la Ciudad de Querétaro, México. *Revista Médica de Chile* 138, 988–993.

García Canclini, N. (2004) Culturas juveniles en una época sin respuesta. *Revista de Estudios sobre Juventud* 8, accessed 30 April 2008. http://ver2.imjuventud.gob.mx/pdf/rev_joven_es/20/Culturas%20juveniles%20en%20una%20%E9poca%20sin%20respuestas,%20N%E9stor%20Garc.pdf

García Lecumberri, M.L. and Gallardo, F. (2003) English FL sounds in school learners of different ages. In M.P. García Mayo and M.L. García Lecumberri (eds) *Age and the Acquisition of English as a Foreign Language* (pp. 115–135). Clevedon: Multilingual Matters.

García Mayo, M.P. and García Lecumberri, M.L. (eds) (2003) *Age and the Acquisition of English as a Foreign Language*. Clevedon: Multilingual Matters.

García Rendón, O.L. (2006) La problemática social de la atención a la vejez en México. Paper presented at the Congreso de la Federación Nacional de Estudiantes y Egresados de Trabajo Social, Escuela de Trabajo Social, Universidad Autónoma de Sinaloa, Mazatlán, Sinaloa, Mexico, October.

Gass, S.M. (1998) Apples and oranges: Or, why apples are not orange and don't need to be: A response to Firth and Wagner. *Modern Language Journal* 82, 83–90.

Gee, J.P. (1999) *An Introduction to Discourse Analysis: Theory and Method*. New York: Routledge.

Gee, J.P. (2001) Reading as situated language: A sociocognitive perspective. *Journal of Adolescent and Adult Literacy* 44, 714–725.

Gee, J.P. (2005) *An Introduction to Discourse Analysis: Theory and Method* (2nd edn). London: Routledge.

Gee, J.P. (2008) *Social Linguistics and Literacies: Ideology in Discourses* (3rd edn). London: Routledge.

Gergen, K.J. (1996) Social theory in context: Relational humanism. In J.D. Greenwood (ed.) *Mark of the Social: Discovery or Invention?* (pp. 213–230). New York: Rowman and Littlefield.

Gergen, K.J. (1999) *An Invitation to Social Construction*. London: Sage.

Giddens, A. (1991) *Modernity and Self-Identity: Self and Society in the Late Modern Age*. Cambridge: Polity Press in association with Blackwell.

Giles, H., Coupland, N. and Coupland, J. (eds) (1991) *Contexts of Accommodation: Developments in Applied Sociolinguistics*. Cambridge: Cambridge University Press.

Gilleard, C. and Higgs, P. (2000) *Cultures of Ageing: Self, Citizen and the Body*. London: Prentice Hall.

Giraldo Rodríguez, L. and Torres Castro, S. (2006) Envejecimiento, vulnerabilidad y maltrato. *México: Instituto de Geriatría*, accessed 9 June 2011. http://www.geriatria.salud.gob.mx/descargas/29.pdf

González de la Rocha, M. (2005) Familias y política social en México: El caso de oportunidades. Paper presented at the United Nations Economic Commission for Latin America (CEPAL) Reunión de Expertos: Políticas hacia las Familias, Protección e Inclusión Sociales, Santiago, Chile, June 28–29.

Gray, J. (2002) The global coursebook in English language teaching. In D. Block and D. Cameron (eds) *Globalization and Language Teaching* (pp. 151–167). London: Routledge.

Green, B.S. (1993) *Gerontology and the Construction of Old Age: A Study in Discourse Analysis*. New York: Aldine de Gruyter.

Gubrium, J.F., Holstein, J.A. and Buckholdt, D.R. (1994) *Constructing the Life Course*. Dix Hill, NY: General Hall.

Guijarro Morales, A. (2001) *El Síndrome de la Abuela Esclava: Pandemia del Siglo XXI*. Granada, Spain: Grupo Editorial Universitario.

Gullette, M.M. (1997) *Declining to Decline: Cultural Combat and the Politics of Midlife*. Charlottesville, VA: University Press of Virginia.
Gullette, M.M. (2004) *Aged by Culture*. Chicago: University of Chicago Press.
Gullette, M.M. (2011) *Agewise: Fighting the New Ageism in America*. Chicago: University of Chicago Press.
Haber, S.H. (1989) *Industry and Underdevelopment: The Industrialization of Mexico* (pp. 1890–1940). Stanford, CA: Stanford University Press.
Hahne, A. (2001) What's different in second-language processing? Evidence from event-related brain potentials. *Journal of Psycholinguistic Research* 30, 251–266.
Hakuta, K., Bialystok, E. and Wiley, E. (2003) Critical evidence: A test of the critical-period hypothesis for second-language acquisition. *Psychological Science* 14, 31–38.
Hall, J.K. (1995) (Re)creating our worlds with words: A sociohistorical perspective of face-to-face interaction. *Applied Linguistics* 16, 206–232.
Hall, J.K. (1997) A consideration of SLA as a theory of practice: A response to Firth and Wagner. *Modern Language Journal* 81, 301–306.
Ham Chande, R. (1999) El envejecimiento en México: De los conceptos a las necesidades. *Papeles de Población* 19, 7–21.
Hareven, T.K. (1995) Changing images of aging and the social construction of the life course. In M. Featherstone and A. Wernick (eds) *Images of Aging: Representations of Later Life* (pp. 119–134). London: Routledge.
Harley, B. (2001) Review of *Second Language Acquisition and the Critical Period Hypothesis*, edited by David Birdsong. *Journal of Linguistics* 37, 633–636.
Harley, B. and Hart, D. (1997) Language aptitude and second language proficiency in classroom learners of different starting ages. *Studies in Second Language Acquisition* 19, 379–400.
Harley, B., Howard, J. and Hart, D. (1995) Second language processing at different ages: Do younger learners pay more attention to prosodic cues to sentence structure? *Language Learning* 45, 43–71.
Harley, B. and Wang, W. (1997) The critical period hypothesis: Where are we now? In A.M.B. de Groot and J.F. Kroll (eds) *Tutorials in Bilingualism* (pp. 19–51). Hillsdale, NJ: Lawrence Erlbaum.
Harper, S. (1997) Constructing later life/constructing the body: Some thoughts from feminist theory. In A. Jamieson, S. Harper and C. Victor (eds) *Critical Approaches to Ageing and Later Life* (pp. 160–172). Buckingham: Open University Press.
Harré, R. and van Langenhove, L. (1999a) The dynamics of social episodes. In R. Harré and L. van Langenhove (eds) *Positioning Theory: Moral Contexts of Intentional Action* (pp. 1–13). Oxford: Blackwell.
Harré, R. and van Langenhove, L. (eds) (1999b) *Positioning Theory: Moral Contexts of Intentional Action*. Oxford: Blackwell.
Hazan, H. (1994) *Old Age, Constructions and Deconstructions*. Cambridge: Cambridge University Press.
Holmes, J. (1997) Women, language and identity. *Journal of Sociolinguistics* 1, 195–223.
Holmes, J. and Schnurr, S. (2006) 'Doing femininity' at work: More than just relational practice. *Journal of Sociolinguistics* 10, 31–51.
Hopkins, A. and Potter, J. (1994) *Look Ahead. Classroom Course. Students' Book 1*. New York: Longman.
Horsch, K., Little, P.M.D., Chase Smith, J., Goodyear, L. and Harris, E. (2002) *Youth Involvement in Evaluation and Research*. Issues and Opportunities in Out-of-School Time Evaluation. Issue No. 1. Harvard Family Research Project, Harvard Graduate School of Education.
Ioup, G., Boustagui, E., El Tigi, M. and Moselle, M. (1994) Reexamining the critical period hypothesis: A case study of successful adult SLA in a naturalistic environment. *Studies in Second Language Acquisition* 16, 73–96.

Jaworski, A. and Coupland, N. (1999) Editors' introduction to Part Five. In A. Jaworski and N. Coupland (eds) *The Discourse Reader* (pp. 407–414). London: Routledge.

Jia, G. and Aaronson, D. (2003) A longitudinal study of Chinese children and adolescents learning English in the United States. *Applied Psycholinguistics* 24, 131–161.

Jia, G., Strange, W., Wu, Y. and Collado, J. (2006) Perception and production of English vowels by Mandarin speakers: Age-related differences vary with amount of L2 exposure. *Journal of the Acoustical Society of America* 119, 1118–1130.

Johnson, J.S. and Newport, E.L. (1989) Critical period effects in second language learning: The influence of maturational state on the acquisition of English as a second language. *Cognitive Psychology* 21, 60–99.

Johnson, M. (2004) *A Philosophy of Second Language Acquisition*. New Haven, CT: Yale University Press.

Kasper, G.E. (1997) 'A' stands for acquisition: A response to Firth and Wagner. *Modern Language Journal* 81, 307–312.

Katz, S. (2001) Growing older without aging? Positive ageing, anti-ageism, and anti-aging. *Generations* 25, 27–32.

Keith, J. (1984) Age in anthropological research. In R.H. Binstock and E. Shanas (eds) *Handbook of Aging and the Social Sciences* (pp. 231–263). New York: Van Nostrand Reinhold.

Kiesling, S.F. (1998) Men's identities and sociolinguistic variation: The case of fraternity men. *Journal of Sociolinguistics* 2, 69–99.

Kramsch, C. (2000) Second language acquisition, applied linguistics, and the teaching of foreign languages. *Modern Language Journal* 84, 311–326.

Lantolf, J.P. and Pavlenko, A. (1995) Sociocultural theory and second language acquisition. *Annual Review of Applied Linguistics* 15, 108–124.

Lantolf, J.P. and Pavlenko, A. (2001) (S)econd (L)anguage (A)ctivity theory: Understanding second language learners as people. In M.P. Breen (ed.) *Learner Contributions to Language Learning: New Directions in Research* (pp. 141–158). Harlow: Longman.

Lantolf, J.P. and Thorne, S.L. (2006) *Sociocultural Theory and the Genesis of Second Language Development*. Oxford: Oxford University Press.

Larsen-Freeman, D. (2000) Second language acquisition and applied linguistics. *Annual Review of Applied Linguistics* 20, 165–181.

Larsen-Freeman, D. and Long, M.H. (1991) *An Introduction to Second Language Acquisition Research*. London: Longman.

Latimer, J. (1997) Figuring identities: Older people, medicine and time. In A. Jamieson, S. Harper and C. Victor (eds) *Critical Approaches to Ageing and Later Life* (pp. 143–159). Buckingham: Open University Press.

Lave, J. and Wenger, E. (1991) *Situated Learning: Legitimate Peripheral Participation*. Cambridge: Cambridge University Press.

Leather, J. (2003) Phonological acquisition in multilingualism. In M.P. García Mayo and M.L. García Lecumberri (eds) *Age and the Acquisition of English as a Foreign Language* (pp. 23–58). Clevedon: Multilingual Matters.

Lechner, N. (2004) Cultura juvenil y desarrollo humano. *Revista de Estudios sobre Juventud* 8, accessed 5 April 2008. http://ver2.imjuventud.gob.mx/pdf/rev_joven_es/20/Cultura%20juvenil%20y%20desarrollo%20humano,%20Norbert%20Lechner.pdf

Lenneberg, E.H. (1967) *Biological Foundations of Language*. New York: John Wiley and Sons.

Leñero Otero, L. (1999) Implicaciones intrafamiliares de la población en la tercera edad. *Papeles de Población* 19, 199–215.

Levy, B.R. (2001) Eradication of ageism requires addressing the enemy within. *The Gerontologist* 41, 578–579.

Long, M.H. (1990) Maturational constraints on language development. *Studies in Second Language Acquisition* 12, 251–285.
Long, M.H. (1997) Construct validity in SLA research: A response to Firth and Wagner. *Modern Language Journal* 81, 318–323.
Long, M. (2005) Problems with supposed counter-evidence to the critical period hypothesis. *IRAL*, 4, 287–317.
López Hernández, L.J. (2007) Historia de la mujer en México. *Mujeres, Derechos y Sociedad* 3, accessed 30 November 2007. http://www.femumex.org/femu/revista/0305/0305art02/art02pdf.pdf
MacWhinney, B. (1998) Models of the emergence of language. *Annual Review of Psychology* 49, 199–227.
Maguire, M.H. and Graves, B. (2001) Speaking personalities in primary school children's L2 writing. *TESOL Quarterly* 35, 561–593.
Makoni, S. (1997) Gerontolinguistics in South Africa. *International Journal of Applied Linguistics* 7, 57–65.
Malacara, J.M. (2006) Los factores psicosociales en la menopausia. *Revista de Endocrinología y Nutrición* 14, 137–140.
Marinova-Todd, S.H. (2003) Know your grammar: What the knowledge of syntax and morphology in an L2 reveals about the critical period for second/foreign language acquisition. In M.P. García Mayo and M.L. García Lecumberri (eds) *Age and the Acquisition of English as a Foreign Language* (pp. 59–73). Clevedon: Multilingual Matters.
Marinova-Todd, S.H., Marshall, D.B. and Snow, C.E. (2000) Three misconceptions about age and L2 learning. *TESOL Quarterly* 34, 9–34.
Martohardjono, G. and Flynn, S. (1995) Is there an age-factor for Universal Grammar? In D. Singleton and Z. Lengyel (eds) *The Age Factor in Second Language Acquisition* (pp. 135–153). Clevedon: Multilingual Matters.
McCann, R.M., Dailey, R.M., Giles, H. and Ota, H. (2005) Beliefs about intergenerational communication across the lifespan: Middle age and the roles of age stereotyping and respect norms. *Communication Studies* 56, 293–311.
McCarthy, M. and Carter, R. (1994) *Language as Discourse: Perspectives for Language Teaching*. Harlow: Longman.
McDonald, J.L. (2006) Beyond the critical period: Processing-based explanations for poor grammaticality judgment performance by late second language learners. *Journal of Memory and Language* 55, 381–401.
Mead, G.H. (1932) *Philosophy of the Present*. LaSalle, IL: Open Court.
Mesthrie, R., Swann, J., Deumert, A. and Leap, W.L. (2000) *Introducing Sociolinguistics*. Philadelphia: John Benjamins.
Mishler, E.G. (1999) *Storylines: Craftartists' Narratives of Identity*. Cambridge, MA: Harvard University Press.
Mishler, E.G. (2006) Narrative and identity: The double arrow of time. In A. De Fina, D. Schiffrin and M. Bamberg (eds) *Discourse and Society* (pp. 30–47). Cambridge: Cambridge University Press.
Montes de Oca, V. (2001) Discourses, voices and visions on the aged in Mexico City. *Indian Journal of Gerontology* 15, 53–66.
Moreno Fernández, F. (1998) *Principios de Sociolingüística y Sociología del Lenguaje*. Barcelona: Ariel.
Moyer, A. (1999) Ultimate attainment in L2 phonology: The critical factors of age, motivation, and instruction. *Studies in Second Language Acquisition* 21, 81–108.
Moyer, A. (2004) *Age, Accent and Experience in Second Language Acquisition: An Integrated Approach to Critical Period Inquiry*. Clevedon: Multilingual Matters.

Mueller, J.L. (2005) Electrophysiological correlates of second language processing. *Second Language Research* 21, 152–174.

Mueller, J.L. (2009) The influence of lexical familiarity on ERP responses during sentence comprehension in language learners. *Second Language Research* 25, 43–76.

Muñoz, C. (ed.) (2006) *Age and the Rate of Foreign Language Learning*. Clevedon: Multilingual Matters.

Muñoz, C. (2008) Symmetries and asymmetries of age effects in naturalistic and instructed L2 learning. *Applied Linguistics* 29, 578–596.

Nelson, T.D. (2005) Ageism: Prejudice against our feared future self. *Journal of Social Issues* 61, 207–221.

Neufeld, G. (1978) Language learning ability in adults: A study on the acquisition of prosodic and articulatory features. *Working Papers on Bilingualism* 12, 45–60.

Neustadter, R. (2002) Review of *Beyond Political Correctness: Social Transformation in the United States*, by Michael S. Cummings. *Contemporary Sociology* 31, 724–725.

Norton, B. (2000) *Identity and Language Learning: Gender, Ethnicity and Educational Change*. Harlow: Longman.

Nussbaum, J.F., Pitts, M.J., Huber, F.N., Krieger, J.L.R. and Ohs, J.E. (2005) Ageism and ageist language across the life span: Intimate relationships and non-intimate interactions. *Journal of Social Issues* 61, 287–305.

Oliveira, O. and Ariza, M. (1999) Trabajo, familia y condición femenina: Una revisión de las principales perspectivas de análisis. *Papeles de Población* 20, 89–127.

Oyama, S. (1976) A sensitive period for the acquisition of a nonnative phonological system. *Journal of Psycholinguistic Research* 5, 261–285.

Oyama, S. (1978) The sensitive period and comprehension of speech. *Working Papers on Bilingualism* 16, 1–12.

Packer, M.J. and Goicoechea, J. (2000) Sociocultural and constructivist theories of learning: Ontology, not just epistemology. *Educational Psychologist* 35, 227–241.

Palmore, E.B. (2005) Three decades of research on ageism. *Generations* 29, 87–90.

Parker, I. (1992) *Discourse Dynamics: Critical Analysis for Social and Individual Psychology*. London: Routledge.

Partida, R. (2004) Trabajadoras de la electrónica en Jalisco: Las abuelas como proveedoras de cuidado infantil. *El Cotidiano* 19, 68–77.

Patkowski, M. (1980) The sensitive period for the acquisition of syntax in a second language. *Language Learning* 30, 449–472.

Pavlenko, A. (2001a) 'How am I to become a woman in the American vein?' Transformations of gender performance in second language learning. In A. Pavlenko, A. Blackledge, I. Piller and M. Teutsch-Dwyer (eds) *Multilingualism, Second Language Learning, and Gender* (pp. 133–174). New York: Mouton De Gruyter.

Pavlenko, A. (2001b) 'In the world of the tradition, I was unimagined': Negotiation of identities in cross-cultural autobiographies. *International Journal of Bilingualism* 5, 317–344.

Pavlenko, A. (2002a) Narrative study: Whose story is it, anyway? *TESOL Quarterly* 36, 213–218.

Pavlenko, A. (2002b) Poststructuralist approaches to the study of social factors in second language learning and use. In V. Cook (ed.) *Portraits of the L2 User* (pp. 275–302). Clevedon: Multilingual Matters.

Pavlenko, A. and Lantolf, J.P. (2000) Second language learning as participation and the (re)construction of selves. In J.P. Lantolf (ed.) *Sociocultural Theory and Second Language Learning* (pp. 155–177). Oxford: Oxford University Press.

Penfield, W. and Roberts, L. (1959) *Speech and Brain-Mechanisms*. Princeton, NJ: Princeton University Press.

Phillipson, C. (1998) *Reconstructing Old Age: New Agendas in Social Theory and Practice.* Thousand Oaks, CA: Sage.
Polkinghorne, D.E. (1988) *Narrative Knowing and the Human Sciences.* Albany, NY: State University of New York Press.
Potter, J. (1996) *Representing Reality: Discourse, Rhetoric and Social Construction.* London: Sage.
Preece, S. (2009) *Posh Talk: Language and Identity in Higher Education.* Basingstoke: Palgrave Macmillan.
Rampton, B. (1995) *Crossing: Language and Ethnicity among Adolescents.* London: Longman.
Rampton, B. (1997) *Language Crossing and the Redefinition of Reality: Implications for Research on Code-Switching Community.* Working Papers in Urban Language and Literacies. Paper 5. London: King's College.
Rampton, B. (1999) Styling the other: Introduction. *Journal of Sociolinguistics* 3, 421–427.
Rampton, B. (2000) Continuity and change in views of society in applied linguistics. In H. Trappes-Lomax (ed.) *Change and Continuity in Applied Linguistics: Selected Papers from the Annual Meeting of the British Association for Applied Linguistics Held at the University of Edinburgh, September 1999* (pp. 97–114). Clevedon: British Association for Applied Linguistics in association with Multilingual Matters Ltd.
Rampton, B. (2001) Language crossing, cross-talk, and cross-disciplinarity in sociolinguistics. In N. Coupland, S. Sarangi and C.N. Candlin (eds) *Sociolinguistics and Social Theory* (pp. 261–296). Harlow: Longman.
Rampton, B. (2006) Language and ethnicity at school: Some implications from theoretical developments in sociolinguistics. Paper presented at a conference at the University of London Institute of Education, May 9.
Reguillo, R. (2001) La gestión del futuro: contextos y políticas de representación. *Revista de Estudios sobre Juventud* 5, accessed 1 May 2008. http://ver2.imjuventud.gob.mx/pdf/rev_joven_es/15/La%20gesti%F3n%20del%20futuro.%20Rossana%20Reguillo.pdf
Ricoeur, P. (1995) *Tiempo y Narración I: Configuración del Tiempo en el Relato Histórico* (A. Neira, trans.). Mexico: Siglo XXI Editores.
Richards, J.C., with Hull, J. and Proctor, S. (1991) *Interchange 3. English for International Communication. Student's Book.* Cambridge: Cambridge University Press.
Robles Silva, L., Vázquez Palacios, F., Reyes Gómez, L. and Orozco Mares, I. (2006) *Miradas Sobre la Vejez: Un Enfoque Antropológico.* Mexico: El Colegio de la Frontera Norte y Plaza y Valdés.
Salguero Velásquez, A. (2006) Identidad, responsabilidad familiar y ejercicio de la paternidad en varones del Estado de México. *Papeles de Población* 48, 155–179.
Salles, V. and Tuirán, R. (1996) Mitos y creencias sobre la vida familiar. *Revista Mexicana de Sociología* 58, 117–144.
Sandoval Ávila, A. (2002) Impacto de la socialización de los hijos de la incorporación de la mujer al trabajo remunerado. *Espiral* 8, 179–207.
Sawchuk, K.A. (1995) From gloom to boom: Age, identity and target marketing. In M. Featherstone and A. Wernick (eds) *Images of Aging: Cultural Representations of Later Life.* London: Routledge.
Scovel, T. (2000) A critical review of the critical period research. *Annual Review of Applied Linguistics* 20, 213–223.
Scherag, A., Demuth, L., Rösler, F., Neville, H. J. and Röder, B. (2004) The effects of late acquisition of L2 and the consequences of immigration on L1 for semantic and morpho-syntactic language aspects. *Cognition* 93, B97–B108.
Schettino Yáñez, M. (2002) *México: Problemas Sociales, Políticos y Económicos.* Mexico: Pearson Educación.
Schiffrin, D. (1994) *Approaches to Discourse.* Oxford: Blackwell.

Schilling-Estes, N. (2004) Constructing ethnicity in interaction. *Journal of Sociolinguistics* 8, 163–195.

Schumann, J.H. (1997) *The Neurobiology of Affect in Language*. Malden, MA: Blackwell.

Selby, H.A. and Browning, H.L. (1992) *The Sociodemographic Effects of the Crisis in Mexico*. Austin, TX: The University of Texas at Austin. Available online at http://www1.lanic.utexas.edu/project/etext/mexico/selby/, accessed 28 January 2008.

Seliger, H.W. (1978) Implications of a multiple critical periods hypothesis for second language learning. In W.C. Ritchie (ed.) *Second Language Acquisition Research: Issues and Implications* (pp. 11–19). New York: Academic Press.

Sfard, A. (1998) On two metaphors for learning and on the dangers of choosing just one. *Educational Researcher* 27, 4–13.

Shweder, R.A. (ed.) (1998) *Welcome to Middle Age! (And Other Cultural Fictions)*. Chicago: University of Chicago Press.

Singleton, D. (1995) Introduction: A critical look at the critical period hypothesis in second language acquisition research. In D. Singleton and Z. Lengyel (eds) *The Age Factor in Second Language Acquisition* (pp. 1–29). Clevedon: Multilingual Matters.

Singleton, D. (1998) Age and the second language lexicon. *Studia Anglica Posnaniensia: International Review of English Studies* 33, 365–376.

Singleton, D. (2005) The critical period hypothesis: A coat of many colours. *IRAL* 43, 269–285.

Singleton, D. and Ryan, L. (2004) *Language Acquisition: The Age Factor* (2nd edn). Clevedon: Multilingual Matters.

Skehan, P. (1998) *A Cognitive Approach to Language Learning*. Oxford: Oxford University Press.

Slabakova, R. (2006) Is there a critical period for semantics? *Second Language Research* 22, 302–338.

Slavoff, G.R. and Johnson, J.S. (1995) The effects of age on the rate of learning a second language. *Studies in Second Language Acquisition* 17, 1–16.

Soars, L. and Soars, J. (2001a) *American Headway 1. Student Book*. New York: Oxford University Press.

Soars, L. and Soars, J. (2001b) *American Headway 2. Student Book*. New York: Oxford University Press.

Soars, L. and Soars, J. (2003) *American Headway 3. Student Book*. New York: Oxford University Press.

Stowe, L.A. and Sabourin, L. (2005) Imaging the processing of a second language: Effects of maturation and proficiency on the neural processes involved. *IRAL* 43, 329–353.

Taylor, D. (1994) Inauthentic authenticity or authentic inauthenticity? *TESL-EJ* 1, accessed 27 November 2007. http://www.zait.uni-bremen.de/wwwgast/tesl_ej/ej02/a.1.html

Thorne, S.L. (2000) Second language acquisition theory and the truth(s) about relativity. In J.P. Lantolf (ed.) *Sociocultural Theory and Second Language Learning* (pp. 219–243). Oxford: Oxford University Press.

Toohey, K. (2000) *Learning English at School: Identity, Social Relations and Classroom Practice*. Clevedon: Multilingual Matters.

Treviño Siller, S., Pelcastre Villafuerte, B. and Márquez Serrano, M. (2006) Experiencias de envejecimiento en el México rural. *Salud Pública de México* 48, accessed 14 June 2011. http://www.medigraphic.com/pdfs/salpubmex/sal-2006/sal061e.pdf

Tulle-Winton, E. (1999) Growing old and resistance: Towards a new cultural economy of old age? *Ageing and Society* 19, 281–299.

Van Boxtel, S., Bongaerts, T. and Coppen, P-A. (2005) Native-like attainment of dummy subjects in Dutch and the role of the L1. *IRAL* 43, 355–380.

Vincent, J. (2003) *Old Age*. London: Routledge.

Vincent, J. (2006) Ageing contested: Anti-ageing science and the cultural construction of old age. *Sociology* 40, 681–698.

Vygotsky, L.S. (1978) *Mind in Society: The Development of Higher Psychological Processes*. Cambridge, MA: Harvard University Press.

Vygotsky, L.S. (1981) The genesis of higher mental functions. In J.V. Wertsch (ed.) *The Concept of Activity in Soviet Psychology* (pp. 144–188). New York: Sharpe.

Weber-Fox, C.M. and Neville, H.J. (1996) Maturational constraints on functional specializations for language processing: ERP and behavioral evidence in bilingual speakers. *Journal of Cognitive Neuroscience* 8, 231–256.

Weber-Fox, C.M. and Neville, H.J. (1999) Functional neural subsystems are differentially affected by delays in second language immersion: ERP and behavioral evidence in bilinguals. In D. Birdsong (ed.) *Second Language Acquisition and the Critical Period Hypothesis* (pp. 23–38). Mahwah, NJ: Lawrence Erlbaum.

Weedon, C. (1997) *Feminist Practice and Poststructuralist Theory* (2nd edn). Oxford: Blackwell.

White, L. (1989) *Universal Grammar and Second Language Acquisition*. Amsterdam: John Benjamins.

White, L. and Genesee, F. (1996) How native is near-native? The issue of ultimate attainment in adult second language acquisition. *Second Language Research* 12, 233–265.

Williams, A. and Giles, H. (1996) Intergenerational conversations: Young adults' retrospective accounts. *Human Communication Research* 23, 220–250.

Wodak, R., de Cillia, R., Reisigl, M. and Liebhart, K. (1999) *The Discursive Construction of National Identity* (A. Hirsch and R. Mitten, trans.). Edinburgh: Edinburgh University Press.

Zermeño, A. (2005) La familia en la génesis del siglo XXI. *Razón y Palabra* 45, accessed 19 March 2008. http://www.razonypalabra.org.mx/anteriores/n45/azermeno.html

Zuengler, J. and Miller, E.R. (2006) Cognitive and sociocultural perspectives: Two parallel SLA worlds? *TESOL Quarterly* 40, 35–58.

Zúñiga Herrera, E. (2004) El proceso de envejecimiento demográfico: Situación y perspectivas. Paper presented at the Congreso Internacional El Reto del Envejecimiento, INAPAM, Secretaría de Relaciones Exteriores, Mexico, 17 June.

Zúñiga Herrera, E. (ed.) (2005) *México: Ante los Desafíos de Desarrollo del Milenio*. Mexico: Consejo Nacional de Población.

Index

Note: n refers to endnotes.

Aaronson 10, 12, 15, 17
Abrahamsson 12, 17
Abu-Rabia 6, 8, 10, 17
accent 8, 10, 12, 39
activity theory 20
Adela 69, 110, 111, 112, 113, 115, 116, 117, 118, 119, 120, 122, 127, 128, 129, 130, 131, 133n, 136, 138, 139
Adler 54
adolescence 18, 35, 39, 40, 50, 52, 53, 54, 115 116, 119, 129, 130, 138, 141; *see also* age categories; life stages
adulthood xv, 40, 47, 54, 119, 122, 129, 130, 133, 141, 143, 147, 148, 150, 154; *see also* age categories; life stages; *and specific stages of adulthood*
adultism 98, 105, 130, 132, 154
age anxiety 52, 73, 130
age categories 18, 40, 50, 51, 53–55, 110, 116, 118, 119, 120, 130, 131, 133, 147, 148, 149, 150, 153, 154, 160; *see also* life stages
age constraints *see* maturational constraints
age discourses xiv, xvi, 1, 41, 44–58, 59, 62, 67, 107, 123, 124, 131, 149, 150, 157
age factor xiii, xv, 1, 3, 7, 12, 13, 14, 15, 18, 19, 24, 25, 62, 152, 158
age identity x, xiv, xv, xvi, 1, 3, 19, 30, 31, 33, 39, 42, 44, 58, 59, 61, 62, 64, 65, 68, 69, 70, 71, 73, 80, 82, 85, 89, 104, 106, 108, 109, 110, 118, 126, 129, 130, 131, 132, 141, 145, 148, 149, 150, 153, 154, 155, 157, 159, 160
age of onset (AO) 5, 7, 8, 9, 11, 15, 16, 17, 26n
age salience 55, 76, 88, 159
age segregation/self-segregation 53, 77, 88, 148, 154

age studies xiv, xv, 45, 156, 158, 159
age theory xiv, 41, 45, 58
age/aging, concept of xiv, 45, 46, 55, 57, 61, 64, 107
age-appropriateness 41, 52, 79, 84, 124, 125, 130, 132, 154
ageism 41, 47, 48, 50, 51, 52, 53, 55, 59, 65, 66n, 77, 79, 80, 84, 88, 98, 107, 108, 116, 117, 120, 121, 124, 131, 154, 155, 157, 158, 160
ageist discourses 41, 48-52, 59, 69, 84, 88, 108, 132, 153, 154, 157, 160
age-related differences x, xiii, 7, 12, 13, 14, 15, 18, 51, 149, 156
aging process x, xiv, 11, 19, 44, 45, 48, 55, 56, 57, 58, 65, 79, 81, 88, 91, 123
Ainlay 55
American culture xii, 53, 54, 66n, 80, 87
American Sign Language 4
Andrews 57, 80
Anglophone culture xii, xiv, 87, 93, 110, 131, 154
anti-ageist discourses 57–58, 59, 88, 100
aptitude 11, 12, 15
Arber 58
Ariès 44, 45, 53
Aristotle 45
Ariza 96, 128
Ashcroft 34, 109n
Atkinson 20, 21
attainment, end-state/linguistic/ultimate xi, xiii, 7, 8, 9, 10, 11, 12, 158
attitudes xii, xiv, 46, 48, 52, 53, 67, 68, 75, 77, 79, 82, 86, 88, 92, 97, 101, 106, 107, 108, 117, 130, 131, 132, 145, 149, 150, 154, 155, 157, 158, 160
attribute 24, 25, 60
Augustine 45
Austin 29

authority 46, 92, 94, 95, 97, 99, 105, 106, 107

Bakhtin 21, 26n, 30
Baxter 37, 60, 127
beliefs x, xiv, 5, 13, 22, 28, 29, 38, 46, 48, 50, 51, 55, 67, 68, 75, 83, 85, 88, 91, 92, 94, 96, 106, 107, 112, 125, 130, 131, 145, 149, 154, 157, 160
Benwell 137, 138
Bergson 45
Berta 69, 110, 111, 112, 113, 115, 116, 117, 118, 123, 124, 125, 126, 129, 130, 131, 153
Bialystok 7, 9, 10, 11
Bijarro 48
bilingualism xi, 8, 13, 74
biology xiii, xv, 1, 3, 4, 6, 7, 9, 14, 15, 18, 25, 35, 40, 42, 45, 48, 55, 56, 60, 61, 66n, 77, 81, 123, 157, 158, 159
Birdsong xiii, 8, 9, 10, 11, 13, 16, 17
Bishop 137, 145
Blackledge xiv, 34, 59
Blanco 128
Bley-Vroman 11
Block xii, 22, 24, 25
Blommaert 29
bodily aging 52, 56, 57
body and biomedical discourses 55–57, 65
Bongaerts 6, 8, 11, 16
Bourdieu 38, 43n, 55, 58, 73, 87, 112, 129, 131, 135, 143, 145, 148, 149, 155
brain 4, 6, 9, 14, 26n, 137
Breen 24, 115
Brigeiro 58
Browning 109
Bruner 62
Burr 29, 30, 62
Butler, J. 36, 60
Butler, R. 48

Calasanti 57, 58
Cameron xiv, 33, 35, 36, 60, 103
Candlin 22, 23
capital, cultural/economic//social/symbolic xv, 38, 39, 43n, 50, 73, 87, 112, 129, 130, 131, 135, 148, 149, 155
Carter 29
childhood xiii, 3, 4, 18, 40, 44, 47, 49, 53, 54, 55, 73, 84, 90, 110, 112, 119, 120, 131, 135, 141, 142, 143, 144, 147, 148; *see also* age categories; life stages

Chomsky 21
Chopra 57
chronological age 18, 40, 45, 55, 81, 93, 110, 130, 132, 153, 156, 160
Cicirelli 49
Cilliers 63
class, middle/social/upper/working xi, xv, 18, 24, 27, 32, 33, 35, 36, 37, 38–39, 40, 42, 43, 58, 62, 86, 87, 109, 128, 138, 143, 153, 157
Clay 50
coconstruction 24, 67, 68, 107, 118, 131, 149, 153
cognitive/psycholinguistic approaches/orientation to SLA xv, 15, 18, 19, 21, 23, 24, 25, 26n, 156, 158
cognitive/psychological/social/affective factors 11, 12, 15, 55, 81, 157
Cohen 85
Cole 57, 82
Collins 38
Combe 108
communities of practice 22–23, 24, 29
competence 4, 9, 12, 13, 20, 21, 41, 42, 49, 84, 99, 100, 103, 110
competing discourses 60, 65, 69, 81, 88, 99, 103, 106, 109, 120, 127, 141, 150
competition model 10, 26n
connectionism 21, 26n
Cook 10, 13
Corbett 146
Coupland, J. 41
Coupland, N. 33, 40, 41, 42, 49, 50, 53, 55, 81, 82, 84, 93, 101, 109
critical period 3, 4, 5, 6, 7, 9, 11, 13, 14, 15, 25
Critical Period Hypothesis (CPH) xiii, 1, 3–18, 25, 26n, 50, 51, 152, 158
crossing 35, 38, 43n
Cruikshank 52, 53, 55, 56, 57, 58, 88
cultural discourses 30, 46, 47, 48, 60, 64, 65, 107, 131, 149, 152, 153, 155, 157
cultural studies 1, 44
Curtiss 4

David 69, 134-148, 149, 150, 151, 151n, 153, 154, 155
Dayrell 140, 148
De Bot 12, 15
death 55, 56, 81, 85, 100, 144
Deats 55

decline discourses/narratives 18, 26n, 46–48, 65, 66n, 71, 81, 87, 88, 89, 99, 100, 105, 120–124, 130, 132, 141–143, 149, 150, 152, 154, 157, 160
decrement 18, 41, 42, 57, 84, 88, 105, 121
deficit 57, 91, 100, 107, 108, 157
DeKeyser 12, 13, 17
dependence/independence 41, 48, 49, 54, 57, 69, 82, 83–85, 88, 99, 112, 123, 141, 143–144, 148, 150
dialogue 21, 26n, 30, 35, 63, 79, 94, 95, 104
discourse analysis 32, 37
discourse and language 28, 29–30
discourse-oriented sociolinguistics 1, 27, 32–33, 39, 42, 45, 152
discourses *see specific discourses*
discursive interaction xv, 1, 27, 29, 30, 31, 32, 35, 43, 45, 65, 152
Dörnyei 12, 15
Dumas 58
dynamic systems 12–13

Eckert xiv, 18, 36, 38, 39, 40, 47, 140
Einstein 45
Ellis 26n
Elsa 69, 95, 96, 110, 111, 112, 113, 114, 115, 117, 118, 119, 122, 123, 129, 130, 131
empty-nest syndrome 50, 54, 120
engagement/disengagement 49, 82–83, 88, 99, 108
English as a foreign language (EFL) x, xiv, 68, 107, 131, 149, 152, 153, 160
environmental account 10, 12, 15
essentialism 18, 30, 60, 65, 66n, 152
ethnic identity 34, 35, 38, 39, 85, 148
ethnicity xiv, xv, 18, 24, 25, 27, 32, 33, 34–35, 36, 37, 38, 39, 40, 42, 43, 51, 58, 59, 62, 68, 85, 86, 87, 89, 109n, 138, 147, 152, 153, 155, 157, 158, 159
ethnography/ethnographic approach 19, 32, 33, 36, 37, 67
Eubank 10, 14
event-related potential patterns (ERP) 9
expectations x, xii, 37, 41, 47, 58, 63, 92, 128, 144
experience of age/aging x, xiv, xvi, 1, 19, 42, 44, 46, 49, 56, 59, 61, 62, 64, 65, 69, 109, 123, 133, 152, 153

Fanon 87
fatherhood 102, 132, 134, 144, 146
fear of aging 41, 56

Featherstone 47, 51, 55, 56, 94
Feixa 140, 144
Felix ix, 69, 71, 89–107, 108, 109, 109n, 110, 112, 116, 118, 120, 121, 123, 129, 135, 147, 150, 153, 154, 155
Felix, S. 10
femininity/feminine identity 35, 36, 37, 39, 138, 155
first language *see* L1
Firth 21, 22
Flege 8, 10, 16
Flores 143
Flynn 10, 11, 14
Fortes 58, 86, 87, 109n
Francis xii
Franco 49
fundamental difference hypothesis 11

Gallardo 8, 17
García Canclini 143
García Lecumberri 8, 11, 17
García Mayo 8, 11, 17
García Rendón 50
Gass 21
Gee xvin, 29, 43n
gender xiv, xv, 18, 24, 25, 27, 32, 33, 35–38, 39, 40, 42, 43, 45, 51, 58, 59, 62, 69, 70, 80, 132, 138, 150, 152, 153, 155, 157, 159
gender identity 35, 36, 37, 38, 39, 61, 68, 85, 89, 105, 106, 108, 126, 127, 129, 130, 132, 147, 148, 150, 153, 155, 158, 159
Genesee 8, 10, 13, 16, 26n
Gergen 27, 28, 30, 31
Giddens 31, 61, 65
Gilda 69, 110, 111, 112, 113, 116, 117, 118, 121, 122, 123, 124, 126, 127, 129, 130, 131, 133n, 136, 139
Giles 41, 53
Gilleard 57
Ginn 58
Giraldo 47
Goicoechea 23
González 54
grammar/grammaticality 8, 9, 13, 16, 17, 117
Graves 18
Gray 137
Green, B. 45
Gregg 10, 14
Gubrium 64, 82

Guijarro 129
Gullette 47, 49, 52, 58, 59, 66n, 71, 120, 131, 132, 154, 159

Haber 47
Hahne 9, 17
Hakuta 11, 17
Hall 18, 20, 22, 25
Ham 49
Hareven 54, 120
Harley 11, 13, 15, 16
Harper 56
Harré 60, 62
Hart 11, 16
Hazan 52, 132
Hector 69, 71–89, 90, 91, 92, 94, 99, 102, 104, 105, 106, 107, 108, 109, 109n, 112, 116, 118, 120, 121, 123, 129, 135, 147, 150, 153, 154, 155
Hepworth 47, 51, 55, 94
Higgs 57
Holmes 36, 37
Hopkins xviii
Horsch 98
Hyltenstam 12, 17

identity *see specific identities; see also* subjectivity
immigrant 8, 10
infancy 6, 148; *see also* age categories; life stages
innate language learning mechanism/ faculty 4, 6, 10
Ioup xiii, 6, 8, 16

Jaworski 33
Jia 10, 12, 15, 17
Johnson, J. xiii, 6, 7, 10, 13, 16
Johnson, M. 21

Kasper 22
Katz 52
Kehat 6, 8, 10, 17
Keith 53
Kiesling 36, 38, 39
Kramsch 20

L1 3, 4, 5, 8, 9, 10, 11, 15, 16
L2 3, 5, 6, 7, 8, 9, 10, 11, 12, 13, 14, 15, 16, 18, 19, 20, 21, 22, 23, 25, 26n, 34, 51, 61, 67, 136, 157; *see also* second language

La Santa 38
language exposure 10, 11, 12, 26n, 74
language proficiency 4, 5, 7, 8, 9, 10, 11, 12, 16, 17, 75, 111, 133n, 135, 136, 156; *see also* native/native-like/ near-native proficiency
language socialization 21
language use xviii, 10, 19, 21, 22, 26n, 29, 34, 35, 36, 43n, 52, 53, 74, 109n, 115
language-learning experience x, xi, xii, xiii, xiv, xv, xvi, 18, 19, 25, 67, 68, 70, 107, 108, 118, 131, 132, 133, 149, 150, 155, 156, 158, 159, 160
Lantolf 19, 20, 21, 23
Larsen-Freeman 18
later adulthood xvi, 48, 58, 69, 71, 89, 107, 108, 109, 120, 121, 124, 129, 133, 153, 154, 155; *see also* age categories; life stages
lateralization 4, 13, 26n
Latimer 57
Lave 22, 23
Leather 12
Lechner 144, 146, 148
Leñero 54
length of residence (LOR) 7
Lenker 55
Lenneberg 3, 4, 26n
Leontiev 20
Levy 52, 84, 85
life course xiv, 13, 18, 41, 42, 46, 47, 50, 52, 53, 54, 58, 59, 64, 72, 76, 80, 81, 88, 103, 118, 119, 120, 121, 122, 123, 124, 130, 141, 142, 143, 148, 149, 150, 156, 159, 160
life stage xiv, 18, 40, 41, 46, 47, 50, 52, 53, 54, 58, 75, 81, 82, 119, 120, 124, 129, 141, 147, 148; *see also* age categories; *and specific life stages*
lifespan 40, 46, 53, 65, 68, 70, 82, 107, 131, 141, 149, 155, 156, 159
linguistic and non-linguistic dimensions/ outcomes xi, xv, 1, 5, 6, 7, 10, 12, 14, 15, 18, 25, 70, 107, 108, 131, 155, 158, 159
Long xiii, 5, 6, 7, 13, 14, 18, 21
López 128
Luria 20

McCann 140
McCarthy 29
McConnell-Ginet xiv, 36, 38, 39
McDonald 13, 17

MacWhinney 26n
Maguire 18
Makoni 12, 15, 45
Malacara 54, 66n
Manuel 11
marginalization 41, 48, 49, 58, 101, 108, 123, 154, 157
Marinova-Todd xiii, 13
Martin 70, 117, 136, 137, 140
Martohardjono 10, 11, 14
masculinity/masculine identity 35, 36, 37, 39, 85, 89, 94, 104, 105, 108, 138, 147, 150, 155
maturational/age/biological constraints xiii, 3, 4, 6, 7, 8, 9, 12, 13, 14, 15, 157
Mead 42
memory 12, 13, 51, 74
Mendiola 48
Mesthrie 32, 35
Mexican culture/society 66n, 69, 95, 97, 110, 120, 124, 125, 127, 129, 154
'middle' adulthood xvi, 110, 120, 121, 129, 131, 132, 133, 153, 155; see also age categories; life stages
middle age xiv, 18, 50, 54, 69, 119, 120, 130, 154; see also age categories; life stages
midlife/midlifers 47, 48, 49, 50, 51, 54, 57, 58, 66n, 69, 110, 111, 112, 113, 120, 126, 129, 130, 131, 132, 133n, 139, 141, 153, 154, 155
Miller 21
Mishler 63
Molis 10, 17
Montes de Oca 56, 58
Moreno 32
mortality xiv, 53, 100
motherhood 37, 54, 69, 75, 111, 128, 129, 132, 134, 135, 141, 143, 146, 156
Moyer 8, 12, 16, 17
Mueller 9, 17
multilingualism 15, 22, 34, 39, 138
multiple critical periods 4, 14
multiple identities 23, 30, 31, 44, 61, 65, 80, 106, 155, 156
Muñoz 7, 11, 17

narration x, 28, 31, 32, 44, 59, 63–64, 65, 84, 88, 125
narrative 17, 19, 28, 31, 33, 34, 37, 46, 47, 49, 50, 57, 58, 59, 61, 62, 63, 64, 65, 67, 68, 69, 74, 80, 81, 87, 89, 92, 94, 96, 97, 98, 105, 109, 109n, 117, 120, 124, 133, 134, 135, 137, 138, 140, 146, 150, 153, 156, 157; see also decline narrative; progress narrative
national identity xii, 34
nationality 33, 34, 80
native/native-like/near-native proficiency 5, 7, 8, 12, 13
Nelson 46, 53, 56
Neufeld 8, 16
Neustadter 99
Neville 9, 13, 16
Newport xiii, 6, 7, 10, 16
Newton 45
Nidia 70, 97, 114, 117
Norton 18, 23, 25, 59, 62
Nussbaum 41, 53

old age xiv, 40, 41, 47, 48, 49, 52, 53, 54, 55, 56, 57, 73, 84, 88, 91, 94, 107, 108, 110, 116, 119, 121, 122, 123, 131, 133, 141; see also age categories; life stages
Oliveira 96, 128
Oyama 6, 7, 16

Packer 23
Palmore 52
Parker 29
Partida 129
passing 57, 79, 81, 88
Patkowski 6, 7, 13, 16
patriarchy 69, 94, 95, 97, 99, 105, 106, 108, 128, 150
Pavlenko 19, 20, 21, 23, 24, 34, 59, 63, 156
peer 20, 36, 37, 39, 53, 62, 138, 140, 145, 146, 150, 154
Penfield 26n
performance 8, 10, 13, 14, 21, 33, 36, 37, 39, 42, 71, 77, 92, 151
Phillipson 49
phonetics/phonology 8, 12, 14, 36; see also pronunciation
Polkinghorne 63, 65
positioning/subject position ix, xiii, xiv, 33, 37, 38, 46, 48, 60, 61, 62, 63, 64, 65, 68, 69, 70, 76, 77, 80, 81, 82, 83, 84, 85, 87, 88, 89, 90, 92, 93, 94, 99, 104, 105, 106, 107, 108, 109, 115, 116, 117, 118, 119, 120, 126, 127, 128, 129, 130, 131, 132, 133, 139, 141, 143, 145, 146, 147, 148, 149, 150, 151, 152, 153, 154

positive aging 47, 57, 58, 59, 65, 80, 81, 82, 87, 88, 106
postmodernism 28, 33
poststructuralism 37, 44, 59, 60, 61–62, 66n
Potter, Jocelyn xvin
Potter, Jonathan 27
power xii, 36, 39, 41, 52, 55, 56, 57, 59, 60, 62, 63, 86, 87, 89, 95, 103, 108, 120, 127, 131, 132, 155
Preece 39, 138
prestige xii, 38, 72, 73, 87, 102, 107, 108, 110, 131, 149, 155
productivity 49, 54, 58, 73, 82, 85, 87, 89, 101, 103, 104, 105, 106, 108, 123
professional identity 69, 85, 89, 104, 106, 108, 126, 130, 132, 155, 156, 159
progress discourse/narrative 47, 71, 73, 87, 89, 120–124, 129, 132, 141–142, 150, 154
pronunciation 7, 8, 10, 12, 16, 17, 91; *see also* phonetics/phonology
puberty/postpuberty/prepuberty xiii, 4, 5, 6, 8, 10, 13, 15; *see also* age categories; life stages

race 34, 38, 45, 51, 87, 109n
racial identity 35
Ramon 70, 77, 78, 79, 116, 117, 118, 121, 136, 137
Rampton 32, 33, 35, 38, 43n
rate of acquisition 7
Redfoot 55
Reguillo 140, 148
relational focus 28–29
responsibility 50, 57, 70, 92, 94, 97, 98, 113, 116, 128, 129, 130, 132, 133, 140, 143, 147, 151, 153, 154
retirement ix, 40, 49, 50, 52, 54, 58, 69, 71, 72, 73, 78, 82, 83, 87, 89, 90, 91, 100, 101, 104, 105, 106, 107, 108, 112, 120, 122, 123, 126, 127, 129, 130, 133n, 133, 134, 141, 153, 155
Richards xvin
Ricoeur 63, 65
Roberts 26n
Robles 50
Ryan, L. xiii, 9, 11, 51
Ryan, P. xii

Sabourin 9
Salguero 96, 97, 112, 144, 145, 147
Salles 96, 97, 104

Sandoval 112, 129
Sawchuk 52
Scherag 14, 17
Schettino 109
Schiffrin 29
Schilling-Estes 35
Schmader 108
Schnurr 37
Schrauf 12, 15
Schumann 12
Scovel 14
second language x, xii, xiii, 3, 22, 74; *see also* L2
second language acquisition (SLA) xiii, xv, 1, 3, 5, 6, 7, 9, 10, 11, 12, 13, 14, 15, 16, 18, 19, 20, 21, 22, 23, 24, 25, 50, 107, 131, 149, 152, 153, 156, 158
Selby 109
Seliger 14
Sfard 23
Shweder 50, 66n, 154
sickness 48, 56, 66n, 128
Simon 70, 93, 94, 96, 97, 98, 114, 117
Singleton xiii, 8, 9, 11, 13, 14, 15, 16, 51
Skehan 10
Slabakova 9
Slavoff 7, 13, 16
Soars, J. xvin, 75, 92, 136
Soars, L. xvin, 75, 92, 136
social construct *see* age; ethnicity; gender; social class
social constructionism 1, 27–32, 60, 152
social dimensions/parameters xiv, xv, xvi, 1, 18, 19, 20, 23, 25, 27, 30, 32, 33, 35, 37, 38, 39, 40, 43, 55, 59, 152, 156, 158, 159
social identity 12, 19, 23, 36, 37, 38, 39, 87, 89, 108, 146, 147, 153, 158
sociocognitive approaches 20–21
sociocultural approaches/orientation to SLA xv, 1, 3, 18, 19–25, 152, 156, 158
sociocultural context 27, 30, 32, 42, 43, 56, 148
sociocultural theory 19, 21, 23
sociolinguistics 1, 19, 22, 27, 32, 33, 38, 40, 41, 42, 44; *see also* discourse-oriented sociolinguistics
Soviet psychology 20
stereotype 37, 41, 48, 49, 50, 51, 52, 55, 65, 84, 94, 99, 132, 160
Stokoe 137, 138

story xvi, 31, 44, 59, 61, 62, 63, 64, 65, 67, 68, 69, 70, 71, 72, 76, 80, 82, 85, 87, 88, 89, 92, 99, 105, 107, 109, 110, 116, 118, 124, 129, 130, 133, 134, 135, 147, 149, 153, 159
Stowe 9
student culture 36, 137, 148, 150
student identity 145, 146, 148, 149, 150, 155
subjectivity 59, 60, 61, 66n, 97; see also identity
syntax/morphosyntax 7, 8, 16, 17

Taylor 115
temporality xv, 55, 63, 65, 82, 158, 159
textbook xvin, 75, 78, 92, 109n, 113, 136, 157, 160
Thorne 20, 23
timetable 4, 120, 124, 125, 130, 154
Tomas 70, 98, 113, 117
Toohey 18, 25
Torres 47
Treviño 47
Tuirán 96, 97, 104
Tulle-Winton 58

Universal Grammar (UG) 10–11
university student x, xii, 39, 61, 69, 90, 107, 113, 120, 131, 133, 134, 136, 137, 138, 139, 141, 143, 144, 145, 146, 148, 149, 150, 153, 155

Van Boxtel 6, 8, 17
van Langenhove 60, 62–63
variable xv, 11, 12, 15, 24, 37, 40, 62
Vincent 56, 57, 58
Vygotsky 20, 21

Wacquant 43n
Wagner 21, 22
Wang 13
Weber-Fox 9, 13, 16
Weedon 59, 60
Wenger 22, 23
Wernick 56
Western culture/society xi, xv, xvi, 1, 18, 40, 41, 44, 45, 46, 47, 48, 53, 55, 56, 58, 59, 65, 66n, 84, 100, 108, 123, 153, 157
White 8, 10, 11, 13, 16, 26n
Williams 53
Wodak xiv, 34

young adulthood xvi, 69, 110, 116, 119, 129, 131, 133, 134, 141, 142, 148, 149, 150, 154, 155; see also age categories; life stages
youth culture 76, 88, 117

Zermeño 54, 129, 130
Zuengler 21
Zúniga 47, 49

For Product Safety Concerns and Information please contact our EU Authorised Representative:

Easy Access System Europe

Mustamäe tee 50

10621 Tallinn

Estonia

gpsr.requests@easproject.com